HOLLYWOOD RENEGADES

HOLLYWOOD

The Society of Independent

by

J. A. ABERDEEN

RENEGADES

Motion Picture Producers

Cobblestone
entertainment

Los Angeles

For orders and information contact the publisher:

Cobblestone Entertainment
P.O. Box 894
Palos Verdes Estates, California 90274

http://www.cobbles.com
1-888-STORYBOOK

This book has not been commissioned, licensed or endorsed by any organization associated with former members of SIMPP, nor is any sanction by such parties implied. Although the sources in this book have been researched for accuracy and completeness, neither the author nor the publisher assume any responsibility for any unintentional errors, omissions, or other inconsistencies herein. Any offense to people or institutions past, present, or future is unintentional.

Book cover design by the Prism Media Company, Los Angeles.

Photo credits include the following: W. Wanger and O. Welles courtesy of the Academy of Motion Picture Arts and Sciences; S. Goldwyn courtesy of Cinema Cavalcade; M. Pickford courtesy of the Berlin Company; A. Korda courtesy of Stephen Mitchell; other images from the author's private collection. All photos and other materials have be published in accordance with international copyright and public domain laws.

Printed by Technical Communication Services, North Kansas City, Missouri.

9 8 7 6 5 4 3 2 1

First Printing - 2000

Cobblestone books may be purchased in bulk at special discounts for sales, promotion, fund-raising, or educational purposes. Special editions may be created to specifications. For details, contact:

Special Sales Department
Cobblestone Entertainment
P.O. Box 894
Palos Verdes Estates, CA 90274.

Library of Congress Cataloging-in-Publication Data
Aberdeen, J. A.
   Hollywood renegades : the Society of Independent Motion Picture Producers / by
J. A. Aberdeen.
      p.   cm.
   Includes bibliographical references and index.
   ISBN 1-890110-24-8 (alk. paper)
      1. Society of Independent Motion Picture Producers—History. 2. Independent
filmmakers—United States—Biography. I. Title.
   PN1999.S63 A24 2001
      791.43'0232'092279494—dc21   00-9588
                                                                           CIP

Contents

PRELUDE

1

Introduction

Hollywood 1939

BY THE TIME the movie moguls celebrated the golden year of the American film golden age, Hollywood had perfected the most complete and complex system of filmmaking in existence. Each major movie company had vast resources that were coordinated in such a way to give the studio authority over every aspect of film, from the beginning of a story idea to the actual showing in theaters. This highly-controlled process was known as the Hollywood studio system.

Decades of merger and consolidation gave rise to eight corporations that dominated the film market—Paramount, Metro-Goldwyn-Mayer, Twentieth Century-Fox, Warner Bros., RKO, Universal, Columbia, and United Artists. In Los Angeles these majors operated the world's most illustrious film factories with a virtual lock on talent contracts. From New York, their corporate offices controlled film marketing and distribution. And across the country, studio-owned theater chains dictated the nation's box office. The studio system enabled the eight film giants to control a combined 95 percent of all industry revenue with a façade of glamour and showmanship that obscured one of the most potent oligopolies in United States corporate history. The domination of the American film market was so absolute that no film could feasibly receive a national release without going through one of the eight major distributors. The system also precluded the work of any filmmaker who wished to operate independent of a major studio.

The grand old studio system survived government legislation, economic depression, organized labor, and wartime conflict. But it was challenged by a group of eight producers—Charles Chaplin, Walt Disney, Samuel Goldwyn, Alexander Korda, Mary Pickford, David O. Selznick, Walter Wanger, and Orson Welles—who despised the en-masse filmmaking of the major studios. The producers had grown weary of the unsuccessful attempts of the government to curb the power of the vertically-integrated corporations. These filmmakers joined together to form an association of independents designed to end the assembly-line studio methodology, and replace it with a new structure based on independent film production and single-film units focused on creating quality entertainment. By the time they had finished, the old-time Hollywood studio system had shriveled and the stranglehold was broken. *Hollywood Renegades* is the story of this group—the Society of Independent Motion Picture Producers (SIMPP).

INDEPENDENT PRODUCTION, AS practiced by SIMPP, meant that a producer would operate a company that would enter into a distribution deal with a Hollywood studio, but remain off of the studio payroll. The filmmakers would finance their own movies, develop their own projects, hire their own talent, and make their own films without any studio interference. When film production was complete, then a major studio would serve as distributor, charging a fee (usually between 15 and 35 percent of the box office), and the independent producer would receive a share of the profits.

These independent producers of old Hollywood were not art-house filmmakers nor champions of avant-garde cinema. They were showmen; their specialty was the "prestige picture"—the A-class movie with large budgets and high profit potential. Unlike the major Hollywood film factories that released upwards of 50 features each year, the independent producers concentrated on only one or two annual releases, leaving the independents in a far more vulnerable position than the large studios which could absorb the costs of a box-office bomb.

"There are two kinds of producers," Sam Goldwyn explained. "One is a film manufacturer who turns out many pictures, some of them good, more of them not so good. I once tried being a film manufacturer but I didn't like it. There were too many pictures going out under my name which were not satisfactory to me. Since then, I've tried to be the other kind of producer, making fewer pictures but each one the best I could make it."

When David O. Selznick went independent, he told his partners, "It is my opinion, generally speaking, and from long observation, that there are only two kinds of merchandise that can be made profitably in this business—either the very cheap pictures or the expensive pictures. . . . If we don't deliver really topnotch product, we are not going to get terms and we are going to take a terrible beating after the first few pictures. There is no alternative open to us but to attempt to compete with the very best."

Most of the producers believed that prestige film production was the only way they could distinguish their material. "I can't afford to make a cheap picture," Alexander Korda, with his characteristic whimsy, was fond of saying. The independents produced only a fraction of Hollywood's total films, but their batting average generated a high-profile reputation among their peers, and their films have become memorable classics.

A case in point was 1939, the year which was known for its top-flight Hollywood studio classics including *The Wizard of Oz* (MGM), *Mr. Smith Goes to Washington* (Columbia), *Union Pacific* (Paramount), and *Dark Victory* (Warner). But among the year's most significant releases were out-of-house productions, by those who, two years later, would found the Society of Independent Motion Picture Producers: Samuel Goldwyn's *Wuthering Heights*, Walter Wanger's *Stagecoach*, and David O. Selznick's epic paragon *Gone With the Wind*. Amidst formidable competition, their films were remarkable both as blockbusters and cinematic benchmarks.

In old Hollywood, just as in modern Hollywood, there were any number of independent-type arrangements, and the various terms fluctuated considerably. In some cases, the independent deals involved financing from the distributor or the use of the studio backlot, which meant that *independence* was a relative ideal. Walter Wanger facetiously defined an independent producer as someone who is dependent on the banks, the press, the distributors, and ultimately the public. Even as independents, the SIMPP producers worked alongside the major studios, frequently borrowed from the studio pools of movie stars, and depended heavily on the studio-owned theater chains. Though they operated within the industry mainstream, they flaunted their production freedom from the studio system and continually sought to undermine the vertically-integrated corporations.

During the 1920s and 1930s, the independent movement tested the limitations the studio system, but the Hollywood giants proved resilient. Part of the difficulty in bringing monopoly charges against the major studios was that the Big Eight stranglehold did not appear as dominant on paper as it was in practice. Only five of the Big Eight owned their own theater chains, for a combined total of about 16 percent of all of the domestic movie theaters. However, the studios turned this minority share into an exhibition monopoly by concentrating their theater holdings in key metropolitan areas which generated the most revenue. In 1939, the Hollywood studios controlled 126 of the nation's 163 most prestigious first-run theaters. Furthermore, the Big Eight companies showed preference to each other's films, allowing them to suppress competition. This gave the major studios the power to arbitrarily shut out any outside filmmaker, independent or otherwise. A big budget independent film was considered a doomed venture without a Big Eight distribution deal. Even the banks refused to loan money to a production company unless the producer secured a major distribution contract first.

Notwithstanding these disadvantages, the independent producers were criticized for their close ties to the studios, and frequently were brought under the same condemnation as the Big Eight. After all, some of the most high-profile SIMPP members were founders and/or owners of United Artists, one the major distributors. Critics of SIMPP claimed that "independent producer" was a self-styled term that misrepresented the true relationship between the film-makers and the studios. To complicate the situation, the trade publications applied the designation "independent" in a rather loose fashion, often to describe a studio filmmaker or performer whose contract provided some amount of creative control.

The independents did not condemn film studios per se; they despised the *studio system* which made assembly-line films and engendered monopoly control. This self-contradiction became a unique dynamic of the SIMPP movement. The producers professed their autonomy from the studio system but maintained close ties with the major distributors in a resentful manner. Consequently, the independent producers spent a great deal of effort trying to distance themselves from the vertically-integrated Hollywood giants. The creation of SIMPP helped the independents to disassociate themselves from the film oligopoly and project an image of defiance in the industry.

The Society believed that its mission was logical: that films should be made, marketed, and shown as individual works—creatively overseen by a single individual. SIMPP sought to make independent production, rather than studio filmmaking, the new paradigm for Hollywood. To do so would require the upheaval of the studio system.

THE SOCIETY OF INDEPENDENT Motion Picture Producers had its origin in the Hollywood antitrust case that enveloped the American film industry in the late 1930s. Acting upon repeated complaints from independent producers and small theater-owners, the United States Department of Justice initiated an antitrust suit against the eight major studios in July 1938. The attorney general accused the studios of creating an illegal conspiracy in restraint of trade by monopolizing production, distribution, and exhibition. The suit, one of the largest antitrust cases ever filed by the government against an industry, took its name after the biggest of the eight defendants, and became known as the *Paramount* case [*United States v. Paramount Pictures, Inc. et al*, 334 U.S. 131 (1948)].

The eight majors were divided into two groups. The theater-owning companies, known as the Big Five, were Paramount Pictures Inc., Loew's Inc. (parent company of MGM), Twentieth Century-Fox Film Corporation, Warner Bros. Pictures Inc., and RKO-Radio Pictures Inc. The Little Three—Universal Pictures Company Inc., Columbia Pictures Corporation, and United Artists Corporation—did not own theaters, but were alleged co-conspirators who upheld a supporting role in the industry, completed the oligopoly, and claimed a portion of the film bounty. The Justice Department demanded that the eight studios cease all anti-competitive practices and that the Big Five "divest themselves of all interest and ownership, both direct and indirect, in theatres and theatre holdings."

With the Hollywood studios on one side, and the independent producers, small theater owners, and U.S. government on the other, industry conflict continued to intensify as the case proceeded to trial in 1940. The independent producers awaited the studio system's day of reckoning, and were stunned when, only one week into preliminary arguments, the studios cut a deal with the government.

Known as the Consent Decree of 1940, the agreement between the Big Five and the Justice Department permitted the studios to keep their theater chains in exchange for the studios' promise to limit certain monopolistic practices. Eager to avoid a lengthy trial with potentially devastating effects, the studios successfully launched the first of a long series of compromises and stall tactics that postponed the independents' triumph for over ten years.

Although several key independent producers participated in the early stages of the antitrust case, the *Paramount* suit before World War II had focused primarily on the woes of the independent exhibitors—the theater chains which were not affiliated with the Hollywood studios. To the independent producers, the advent of a consent decree proved that they could not trust the government and the independent theaters to enact a judgement equitable to all independent parties. The situation worsened when the independent exhibitor organizations grew dissatisfied with the Consent Decree of 1940, and began to make their own deal with the Big Five—to the disadvantage of the independent producers.

Alienated by their exhibitor allies, and with the antitrust case reaching a standstill, the independent producers combined to form the Society of Independent Motion Picture Producers. Organized secretly in 1941, then publicly announced in early 1942, the group intended to do collectively what no independent producer could do as a maverick—end the Hollywood studio monopoly of the American film industry.

Most of the SIMPP founders had years of filmmaking experience fighting for creative and economic freedom. When they joined together in their collective effort, some of the producers were at the peak of their influence in Hollywood, while others were at important crossroads in their careers.

Charlie Chaplin, the screen's most highly-regarded comedian, was also one of the most versatile talents in Hollywood. As writer, director, and actor, he had grown accustomed to lavishing years of painstaking effort on each of his features. As independent producer, Chaplin worked at his own pace without having to answer to any studio boss. His pioneering achievements in independent production showed other artists how to use their own companies to maintain complete creative control.

Walt Disney, the cartoon filmmaker from the midwest, established his studio as Hollywood's preeminent animation house with an uncompromising attitude toward independence that gave him the freedom to take the animated cartoon to artistic and commercial prominence. Disney overturned box office figures with *Snow White and the Seven Dwarfs* (1937), and, during Hollywood's golden age, was one of the most venerated and decorated filmmakers in the American cinema.

Samuel Goldwyn, the oldest producer of the group, was one of the founding fathers of Hollywood, and an instrumental figure in the early history of both Paramount and Metro-Goldwyn-Mayer. He opted out of the studio executive class, motivated in part by his "lone wolf" nature as well as his inability to deal with partners. A one-time Hollywood mogul archetype, he reinvented himself as an independent producer, forming a production company that became the model for the independents who followed.

Hungarian cosmopolitan Alexander Korda was one of Hollywood's promising imported directors who turned his back on the American studio system to become an empire-builder overseas. Settling in London, he intended to make his independent production company the most important studio outside the United States, before setting out again to conquer Hollywood.

Mary Pickford was one of the screen's most remarkable figures who embraced a mixture of acting presence, filmmaking ability, and astute business aptitude that was almost otherworldly. She used her screen idol status to become her own producer, and ultimately her own company boss, while remaining one of the most outspoken proponents of independent production.

David O. Selznick was the son of industry pioneer Lewis J. Selznick, and the beneficiary of a childhood immersion in independent film production. Working within the major Hollywood studios, he became a supervisor, and later studio production head, before heading his own independent production company.

Walter Wanger, a tweed-suited college graduate with a background in theater, also successfully worked his way up the studio chain of command before getting out at the top. His style and mannerisms evoked the image of consummate Hollywood film producer, and lent itself well to both his studio occupation and his independent producer mantra.

The final founding member of SIMPP was Orson Welles, then a virtual newcomer to the film industry. The writer-director-actor attained unprecedented public attention in theater and radio. Then, at age 24 Welles produced his extraordinary film debut *Citizen Kane* (1941). He was a skilled producer and an influential member of SIMPP, but his revolutionary film directing has overshadowed his many important contributions to the industry.

The formation of the Society of Independent Motion Picture Producers became a turning point in the *Paramount* antitrust case.

SIMPP lobbied within the industry, and recruited other producers who tired of the studio restraints, including Howard Hughes, Hal Roach, Leo McCarey, Sol Lesser, James Cagney, Bing Crosby, John Huston, Preston Sturges, Sam Spiegel, and Stanley Kramer. Gradually the focus of the *Paramount* case shifted away from the independent exhibitors as SIMPP began to steer the events of the antitrust suit in favor of the independent producers.

They continually petitioned the government during the trial, but concluded that the most effective way to impel change would be to take the case to the people. The SIMPP founders used their house-hold-name status as a weapon against the studios—gobbling up headlines, attracting attention from national media, and generating public awareness of the leviathan behind the Hollywood glitter machine.

SIMPP also waged an all-out war on the most controversial old-time studio practice known as block booking. Under block booking arrangements, a distributor would sell its films in packages on an all-or-nothing basis—usually requiring theaters to buy several mediocre pictures for every desirable one. Because the studios made mass-produced films, they also sold them in bulk.

Block booking was wholly unacceptable to the independent producers for a number of reasons. To begin with, block booking made it difficult for the independents to acquire film bookings when theaters were required to purchase all the studio films they needed in a single package. But even worse, the independents found that their films were being used by the distributors to pawn off low-budget studio B-pictures. The producers believed that block booking encouraged slack filmmaking by forcing inferior films on the theaters and the moviegoers. The SIMPP members brought this obscure practice to the fore until the courts finally abolished block booking—which has remained illegal to this day.

SIMPP continued to intensify its antitrust activity throughout the 1940s. The group filed an *amicus curiae* that enabled friend-of-the-court collaboration between the Society and the Justice Department, and turned SIMPP into one of the most active participants in the antitrust suit. The producers also hired Ellis Arnall, the trustbusting former governor of Georgia, to serve as Society president, bringing with him his political connections and progressive antitrust agenda.

Finally, the 1948 Supreme Court decision provided the independent producers with victory. The Big Eight were declared guilty of conspiracy. The Hollywood studios were forced to sell their theater holdings, and all film companies were prohibited from oppressive practices like block booking. The success of the *Paramount* case signaled the demise of the studio era. In the years prior to the decision, the major studios had softened to independent production; and once block booking and theater owning were eliminated, the studios turned to the independent producers for their films. By the mid-1950s, the majority of major distributor releases were provided by independent production companies, as SIMPP had envisioned years earlier.

Interestingly, following the disintegration of the studio system, SIMPP itself unexpectedly declined. Though SIMPP helped make independent production the dominant form of filmmaking in Hollywood, ironically the movement grew too rapidly, and SIMPP as an organization did not expand accordingly. The Society's influence was undeniable, and its triumph over the studio system was monumental, but the independent producers lacked cohesion. Without the antitrust fight to unify the organization, the members lapsed into their natural state as stubborn, idiosyncratic, and disagreeable partners. After the studio opposition collapsed, the independent organization eroded, going from industry headline to film history footnote. In 1958 as the last of the major studio theaters chains was completing divestiture, SIMPP operations were curtailed and absorbed by one of the most successful independents, Walt Disney Productions.

RESEARCH FOR *Hollywood Renegades* is based on documents that have remained unpublished in the years since the demise of SIMPP. The author has uncovered extensive SIMPP material among the collections of the founding members, particularly David O. Selznick, Mary Pickford, Walter Wanger, and Walt Disney.

Original court records also helped flesh out the history of the organization from an antitrust standpoint. The trade publications and numerous publicity events of the SIMPP members have proved valuable by illustrating the influence of SIMPP in the public arena. The sheer amount of exposure the Society received within the industry and in national publications of its day has made the forgotten nature of the group even more fascinating from a historical perspective.

While some of the works of past biographers mention the trust-busting efforts of individual producers, no previous film history has studied the collective efforts of the independents who joined together to protest the studio system. *Hollywood Renegades* discusses the steps that the SIMPP members took to end the studio lock on American film production.

The existence of SIMPP allowed the producers to romanticize their position in Hollywood history, as most of them viewed their struggle with the studio system on an epic scale worthy of a scenario from one of their own films. While many of the non-antitrust activities have been outlined in this book—such as the blacklist, censorship, and the advent of television—*Hollywood Renegades* focuses on the monopoly war that served as the primary objective of the SIMPP organization. The history of the Society of Independent Motion Picture Producers provides a revealing look at the independent film movement and the transition of the American cinema away from the studio era.

The story of SIMPP also demonstrates a common historical pattern (and one of the most potent ironies about independent film-making)—the inevitable tendency of the independent victors to replace a defeated monopoly with a new monopoly of their own. Even the major studios all once had renegade roots. The studio czars who resisted SIMPP were all former independents themselves. Adolph Zukor, William Fox, and Carl Laemmle were one-time trustbusters who battled the Motion Picture Patents monopoly organized under Thomas Edison in 1908. A generation before SIMPP, "outlaw" independent companies like Paramount, Fox, and Universal moved out west, established Hollywood, and them went on to create an even more sophisticated monopoly that discriminated against other independents.

Hollywood Renegades traces the history of the independent movement back to the silent era in order to elaborate on the rise and fall of monopolies which characterized SIMPP. Chapter 2 provides this overview, without being overly meticulous, while chapters 3 and 4 discuss the antitrust setting that led to the formation of the Society of Independent Motion Picture Producers in chapter 5.

This book also discusses the manner in which the studios themselves adopted the ideology of the SIMPP producers. By adjusting to the methods of the independents, the studios reemerged in conglomerate fashion. The author argues that the independent movement led by SIMPP provided the blueprint for the rise of the diverse media companies of modern Hollywood, as embodied in the corporate progeny of SIMPP founder Walt Disney. *Hollywood Renegades* also shows that certain trends, like the rise of the blockbuster-driven industry mentality and the application of corporate synergy, are not recent entertainment developments, but ones which were popularized years earlier by the SIMPP producers.

While brief career profiles the SIMPP members are provided throughout the text of this book, *Hollywood Renegades* avoids the anecdotal filmmaking exploits of each producer in the interest of focusing on new historical information concerning the Society of Independent Motion Picture Producers. For readers who desire more specifics on the filmmakers featured in this book, the author's supplementary research material has been collected by the publisher Cobblestone Entertainment on its website located at *http://www.cobbles.com*.

The online SIMPP database is provided free of charge to promote film scholarship on the independent movement of the cinema. The website provides sources and additional information on many other aspects of this vast and fascinating topic which could hardly be accommodated in any one volume.

PART I

Hollywood Before SIMPP

2

"Bust the Trust— Go Independent"

Monopoly and integration became unavoidable trends from the earliest days of the film industry. The need for large companies to create a predictable commercial pattern out of the inherent uncertainties of the movie business gave rise to the ever-increasing size of the film corporations themselves. However, in each era of movie consolidation, an independent movement consisting of innovative outsiders has always been present to challenge the power structure of the industry.

In December 1908, the motion picture inventors and industry leaders organized the first great film trust called the Motion Picture Patents Company, designed to bring stability to the chaotic early film years characterized by patent wars and litigation. The Edison Film Manufacturing Company, the Biograph company, and the other Motion Picture Patents members ended their competitive feuding in favor of a cooperative system that provided industry domination. By pooling their interests, the member companies legally monopolized the business, and demanded licencing fees from all film producers, distributors, and exhibitors. A January 1909 deadline was set for all companies to comply with the licence. By February, unlicenced outlaws, who referred to themselves as *independents* protested the trust and carried on business without submitting to the Edison monopoly. In the summer of 1909 the independent movement was in full-swing, with producers and theater owners using illegal equipment and imported film stock to create their own underground market.

With the country experiencing a tremendous expansion in the number of nickelodeons, the Patents Company reacted to the independent movement by forming a strong-arm subsidiary known as the General Film Company to block the entry of non-licenced independents. With coercive tactics that have become legendary, General Film confiscated unlicenced equipment, discontinued product supply to theaters which showed unlicenced films, and effectively monopolized distribution with the acquisition of all U.S. film exchanges, except for the one owned by the independent William Fox who defied the Trust even after his licence was revoked.

Many of the early independents were resilient film exhibitors who ventured into production when they found their supply of film threatened. Carl Laemmle (Independent Motion Picture Company or IMP), Harry E. Aitken (Majestic Films), and Adolph Zukor (Famous Players) were among the pioneering independents who protested the Trust, and then laid the foundation for the Hollywood studios. Having entered the business through exhibition, they determined that they liked production better, and got out of the theater business as the nickelodeon boom ended around 1911.

When the independents started to band together, they began to display their own monopolistic tendencies in a remarkably short time. In 1910 several of the most prominent independents including Laemmle and Aitken, organized a consortium called the Motion Picture Distributing and Sales Company in a preemptive attempt to take control of the film industry. Commonly known as the Sales Company, the independent organization used its consolidated strength to match the influence of Patents Company. Non-affiliated independents complained against the discriminatory practices of the so-called independents and the Sales Company. "Is the independent market controlled by a trust too?," one trade advertisement from January 1911 protested. "Don't be bamboozled by the cry of independence and business freedom."

Even amongst themselves, the independents struggled to maintain harmony in their union. Disagreements between independents divided the Sales Company, and splintered the independent market into smaller factions—some of which would develop into the major studios of Hollywood. The division came in early 1912 when Harry Aitken at Majestic lured Mary Pickford away from IMP, capturing Laemmle's biggest star. While independents had commonly raided the Patents companies, Laemmle took offense at the outlaws stealing from each other.

Laemmle tried to pull rank on Aitken, offering Majestic substandard distribution terms at the Sales Company. Instead, Aitken withdrew and convinced ten other companies to join him to form the Film Supply Company of America which became known as the Mutual Film Corporation in March 1912. The remnants of the weakened Sales Company also adopted a more intuitive-sounding tradename, and reorganized on June 8 as the Universal Film Manufacturing Company.

This early history of independent film provides revealing examples of characteristics that carried over into later independent movements. Obviously, as demonstrated by the Sales Company, once the independents achieved relative stability, they used their leverage to oppress the next wave of independents, proving that the film industry could never remain free for long without the threat of monopolization.

Also the disaffection of the Sales Company illustrated the inability of independents to get along with each other, particularly as they became more established. The independents were highly competitive by nature, and when their common enemy the Patents Trust weakened, the independent association degenerated into squabbles over property, distribution, and profits. While many waves of independents would come and go over the years, the hostility existing between independents reoccurred—notably at United Artists and also at the Society of Independent Motion Picture Producers.

MANY OF THE SIMPP producers traced their independent filmmaking roots to director D. W. Griffith who defected from the Trust, only to find similarly hostile conditions with the outlaws who began to represent the status quo. Harry Aitken lured the famed director away from Biograph in December 1913, and brought Griffith to Mutual to make some of his early features. Unfortunately Aitken and Griffith ran into problems with Mutual when cost overruns on Griffith's Civil War epic alarmed the studio. Aitken was forced to reimburse the company, taking his and Griffith's production independent. As it turned out, the film *The Birth of a Nation* (1915) became one of the most profitable blockbusters in film history. It showed that filmmakers could protect their creative vision by going independent, and insure a hefty box office reward without having to put up with studio interference. The Edison Trust was not yet dismantled, and already the filmmakers were rebelling against the new studio regime.

After Mutual had ousted Aitken, the studio lured Charlie Chaplin away from Essanay, one of the Patents Trust companies, to make two-reel comedies under the Lone Star Mutual banner. Fourteen months and 12 films later in 1917, Chaplin left Mutual to become an independent producer and start making feature films.

Meanwhile Harry Aitken, who accumulated a personal fortune from *The Birth of a Nation*, masterminded the July 1915 agreement to organize the illustrious Triangle Pictures Corporation. Auspicious but ill-fated, Triangle was envisioned as a prestige studio based on the producing abilities of ace filmmakers D. W. Griffith, Thomas Ince, and Mack Sennett. The studio suffered from bloat, and lost all three of its principle producers in 1917. Triangle gradually dwindled, and was swallowed by the emerging Hollywood studios. The triangle-shaped Culver City lot was sold to Goldwyn Pictures, later to become the home of Metro-Goldwyn-Mayer. Triangle's high-profile contracts were absorbed in the rise of Paramount, and Aitken became a forgotten would-be mogul.

As the independent outlaws flourished, the Motion Picture Patents Company was also hit with antitrust charges by the United States government. In October 1915, the courts determined that the

Patents Company and its General Film division acted as a monopoly in restraint of trade, and later ordered it disintegrated. But clearly by the time the decision was handed down, the independents had already outmaneuvered the Trust. The Edison monopoly had taken a retrogressive stance to the innovative industry reforms introduced by the outlaws.

At a time when the American independents and foreign filmmakers were creating feature length movies, the Trust clung to the familiar short-film format. Generally speaking, the Patents Trust also resisted turning their stock actors into recognizable performers, while the outlaws like Laemmle and Zukor were developing the star system into a powerful marketing tool. Furthermore, by moving their studios out west, the outlaws were not only capitalizing on California's optimal year-round outdoor shooting conditions, they were also pioneering a division between the east-coast business headquarters and the west-coast production operation that became another trademark of the Hollywood studio system. Historians of early film have pointed out that each of these innovations originated within the ranks of the Patents Company. However the unwillingness of the Trust to adapt to the changes cleared the way for the rise of the Hollywood studio system while the Edison monopoly perished.

Perhaps the most fundamental transformation that shifted the balance of power from the Motion Picture Patents Company to the emerging Hollywood studios was the Hodkinson system of distribution. Previously, the antiquated distributing methods of the Patents Company limited industry growth, and made it difficult for producers to recoup profits and improve film product. The Hodkinson method took the haphazard film market and created a dynamic distribution revolution that made large scale film production.

During the pre-studio era, movie releases were generally handled in one of two ways—either by *states rights* or by *road show*. In the states rights method, producers sold their films on a territorial basis to a local salesperson who extracted as much money as possible from the movie until the worn and scratched film print literally fell apart from sheer use. States rights had been the most logical way for a producer to tackle a nationwide release. Copyright holders sold the actual copies of their movies; films were sold by their length, usually ten cents per linear foot of film. It was also ideal for short films that had brief stays in the nickelodeons. But for feature film distribution, states rights proved ineffective. The producer made money on the initial sale of the film print, but the states rights salesperson reaped the largest rewards. Producers had slim profit margins while many films failed to return their costs.

For a road show release, the film was treated as a special theatrical engagement. The producer would contract directly with a movie theater—usually at the largest and most prestigious of theaters—to show the film with reserved seating and inflated admission prices. With only a couple of showings per day to emphasize the film's prestige attraction, the road show method was one of the most profitable ways to debut a feature. Road show box office went straight to the producer, but by its very nature, a road show could only be performed only on a regional basis.

Many silent films utilized a combination of road show and states rights. For instance, *The Birth of a Nation* road show engagements allowed Griffith and Aitken to skim the cream from the most lucrative urban markets, and helped generate mass appeal that would interest more states-rights salesmen to handle the film. This made actual box office figures impossible to determine, and gave rise to the exaggerated gross estimates for *The Birth of a Nation* that kept Griffith's film on the all-time box office champion list for more than 50 years.

The road show method never really went away during the studio era. But states rights was completely displaced by the Hodkinson distribution method which gave studios control over distribution.

The person responsible for this radical shift in the industry was William Wadsworth Hodkinson, an independent who defected from the Trust. Though not really a producer himself, Hodkinson was nevertheless a film visionary who revolutionized the business with a distribution masterstroke that became standard practice. His story illustrates the downfall of the Patents Company, the coming of age of Hollywood studios, and how his distribution method, so ideally suited to independent film production was hijacked by the rising Paramount Pictures to become a system of oppression.

W. W. Hodkinson opened his first film exchange in Ogden, Utah in 1907, at the age of 26. Within a few years he became Special Representative to the General Film Company representing the Trust in Salt Lake City and Los Angeles. He envisioned a nation-wide distribution structure that would make states rights obsolete, and provide profit-sharing with producers to encourage filmmakers to concentrate on higher quality films that would yield higher box office.

Under the Hodkinson system, the distributor would provide a cash advance to an independent producer to cover the costs of pro-ducing each feature film. The distributor then received the *exclu-sive* rights to the finished movie, using a network of exchanges to control distribution and marketing, and even offering to pay for the producer's film prints and advertising. Hodkinson kept 35 percent of the box office as a distribution fee, and gave the rest of the prof-its back to the producer. Hodkinson discovered that by financing film producers, the distributor was guaranteed a steady stream of high-class pictures without ever having to operate a film camera, while the producers themselves made much more than they would under the states rights system. The Hodkinson distribution system proved so advantageous for all involved that, with slight modifica-tion, it has remained in full practice in Hollywood to this day.

In April 1911, Hodkinson began to implement his system by reorganizing the San Francisco area for General Film. The test mar-ket generated fantastic results, but in 1912 W. W. Hodkinson encountered resistance from the Trust which refused to enact his new procedure in other regions.

In November 1912 he made two comparative charts "predicting, in one chart what the future of the picture industry would be, espe-cially that of General Film, if my methods were adopted national-ly; and what would happen if they were not." He traveled to New York, for a frustrating encounter that extended until February. San Francisco representatives sent telegrams in favor of Hodkinson's reforms. He persuaded two leaders of the General Film Company, but his policy was refused by the Patents Company members as a whole.

During this trip to New York in late 1912, Hodkinson established ties with some of the important independents including Adolph Zukor, who was then struggling under the states rights method, and was the kind of producer who would benefit greatly by this new distribution procedure. In May 1913 the president of General Film, under pressure from the Trust members, rejected Hodkinson's proposal, and even asked him to undo his successful San Francisco reforms. Hodkinson declined "knowing that it would mean my dismissal from my position—which it did."

Hodkinson formed the Progressive Company, a west coast-based operation that distributed films for a number of independent production companies like the Famous Players Film Company (formed by Adolph Zukor in 1912) and the Jesse L. Lasky Feature Play Company (founded in 1913 by Lasky, his brother-in-law Samuel Goldfish, and first-time director Cecil B. DeMille).

Hodkinson decided to expand his west coast business into a national organization in early 1914, but discovered another east coast company with the same name as his own Progressive Pictures. When he went to New York in 1914, he changed his company's name to Paramount Pictures—allegedly searching through the P-section of the phone book for another alliterative name, and sketching a new company logo himself on a pad of desk-blot paper. Paramount Pictures, Inc. was organized on May 8, 1914. One week later the three most important producers, including Zukor and Lasky, signed five year contracts to distribute their films.

Hodkinson claimed that the producers initially considered Hodkinson's new distribution method foolish—and entered into the long-term five-year deals before they discovered the ingenuity of Hodkinson's unconventional selling approach. The producers then realized that under Hodkinson's plan, the distributor was in a far more powerful position, controlling the sale of the films, and taking its distribution fee before the producer. Though the producers were far better off than they were under states rights, they resented the amount of profits they shared with the distributor. This tension

between the producers and distributors became one of the fundamental conflicts for the SIMPP independents in later years. And
even though Zukor himself was once an independent producer on
the losing end of an unfavorable distribution deal, he seemed to
harbor no sympathy for the next generation of independents who
struggled as he had before he become a tycoon.

Zukor even tried to get out of his contract once he realized how
effectively distribution controlled the film market. W. W.
Hodkinson, as president of Paramount Pictures, refused to release
Zukor from his contract. Zukor, after he had been humiliatingly
rebuffed, confided in Jesse Lasky. "The man has ice in his veins,"
Zukor said of Hodkinson. So Adolph Zukor devised a plan, involving his friend Lasky, that would turn the tables on Hodkinson.

Only one year into his five-year contract—and desperately
wanting out—Zukor surprisingly renegotiated a new 25 year deal
with Paramount on March 1, 1915. By May, Zukor and Lasky had
sold a 51 percent interest in their production companies to
Paramount Pictures. This made Zukor sneakily subordinate to
Hodkinson's Paramount; but it also made Zukor and Lasky cash-
rich franchise holders, and opened up a newly extended line of
credit that allowed them to secretly accumulate Paramount stock.

Within one year, Zukor and Lasky together acquired a majority
of the capital stock of Paramount Pictures, Inc., and ousted the
Hodkinson regime. New directors were elected, followed by the
forced resignation of W. W. Hodkinson and his treasurer Raymond
Pawley on June 13, 1916. Zukor instituted his own president Hiram
Abrams as the new head of Paramount. On July 19, 1916, Zukor
and Lasky merged their companies with Paramount, and created the
Famous Players-Lasky Corporation, a $12.5 million producer-
distributor—the largest film company at the time.

Hodkinson, who did not completely sever his ties with
Paramount until 1924, had always advocated the complete separa-
tion of production, distribution and exhibition. After the coup at
Paramount, Hodkinson remained active as a distributor, forming
Superpictures Incorporated in November 1916 with Raymond
Pawley. He also served as president of the Triangle Distributing

Company before leaving to form the W. W. Hodkinson Company, later reorganized as Producers Distributing Company. PDC, which lasted until 1929, played an important role during Cecil B. DeMille's short-lived but ambitious plans as a full-fledged independent filmmaker in the late 1920s. Hodkinson later served as an airplane manufacturer, then as a commercial aviator in Central America until a series of accidents forced his company out of Guatemala in 1936. Over the years Hodkinson made occasional appearances in the industry, protested vertical integration throughout his life, and died in 1971.

BY COMBINING PRODUCTION with an efficient distribution system, former independent Adolph Zukor inaugurated a new era of studio consolidation. He also redirected the development of the studio system by elaborating on the Hodkinson distribution system with several of his own innovations.

To begin with, Zukor refined the classification of movies based on prestige factors: budget, movie stars, subject matter. His grading scale of A-pictures, B-pictures, and so-on, dictated everything from production value to marketing strategy.

The distributor also had a corresponding grading system for theaters which rated each movie house according to its size, location, and reputation. This gave rise to the studio policy known as *run-zone-clearance*, which brought strict organization to the national film market. The country was broken down into zones, and in each zone the largest theaters were given access to the most desirable films first. Each film went through a succession of releases, known as runs—first run, second run, subsequent run, etc. To maintain order in the system, the distributors set a mandatory time lapse between runs known as clearance. The first-run market, which received the newest films and charged the highest admission prices, was the most desirable run. Each film became less valuable as it made its way through the various runs into the rural areas and neighborhood theaters. In cities where a sophisticated run-zone-clearance was established, a movie could go through up to eleven runs, taking a year to complete the full theatrical distribution cycle.

Adolph Zukor has also been credited with originating the signature practice of the studio era—block booking. He realized that by selling his films in packages, a movie theater that wanted one of his A-pictures could be forced to buy several inferior B-pictures. This created a guaranteed market for even the most mediocre studio films, as theaters were compelled to buy the films sight-unseen. The practice evolved over many years and became the rallying-point for SIMPP producers who denounced block booking as a discriminatory, oppressive distribution method that was used to eliminate competition.

Allegedly Adolph Zukor originated block booking in reaction to the enormous popularity of the films featuring his contract star Mary Pickford. Zukor may have also been inspired by industry reports in 1915 that Essanay was having such unprecedented success with Charlie Chaplin comedies that his two-reel shorts were frequently carrying the sale of the accompanying Essanay feature. Zukor decided to sell each Pickford movie in a package of Famous Players-Lasky films, so that her famous golden curls could be used to foist unwelcome block booking baggage on the theaters. Soon all Paramount films were sold in blocks, and block booking rapidly spread throughout the other Hollywood studios. The independent-minded Pickford threatened to leave Famous Players-Lasky until an anti-block booking provision was written into her contract. She remained one of the most outspoken critics of block booking, and later became a founder of the SIMPP movement. She spent decades trying to eliminate the oppressive practice that was spawned by her immense popularity.

Other empire builders were at work in the film industry, including William Fox, Marcus Loew, Samuel Goldfish (a.k.a Goldwyn), and Carl Laemmle, but Zukor's Paramount-Famous-Lasky Corporation remained the preeminent distributor during the silent era. Zukor also remained the representative film baron of his generation—the self-made immigrant garment dealer who first became an outlaw filmmaker then a Hollywood mogul. "Zukor has been portrayed as a modern combination of Napoleon and Machiavelli with dashes of oriental subtlety;" wrote businessman-turned-film-chronicler Benjamin B. Hampton, "or as an inspired genius, who, while selling furs in New York and Chicago shops, shrewdly planned to make himself dictator of the entertainment world and ruthlessly forced his way to the top."

The theater chains resented the amount of power commanded by Famous Players-Lasky. Contracts with exhibitors frequently gave the producer-distributor the authority to set admission prices, stipulate clearance, and sometimes even select the play date. The devastating effects of block booking also intensified the animosity the exhibitors felt toward the Hollywood studios. So in retaliation, the exhibitors decided to form their own studio. Twenty-seven major theater chains invaded distribution in April 1917 when they amalgamated their holdings into the First National Exhibitors Circuit. Within two years First National expanded to over 600 theaters, creating the most important rival to Zukor. The rise of First National created the most competitive commercial war since the fall of the Patents Trust and became a windfall for independents.

First National attracted some of the industry's top producers with lucrative contracts that also offered creative freedom. High-profile actors, directors, and other artists were offered independent producer status, which most integrated distributors like Zukor had been unwilling to grant. First National adopted the Hodkinson system of distribution, utilizing it in the manner which it was created: for independent film production.

In April 1918 First National signed an eight picture deal with Charlie Chaplin, outbidding Jesse Lasky at Paramount. No longer an employee as he had been before at Mutual, Chaplin became an independent producer with his own filmmaking facility on the corner of Sunset Boulevard and La Brea Avenue in Hollywood. First National advanced Chaplin money to cover production costs, paid for his prints and advertising, and after a 30 percent distribution fee, profits were split equally.

While in preparation for the first Chaplin release, First National delivered shockwaves by luring Mary Pickford away from Paramount. Already semi-independent at Famous Players-Lasky, she left the studio became an independent producer releasing through First National at $675,000 for three features with 50 percent of the profits.

With Famous Players-Lasky and First National in deadlock for industry control, independent production briefly flourished. Competition pushed contracts sky-high, and inflated actors' salaries.

Displeased with the chaotic conditions, Zukor felt that the only way to bring stability back to the industry was to create a fully-integrated studio that controlled production, distribution, and exhibition. The trade press reported rumors of a merger between Famous Players-Lasky and First National, designed to monopolize the industry by subjugating the independent production companies. In addition to the obvious salary caps for artists, the proposed merger would undermine their independence, and undo advances for creative and commercial freedom in an industry already dominated by big business. Instead, the independent producers decided to stage a revolt, which resulted in yet another major corporation in the Hollywood distribution game.

Just days before the alleged $40 million Paramount-First National merger could be announced in January 1919, several of the most prominent producers decided to preempt the deal with their own announcement that they would form their own distribution operation. Charles Chaplin, Mary Pickford, Douglas Fairbanks, and D. W. Griffith organized the United Artists Corporation to distribute films for independent producers. In an official statement to the press, the United Artists members declared that one of the missions of the new studio would be to protect the industry from the ravages of block booking. "We also think that this step is positively and absolutely necessary to protect the great motion picture public from threatening combinations and trusts that would force upon them mediocre productions and machine-made entertainment."

All along, the majors studios denied that there were ever any plans to merge Famous Players-Lasky and First National. And indeed no merger took place, especially not while the independents were further entrenched at United Artists. But the independent revolt did not stop Zukor's ambitions of going vertical. As the largest producer-distributor in the industry, he decided to complete his empire by establishing his own theater chain.

Zukor reentered exhibition by purchasing theaters which were then organized into a Paramount division called Publix Theatres Corporation. In an effort to weaken his main rival First National, Zukor employed an extreme form of block booking and threatened to build next door to existing theaters to get many of the First National affiliates to sell their screens to Paramount. It had been less than a decade since Edison's General Film Company used similarly extreme measures to protect their own monopoly. Now Zukor was on his way to creating the largest movie theater combine ever.

Fatal injury came to First National when the dominant Chicago-based Balaban & Katz theater chain left First National to join the Publix circuit. By the end of the silent era, Paramount-Publix controlled over 1600 domestic theaters, with estimates as high as 2000 total movie houses. The studio had a theatrical presence in all but five states, with a virtual monopoly in Canada, as well as theaters in major European cities.

However no single company, not even one the size of Paramount, could dominate every zone in the United States. Other theater-owning studios like Loew's and Fox followed the vertical-integration lead of Zukor and held near monopoly control in other parts of the country. With First National severely weakened, Famous Players-Lasky became more collaborative with the other major distributors to avoid the deadlock that had ensued during the First National days. The Hollywood studios, like the Motion Picture Patents Company before, proved that when main rivals became mutually-supportive, they proved far more dangerous to the industry.

Describing Zukor at the height of his power in Hollywood, biographer Will Irwin estimated Paramount assets at $149 million. "Adolph Zukor had now rounded this strange business of his into final form. . ." Irwin wrote in his 1928 book *The House that Shadows Built*. "The day of the independent producer has passed. The industry, after all its kaleidoscopic shiftings, has settled down into seven or eight corporations or groups, all of which manage their own distribution and possess or control their own theatres. . . . His creation stands rounded and complete."

THE INDEPENDENT PRODUCERS were hardly extinct, however, due largely to the existence of United Artists as a safe harbor for independent film production during the era of studio consolidation. United Artists adopted the Hodkinson distribution system, but lowered its distribution fee to 25 percent or less. Unfortunately, by weighting the terms in favor of the producer, UA's distribution capacity was always in a weakened state.

There was one more main deviation from the Hodkinson system, which caused many long-term problems for UA—the general policy of the studio to not provide production financing to producers. Whereas Hodkinson revolutionized the industry by giving cash advances to spark production, UA started out as a distributor for only the most established of independents who could finance their own films. This discouraged many new independent production companies, resulted in a failure to lure many would-be independent talent, and relegated the studio to a perpetual state of product deficiency.

The early history of the studio was particularly unsettling, as the studio lacked the number of releases needed to support a major enterprise. UA's president Hiram Abrams, Zukor's former right-hand man, endeavored to overcome many of the independent distributor's shortcomings, and, according to studio insiders, worked himself into a premature death in 1926. Chaplin claimed that Adolph Zukor himself even offered to manage the troubled enterprise. When he was turned down, rumors persisted that United Artists would not last and that the company would soon be absorbed by a major studio—most likely Paramount.

United Artists sustained itself by bringing in other high-profile independents, including Samuel Goldwyn and Joseph M. Schenck, who provided the distributor with a dependable supply of films. Many of these producers settled on the studio lot that Mary Pickford and Douglas Fairbanks had purchased together after forming UA. Formerly known as the Jesse Durham Hampton Studio, the lot property on Santa Monica Boulevard and Formosa Avenue in Hollywood became the Pickford-Fairbanks studio, and then was renamed the United Artists Studio though it was operated as a completely separate entity from United Artists the distribution company.

The independents also kept pace in the consolidating industry by forming the United Artists Theatres Circuit, Inc. in June 1926. They purchased first-run theaters in Los Angeles, Chicago, and Detroit, and even entered into partnerships in seven east coast Loew's theaters and two of Paramount's Times Square crown jewels, the Rivoli and Rialto. Their goal was never to rival the largest of exhibitors, but to protect their interests which were constantly threatened by studio consolidation and exhibitor monopolies. United Artists found that the major studios were willing to book the independents' films in many parts of the country in exchange for United Artists' promise to limit its own theater expansion.

The United Artists Theatres, and other cooperative efforts between the independents and the other distributors—arguably a matter of survival for the independents—gave credence to the later antitrust allegations that charged United Artists as a co-conspirator with the major studios. But at the same time, United Artists was also accustomed to disrupting the balance of power when necessary. For instance in the late 1920s, the independent producers opposed the monopoly of Fox's notorious West Coast Theatres circuit that dominated the Pacific states. On November 6, 1930, Joe Schenck and Sam Goldwyn issued a statement signed by the United Artists compatriots Mary Pickford, Douglas Fairbanks, Charles Chaplin, Norma Talmadge, Gloria Swanson, Eddie Cantor, Al Jolson, D. W. Griffith, and Ronald Coleman. They denounced the Fox West Coast monopoly as "greedy and short-sighted." Fox responded by boycotting all United Artists films, therefore cutting the independents out of many zones. Goldwyn publicly threatened to show his movies "in halls and armories" rather than give in to Fox. When the United Artists theaters began an aggressive expansion in areas of California, Fox settled with the independents in

1931.

The independent producers never had the corporate unity to transform United Artists into another Paramount. The producers differed on many fundamental issues, including the purpose of the distributor. Charles Chaplin viewed United Artists more as a service organization "for the purpose of exploiting our pictures without block booking from other sources," frustrating the other producers like Mary Pickford who had a more expansive agenda for the company. Chaplin decided not to take part in the United Artists Theatres (although he did join in the fight against Fox West Coast). The UA theater circuit always remained a separate corporate identity from the distributing company, thus denying United Artists the corporate leverage of the vertically integrated studios.

Meanwhile, the industry trend toward monopolization continued in full force. Metro-Goldwyn-Mayer was created by Loew's Inc. in a succession of mergers between 1919 and 1924. William Fox also searched for takeover targets as he continued to expand his film empire. In 1928, one year after William Fox declared, "I shall devote my life to prohibiting any man or group of men from forming a monopoly that would tend to prevent the motion pictures from growing to its full height," he attempted to merge Fox and Loew's in a $200 million deal that met with antitrust opposition.

The Warner brothers were also on the rise as producer-distributor-exhibitors. They absorbed one of the last American remnants of the Trust in 1925 when they acquired the moribund Vitagraph—which itself was a combination of three other Patents members Lubin, Selig, and Essanay—known as VLSE in the late 1910s. Warner Bros. renamed the subsidiary Vitaphone, and set out to revolutionize the industry with sound films. The talking pictures boom provided Warner Bros. with a cash infusion to embark on its own theater buying spree by taking over what was left of the First National chain. The First National studio lot in Burbank became the Warner Bros. headquarters.

The Radio Corporation of America also entered the film business as a vertically-integrated competitor to Zukor. RCA, already a giant in the entertainment market as owner of the National

Broadcasting Company and the Victor Talking Machine Company, merged the Film Booking Office Pictures Corporation with the Keith-Albee-Orpheum theater circuit in 1928 to form RKO.

Zukor, matching his competitors unit for unit, then proposed a merger with Warner Bros. and the Columbia Broadcasting Company, to be known as Paramount-Vitaphone. In what would have created a massive new amusement company with over 2,400 theaters, Zukor proceeded with the first phase of the deal by acquiring 50 percent of CBS in an atmosphere of wild stock speculation in September 1929.

The stock market crash and the Great Depression brought the studio consolidation to a reevaluation point. Both the Fox-MGM and Paramount-Warner-CBS deals disintegrated, while RKO never entirely recovered from the economic upheaval that took place in its infancy. However, the Hollywood casualties on Black Monday were not immediately severe, as the studios were experiencing an unprecedented boom in theater attendance that held strong through 1929 and 1930, and at first made the studios seem depression-proof. Only as movie patronage declined, were the largest of movie empires hit the hardest. The theaters, so lucrative and profitable in times of prosperity, burdened the vertically-integrated studios, and threw the largest studios into debt. Paramount, Fox, and RKO, the three entertainment giants set to dominate the future of American amusement, were each sent into receivership in the early 1930s.

Many of the UA founders faced setbacks coincidental with the onslaught of the depression. D. W. Griffith produced several expensive box office flops in the early sound era. His final film, *The Struggle* (1932), another box office failure, threw his production company into debt, costing him his stock in United Artists, and ending his illustrious career in film.

Mary Pickford, who never lost money on a single film in the 1920s, retired as a performer in the early 1930s after her talking films were met with a mixed reception. She concentrated on administrative duties at UA, and planned to return as an independent producer when UA product ran low. Even more sporadic was Douglas Fairbank's later career, on the wane with the coming of sound, ostensibly over at the time of his divorce from Pickford in 1935.

The most active (relatively speaking) of the United Artists founders was Charlie Chaplin, the only successful Hollywood producer of non-talkies in the sound era. His latest film, *City Lights* (1931) had provided UA with a blockbuster-level hit; but at the rate of only one feature every four or five years, Chaplin's output could hardly carry the studio. With the founders of UA in repose, most of the United Artists releases were shouldered by Sam Goldwyn and Joe Schenck.

Schenck helped reignite the independent production movement in the 1930s when he cofounded Twentieth Century Pictures with Darryl F. Zanuck, former head of production at Warner Bros. Twentieth Century Pictures was organized in April 1933 as a showcase for the talented 30-year-old producer who resigned from Warners after a salary dispute earlier that year. Zanuck turned down several lucrative offers from other studios in order to devote his efforts to producing quality movies on an independent basis. Twentieth Century signed a distribution deal with United Artists in July 1933, and quickly became the most prolific supplier of films for the company.

Unfortunately the new independent took a detour straight into the major studio camp when Zanuck became outraged by United Artists' refusal to reward Twentieth Century with UA stock. Schenck, who had been a UA stockholder for over ten years, resigned from United Artists in protest of the shoddy treatment of Twentieth Century, and Zanuck began discussions with other distributors. In May 1935, when Sidney Kent at Fox Film asked the independent to lead the ailing Fox studio, Twentieth Century Pictures and Fox Film merged. The independent company, barely two years old, received top billing; Kent remained president, Schenck became chairman, and Zanuck found himself head-of-production of the new Hollywood powerhouse—the Twentieth Century-Fox Film Corporation.

In addition to the product crisis at United Artists caused by the exit of Twentieth Century, further injury was brought against the UA owners when, in order to buy out Schenck's stock holdings, they were forced to trade away the United Artists Theatres, which became part of Twentieth Century-Fox's massive theater circuit, and further strengthened the Fox West Coast chain monopoly.

Even though Twentieth Century, one of the most promising independent companies, had abandoned the independent movement, Darryl Zanuck's initial step of leaving Warners to form his own company had a trigger effect on other studio executives and creative personnel who desired to go independent. David O. Selznick and Walter Wanger, both of whom had considerable production experience at the two preeminent movie factories Paramount and MGM, became independent producers. Walter Wanger left his production unit at MGM in 1934. The following year David O. Selznick did the same with the formation of Selznick International Pictures.

These studio producers had enjoyed a degree of power and freedom, but ultimately they found their production methods at odds with the factory-like studio environment. "Pictures lose their individuality if too many people are engaged in making them," Wanger told the press when he went independent. "A small compact unit has a greater chance to discover faults in the story, the scenario, the direction, the acting, the cutting, when just enough people to make the picture are engaged in it."

The principle members of United Artists in the mid-1930s—Charles Chaplin, Mary Pickford, Samuel Goldwyn, Alexander Korda, Walter Wanger, David O. Selznick, and Walt Disney—later formed the nucleus of the Society of Independent Motion Picture Producers. But the harmony between these volatile filmmakers did not last long during this turbulent period of UA history. The partners argued bitterly, ultimately unable to agree on a consistent company strategy and standard distribution terms. In turn, each producer left the studio to find better deals elsewhere. Only Chaplin, Pickford, and Selznick were still at United Artists at the time that SIMPP was formed in the early 1940s. All of the producers buried their differences when they came back together to organize SIMPP in a unified protest over film monopolization.

Other major studios in the late 1930s, particularly RKO, took notice of the potential profitability of independent production, and began to offer distribution deals with independent producers. Walt Disney, who had released his animated films with United Artists since 1932, signed with RKO in 1937 shortly before his independent production *Snow White and the Seven Dwarfs* became the box-office champion. MGM snatched up the distribution rights to David O. Selznick's *Gone With the Wind* (1939), the film which redefined the limits of profitability for epic blockbusters.

Samuel Goldwyn also entered into an independent distribution deal with RKO in 1940 following his acrimonious break with United Artists. His inability to cooperate with the other less-active producer-owners of UA led to the atmosphere of antagonism at United Artist in the late 1930s. Over time, he had also accumulated a half ownership of the Pickford-Fairbanks property in Hollywood which he audaciously renamed the Samuel Goldwyn Studios in 1939. He encouraged independent production by renting office space and production facilities to independents who had secured distribution deals with the major studios, but who preferred not to work within close proximity of the distributor's lot.

Perhaps the most significant challenge to the studio system was the rise of the producer-director. In contrast to the considerable authority of the pre-Hollywood era film directors like Griffith and Ince, most of the directors at the major studios in the 1920s and 1930s were reduced to hired-hands. The studio system by its very nature had compartmentalized and restricted the role of the director, and concentrated the creative power in the hands of the film executives who oversaw production from script to editing. As the studio system itself was strained by the economic chaos of the early 1930s, some directors demanded, and received, greater creative freedom at the studios. Directors who had a strong artistic vision, but who also were commercially reliable, worked their way out of mere contract-director status, to head their own semi-autonomous units at the major studios—Frank Capra, John Ford, Howard Hawks, Gregory La Cava, Ernst Lubitsch, Leo McCarey, Mervyn Le Roy, Tay Garnett, William Wellman, and Cecil B. DeMille. As producer-directors, their work seemed to show a continuity of style, and allowed their films to transcend the studio assembly-line.

The studio bosses knew that for many of the independent-minded directors there was only a short jump between unit production under the studio and independent production away from the majors. To avoid an independent production exodus, more studios offered producers and directors a degree of creative freedom and profit participation in their films.

Frank Capra's career best illustrated the rising power of the producer-director that pushed the limitations of the studio system in the 1930s. Capra rose to prominence as a contract director at Columbia Pictures with his successful mixture of populist drama and sentimental comedy that defined depression-era attitudes and elevated Harry Cohn's studio from Poverty Row status to one of the Big Eight majors. Capra was suitably rewarded with his own production unit and an unusually high level of creative freedom. Producing about one picture a year, the Capra unit made quality, event pictures, not unlike the prestige films of Capra's independent producing counterparts. After the success of *It Happened One Night* (1934), his new five-picture contract with Columbia gave him 25 percent of the net profits, and even contained an anti-block booking provision that required all Capra films to be sold individually, beginning with *Mr. Deeds Goes to Town* (1935).

Capra had adopted a "one man, one film" mantra which later generations would dub the *auteur* theory, which claimed that a film, like any other important work of art, should be largely the product of a single creative vision and not the offspring of a studio committee. He believed producer-director setups to be the answer to the generic, manufactured Hollywood film. He blamed the complacency of the well-paid contract directors for selling out their artistic responsibility to the studios. Ultimately, Capra concluded, the ideal position for ambitious, creative filmmakers was in independent production.

With the market for independent films heating up, in 1936 Capra tried to force the cancellation of his contract by protesting Cohn's persistent controversial marketing practices. Capra initiated a bitter lawsuit against the studio, and laid plans for his own independent company. But Columbia reconciled with Capra, and he fulfilled his contract with *You Can't Take It With You* (1938), his highest grossing Columbia picture, and *Mr. Smith Goes To Washington* (1939), his signature film, which he initially contemplated as an independent production.

In July 1939 Frank Capra joined with his chief collaborator, screenwriter Robert Riskin, to form Frank Capra Productions, and landed a one-picture distribution deal with Warner Bros. The highly-favorable terms, a 20 percent distribution fee and all rights to the film returning to Capra after five years, were an indication of the softening attitude of the majors toward independent films. Back at Columbia, Harry Cohn compensated for the loss of Capra by extending unit-production deals to other filmmakers like Leo McCarey and Howard Hawks.

The inroads made by the producer-directors in Hollywood the 1930s helped pave the way for later artistic, single-minded producer-directors like Orson Welles and Alfred Hitchcock. The movement was also closely related to—and in many respects, identical with—the independent production trend that was rising in opposition to the studios.

Even though Warners, RKO, Universal, Columbia and others were opening up to independents, the anti-competitive practices of the major studios still put limitations on the independents in general. Block booking (selling films in bulk) and unit production (lavishing individual attention on films) were concepts in diametric opposition. The filmmakers realized that if they were to secure their freedom in the industry, and if they ever wanted to see the elimination of the studio system, they would need to join the antitrust movement.

3

Box Office Poison

THE BLOCK BOOKING controversy began long before SIMPP, as many industry groups protested the arbitrary manner that the major distributors forced the sale of unwanted pictures. Over time the practice became more sophisticated, as each studio had their own manner of block booking. Eventually the blocks included not just features but a full range of short subject cartoons and newsreels. This mature form of block booking, called "full-line forcing," gave the studios a pre-sold market for all of their pictures, and kept their various production departments working at capacity. Since the films were usually blocked before they were produced, theaters had to make their booking decisions with the barest of information provided by the distributor. This practice known as "blind bidding" forced exhibitors to purchase films sometimes knowing little more than the title of the movie, the cast, and perhaps a brief story tagline.

Most film blocks contained about 20 or more features, but some theaters complained that in the most extreme cases one block had predetermined the playbill for an entire year—with movies they were forced to buy left unshown. The practice was devastating to the small theater owner who had to compete with the studio-owned theater chains that were exempt from block booking. Gentlemen's agreements between studios meant that the first-run theaters could pick the best films from each other without being forced to buy the accompanying range of B-pictures.

Block booking was also particularly frustrating to the independent producers who distinguished their films by quality rather than volume, only to watch in disgust as their highly-individual A-pictures became the selling feature of a block of studio programmer pictures. Independents complained that their films were being fettered by the pre-packaged studio deadweight. But in an industry dominated by vertically-integrated companies, the producers were in a hopelessly disadvantageous bargaining position.

As with any controversy, block booking was a two-sided issue. The Hollywood studios affirmed that block booking was comparable to the concept of wholesaling and bulk-buying that was a staple of American free enterprise. To Adolph Zukor, a survivor of the haphazard film buying system of the old Patents Company, block booking represented movie distribution in its most efficient and evolved state. W. W. Hodkinson, always a critic of industry monopoly, called block booking a corrupted form of the distribution system he pioneered.

The major distributors asserted that block booking actually resulted in better films because the guaranteed cash-flow allowed the studios to take more risks on individual movies that did not have to survive on their own legs. Of course the opponents of block booking claimed the opposite, that block booking impeded overall film quality and that it gave no incentive to improve each film while they were being marketed sight-unseen. Curiously, both sides pointed to the resulting films to support their arguments: the studios praised the worldwide popularity of Hollywood films in general, while the independents noted the overall scarcity of truly remarkable films.

Many civic and public interest groups who became aware of block booking opposed it for censorship reasons. The public-advocates voiced concerns that, under block booking, nothing prevented the self-regulated movie industry from forcing upon the neighborhood theaters (and therefore Middle America) various films of questionable moral value. They likened it to a potentially poisonous food or drug that was being sold without a label. These groups threatened Hollywood with one of its primal fears—outside censorship.

Therefore the battle for block booking had moral and artistic implications as well the obvious economic issues. While the mass-production studio system was in full-swing, block booking was arguably the focal point of the Hollywood studio power-base, one which the major distributors protected at all costs, and eventually fought to a bitter end. The independents identified the indulgence of block booking as the root of the industry evils.

PARAMOUNT'S ANTITRUST PROBLEMS began when the Federal Trade Commission investigated block booking in 1921. In a complaint filed on August 30 of that year, the FTC charged Famous Players-Lasky with restraint of trade by forcing exhibitors to buy unwanted films. Though the case focused on block booking, the investigation also brought studio-ownership of theaters under fire, and accused Famous Players-Lasky of using theater acquisition to intimidate exhibitors into block booking arrangements for Paramount movies.

For example, in one exhibitor grievance from Middleton, New York, an independent theater owner claimed that when his movie house rejected a five-year block booking deal with Paramount, the distributor used predatory tactics to run the exhibitor out of business. The theater owner withstood threats and goon-squad intimidation, in descriptive accounts befitting of the old Edison Trust. Finally, Paramount built a movie house across the street in Middleton, and resorted to temporary price cutting and overbuying in order to destroy competition.

After 17,000 pages of testimony and 15,000 pages of exhibits, the FTC concluded in 1927 that block booking was indeed an unfair trade practice. The case *Federal Trade Commission v. Famous Players-Lasky Corporation, et al* resulted in a cease and desist order for block booking on July 9, 1927, as well as a demand for reform on Paramount theater purchasing. The three respondents—Famous Players-Lasky Corporation, Adolph Zukor, and Jesse L. Lasky—were given 60 days to comply with the findings or to provide the FTC with written explanations.

Famous Players-Lasky ignored the cease and desist order. Unable to embrace reform, the studio decided to stall. When their report to the FTC came due, the three respondents were granted two extensions to the original 60-day limit.

On April 15, 1928 the Paramount-Famous-Lasky Corporation finally submitted its final report of compliance to the Federal Trade Commission. The studio was perched in a position of economic strength, and getting bigger all the time through merger. They disputed the charges, and even denied that Paramount practiced block booking as it had been described by the FTC. Famous Players-Lasky's defiance attracted attention in the press, and was interpreted as a sign of arrogance. The FTC rejected the report, and announced that they would resort to government antitrust action to force compliance.

Almost exactly a decade before the *Paramount* case in the 1930s, the Hollywood antitrust shadows were already in place in the *Famous Players-Lasky* case in the late 1920s. The stalling tactics of the major studios, the complaints of the independents, the charges of industry conspiracy, the veil-piercing allegations that personally accused the studio executives—all of this would return in the *Paramount* case in which SIMPP became involved.

Giving credence to the charges of collusion between the major distributors, the Hollywood studios handled these difficulties by joining together to address the industry grievances without government involvement. The American film business had already developed a tradition of self-regulation. When Hollywood was faced with censorship threats in the scandal-ridden early 1920s, the major film companies formed the Motion Picture Producers and Distributors of America, Inc. in 1921. The MPPDA, also known as the Hays Office under its first president Will Hays, administered a code of self-censorship favored by the industry leaders at large, and quickly became the representative organization of the major studios. To maintain a voice in industry matters, some of the most important independent producers joined the MPPDA, expanding the organization from nine founding members to 23 companies by 1927.

When the antitrust investigation of the early 1920s threatened the major studios, the studios organized the Board of Arbitration in July 1922. Formed as an outgrowth of the MPPDA, the Board of Arbitration aided film booking by dividing the domestic market into 32 territories, each with their own Film Board of Trade. Each regional board had six representatives—three from the producer-distributors, three from the local theater owners—and was designed to settle disputes between the studios and the exhibitors outside of court. The MPPDA not only hoped that this conciliatory gesture would keep the government antitrust watchdogs at bay, they also realized that legal disagreements were crippling the film market. A court injunction could kill an entire run in a territory; but with the arbitration system, decisions were promised in ten days. By 1928, over 50,000 disputes were settled without court involvement.

However the Film Boards of Trade made the block booking debate even more acute. Arbitration had many benefits for the exhibitor, but clearly the system protected block booking and blind bidding. The exhibitors who protested block booking had little legal recourse under the arbitration method. Many independent theater chains discovered that a private dispute with one distributor, resulted in suspension that was tantamount to a boycott from all other major companies associated with the Motion Picture Producers and Distributors of America.

As the Federal Trade Commission attacked Famous Players-Lasky in the 1920s, the exhibitor complaints indicated that a much bigger problem was afoot in the industry, and seemed to point to a conspiracy in Hollywood that monopolized the entire domestic film industry. When the FTC rejected Famous Players-Lasky's compliance report in April 1928, they resolved to go after the entire studio system. Action came within days.

On April 27, 1928, the Department of Justice filed two antitrust cases, which were combined into one equity suit by 1930. The government accused the Paramount-Famous-Lasky Corporation and nine other MPPDA members of monopolizing ninety-eight percent of domestic film distribution. The case also intended to challenge the validity of compulsory arbitration by prosecuting the 32 territorial arbitration boards for conspiracy in violation of antitrust law. In October 1929, the Federal District Court in New York City declared compulsory arbitration illegal, but refused to sanction reforms that would eliminate block booking. The studios and the government were each dissatisfied, and when the judge handed down the decision in early 1930, both sides appealed to the Supreme Court (a situation that would also repeat itself 17 years later in the *Paramount* case). In the Supreme Court decision rendered on November 25, 1930, the ten Hollywood distributors were found guilty of violating antitrust law, and block booking was identified as the fundamental problem.

The days of block booking appeared to be at an end, but the Supreme Court decision in the *Famous Players-Lasky* case was never enforced because of the economic troubles of the Great Depression that surmounted the industry in a short period of time. As the Hollywood studios suffered deep fiscal losses, the Roosevelt administration felt it was not in the best interests of the national economy or the public's morale to hobble such a vital industry while it struggled financially. In 1933 the MPPDA participated in a much-contested deal with the United States government by seeking sanctuary under the National Industrial Recovery Act. The government agreed to nullify the court decree, and call-off the antitrust case, in exchange for the studios' promise to adopt a progressive attitude toward labor unionization.

After years of antitrust conflict, the government temporarily gave its blessing to block booking and vertical integration while the financially vulnerable Hollywood studios got back on their feet. The NIRA even allowed the Motion Picture Producers and Distributors of America to draft its own written code that officially endorsed a number of monopolistic practices, including block booking and blind bidding. The studios were protected until the National Industrial Recovery Act was declared unconstitutional by the Supreme Court in 1935. By that time, not only had the studios successfully postponed the antitrust case, the Big Eight had further evolved their oligopoly which operated to the detriment of the independent exhibitors and producers.

DESPITE THIS TEMPORARY SHIELD from the government, the studios had to take additional measures to safeguard block booking. In the early 1930s during a period of growing public concern over on-screen morality, the exhibitors had blamed block booking for the increase in so-called objectionable movies, and brought their grievances to the attention of civic organizations like the influential Catholic Legion of Decency which was formed in 1933 and comprised of numerous non-Catholic religious and public-interest groups.

Many of the independent theater owners and managers had an ulterior motive besides public concern; that is, they hoped the outrage of civic leaders would help pressure the distributors into better concessions for the theaters. The theaters asked the distributors to allow a "cancellation privilege" that enabled the exhibitor to reject a certain number of films in each block. This, the theaters told the public-advocacy groups, would allow the exhibitors to ferret out Hollywood's inappropriate material before it reached the public. The theaters petitioned the distributors for a cancellation privilege as high as 40 percent, but only a few distributors granted a cancellation privilege at all, which fluctuated between 5 and 15 percent, and was closely monitored under very limited circumstances in various parts of the country. The distributors even commissioned a nationwide study which tracked the films canceled by theaters to show that the exhibitor choices did not demonstrate a consistently high standard of morality, but, rather, the theaters invoked the privilege solely for commercial purposes.

Nevertheless, the National Legion of Decency (as it was known after April 1934) concluded that block booking could not coexist with the Hays Office's lax enforcement of the production code. In one of the most successful public crusades in film history, the Legion of Decency threatened a national boycott and private censorship in 1934 until the MPPDA improved the situation. In response, the Hays Office revitalized its production code under Irish-Catholic Joseph I. Breen, with strictly enforced standards and stiff penalties for producer-distributors. Mary Pickford told the press that the pressure from the Legion of Decency rescued the industry from outside censorship—but unfortunately it also saved the practice of block booking. In exchange for the MPPDA's commitment to keep objectionable material in check, the National Legion of Decency agreed not push for government antitrust intervention.

Nevertheless other public-advocacy groups continued to protest block booking. In October 1934, a coalition of 35 national organizations, including the Motion Picture Research Council, the American Legion, B'nai B'rith, Parents and Teachers associations, Lions Clubs, Boy Scouts of America, and the YMCA, urged Congress to submit legislation at the next session to abolish block booking and blind selling. They also formed a lobbying committee to keep the pressure on as the controversy swelled.

In May 1935, coincidentally the same month that the NIRA was declared unconstitutional, two block booking bills made their way to the United States Congress. Senator Matthew M. Neely of West Virginia proposed the Anti-Block Booking and Blind Selling Bill on May 13, 1935 for hearings in early 1936. Earlier, in the House, Indiana representative Samuel B. Pettengill originated a sister proposal.

Block booking legislation was not new to Cogress. Anti-block booking bills had been sponsored intermittently since December 1927, when the Federal Trade Commission's cease and desist order proved ineffectual. Over the years, block booking restrictions had at times been passed by the Senate, but were consistently rejected by the House. Though ultimately unsuccessful, the Neely-Pettengill bill became the most important anti-block booking measure before the advent of the *Paramount* case. According to the proposal, blocks of any size should be forbidden, as well as well as any conspiracy that offered film discounts to buyers of more than one movie. According to the Senate Report, one of the principle reasons for the bill was to provide relief to the independent producers and exhibitors.

At initial glance, the Neely-Pettengill bill seemed an ideal rallying point for all independents. However a provision designed to undermine blind bidding alienated many of the producers. Since many distributors sold their movies before they were produced, theaters complained that the sparse information upon which the theaters based their purchases was altered during the production process. In a well-intentioned effort to improve the bargaining position of the theaters, the Neely-Pettengill bill required all films to be presented to exhibitors with a "complete and true synopsis" of the movie, including plot details, scene analysis, and character information. Any person who sold a film without a synopsis, or knowingly provided false data, would be subject to fine or imprisonment.

Requiring all Hollywood producers to adhere to a detailed synopsis throughout production was a laughable concept in the major studios which relied on test screenings and reediting to hone their movies before each release. The independent producers also found the provision objectionable. While some independents were known for a methodical approach to film production, many of the creative producers resorted to on-the-fly filmmaking, molding the productions with quick decisions and last minute changes. The unpopular provision left most independent producers apprehensive of the bill, and made Neely an easy target for the Hollywood resistance.

MPPDA general counsel Charles C. Pettijohn, who had risen to prominence defending the arbitration system during the 1920s, attended the Congressional hearings to lambast the Pettengill bill's story synopsis requirement. Pettijohn brought with him quotes from filmmakers Jesse L. Lasky, Harold Lloyd, Louis B. Mayer, and Ernst Lubitsch to attest to the frequency of story changes and the importance of flexibility in film production. Particularly damaging was a statement that David O. Selznick had made, which Pettijohn reported to the sub-committee: "To compel any Producer to be bound in advance of Production to standardized, machine-like production of motion pictures is too abhorrent to ever contemplate." Selznick said that if story changes were a crime, then he would be one of the first to be held in contempt. It was an uneasy situation for Selznick, who despised block booking and blind bidding but genuinely disagreed with the Neely-Pettengill bill. Selznick had only recently turned independent, and, to his frustration, now found his words being used by the MPPDA to defend the monopolistic practices of the studios from which he had defected.

Block booking ignited the industry in the late 1930s, as Senator Neely's bill proceeded into sub-committee. A scathing pamphlet, "What Do You Know About Block-Booking," published anonymously by the MPPDA, was condemned by *The Christian Century* for "irrelevant and misleading statistics" designed to protect block booking.

Another booklet called "What Price Neely Bill?" consisted of a transcription of a talk given by C. C. Pettijohn at a Big Eight conference where he charismatically defended industry self-regulation instead of government edict. Pettijohn, speaking at the end of 1939, extolled the number of recent high-class studio releases, using films from that banner year as evidence that Hollywood did not need government fixing. He lavished considerable praise on the brand new blockbuster *Gone With the Wind* (1939), but neglected to acknowledge the independent producer who vehemently disapproved of the studio system, and who grew increasingly frustrated as the press grouped the independents and studios in the same category.

The Senate Interstate Commerce Committee ordered hearings on block booking in 1939. Again C. C. Pettijohn represented the major studios, and asserted that movies "cannot be sold one at a time if this business is to exist." He offered alternative suggestions like awarding local church and school boards with input in selecting the films in each block, or giving theaters their much-desired cancellation privilege at as much as 20 percent. The government rejected all proposals.

The studios requested that their contract actors join the movie fight and use their celebrity status to uphold block booking by attacking the story-synopsis requirement of the bill. Some Hollywood stars made personal appearances before the Washington committee, as reporters and guests packed the hearing room to get a glimpse of Robert Taylor, for instance, testifying against the Neely bill. The studios also encouraged the contract performers to write to Congress in protest of the bill. Many of the letters followed a generic format that was circulated by the studio managers. The "Sample Letter for Actors and Actresses" read as follows:

> As an active member of the motion picture industry I wish to enter a protest against the law proposed by Senator Neely. In my opinion the Bill, should it be passed, will do a great deal of damage to the picture industry and to all of us connected with it.
>
> Although its purpose is said to be to protect exhibitors, its effect, I believe, would be exactly the reverse. Anyone who has ever worked in films knows that only after the actors are assembled on the set and production starts do the full potentialities of the story become evident. Then a director or producer is free to make changes which usually result in an improved production.
>
> Passage of this Bill would offer so many major obstacles to the production end of the motion picture industry that it undoubtedly would result in the ultimate leadership in this branch of the entertainment field to be transferred to foreign lands. The loss of this leadership not only would effect the industry itself, but would result in wide-spread unemployment of all branches of the business.
>
> May I urge that this measure be killed once and for all.

Eleven year old Shirley Temple and the teenage Mickey Rooney were among the many high-profile stars who submitted letters to relay their disapproval of the Neely legislation.

However there were performers who harbored prejudice against block booking. Some even raised concerns while under contract in the 1930s. James Cagney and Bing Crosby protested block booking as a contributing factor to the factory-like atmosphere of studio filmmaking; later on both joined SIMPP to help oppose the controversial practice during the 1940s.

The Senate Committee eventually issued a favorable report that resulted in a 46 to 28 vote that passed the Neely Anti-Block Booking and Blind Bidding Bill in the Senate on July 1939. The measure was sent to the House, where, despite the momentum of the bill, it was not expected to pass. The studios repeated the letter-writing campaign and parade of stars for the House Interstate Commerce Committee. The Committee called the bill "unworkable," and unanimously recommended to dispose of it. As expected, the controversial bill died in the House of Representatives just as previous block booking reform had in earlier instances.

By the time the Neely bill was shelved in June 1940, the Roosevelt administration had already fired up the *Paramount* case (discussed in chapter 4). That month, the Justice Department took the Big Eight to court, seeking both the abolishment of block booking and the end of studio-owned theater chains.

Though the independent producers had had reservations about the Neely bill, they viewed the *Paramount* suit with great expectations. Ever since the *Famous Players-Lasky* case in the early 1930s, the independent producers spent a great deal of their time defending themselves from allegations that drew United Artists into the fight, rendering themselves ineffective in the antitrust war. The Neely bill made this worse, as the independents were linked even more closely to the studios. This need to distance themselves from the studio system convinced many of the independents that they needed their own trade organization.

Another important result of the block booking fight was the amount of publicity the studio practice received in the 1930s. Outside of the industry and a few public-advocacy groups, block booking remained largely unknown to the public until after 1939. The booklet called "Let's Kill the Movies! No Let's Kill the Neely Bill," which was funded by the major studios, boasted a circulation goal of over one million copies. A counter-pamphlet, distributed by the Allied States Association of Motion Picture Exhibitors, tried to inform the public and national interest organizations about the "false and misleading information" of the Big Eight. Both sides used misleading slogans like "Neely Bill means higher theatre admissions," or "Neely Bill means the end of bad pictures." This helped generate public awareness for the issue, which the Society of Independent Motion Picture Producers would later use as a springboard to bring the antitrust battle into the households of America.

4

Hollywood Trust

PARAMOUNT, LOEW'S (MGM), Warner Bros., Twentieth Century-Fox, and RKO emerged from the Great Depression as the Big Five theater owners in an industry dominated by eight major studios. Though some of the film barons like Adolph Zukor, William Fox, and Carl Laemmle lost a considerable amount of individual stature in the economic crisis, the Big Eight corporations secured an overall position of strength by fostering cooperative inter-studio relations.

Metro-Goldwyn-Mayer was perhaps the unrivaled studio in terms of management and financial stability due to its conservative theater expansion, while Paramount remained the largest by far in terms of size and vertical muscle. Under the leadership of the new president Barney Balaban, the Paramount-Famous-Lasky company came out of receivership in July 1935 with a new business structure and a new corporate identity—Paramount Pictures, Inc.

"A railroad receivership is child's play compared to this vast, multiheaded company," one of the trustees said of Paramount and its 194 corporate subsidiaries. In addition to the national and international distribution network, Paramount operated studios in Hollywood, Astoria (Long Island), and Joinville (near Paris). The Paramount movie circuit, at this time with 1400 domestic theaters, exceeded the size of all other Big Five theater chains combined.

With so many theaters to fill, Paramount—indeed all of the Big Five—relied on the film output from all eight of the major distributors, giving rise to the accusations of favoritism and collusion between the Hollywood studios. Even the movie theaters of the Big Five were suspiciously concentrated geographically, with each studio maintaining a lock in certain areas of the country. Paramount, for instance, dominated New England, the deep south, the upper midwest, and Canada; Loew's controlled many of the runs in metropolitan New York and the outskirts of Connecticut and New Jersey; Warner Bros. Secured the mid-Atlantic region; Fox held the Pacific states and several important western cities; and RKO, the smallest of the Big Five, had parts of New York and Ohio. Although the Big Five claimed that a nationwide conspiracy of this kind was preposterous, many of the independent exhibitors believed that the undefined boundaries were intentionally maintained by the theater-owning studios and a few large non-affiliated theater chains.

In territories where more than one chain dominated, theater pooling also became popular. In a theater pool, two or more competitive chains—usually two dominant studios—agreed to combine their theaters into one super-chain where all profits were kept in a large single pool, later to be divided according to a predetermined percentage.

For example, in one of the most notorious pools, Paramount and RKO combined their theaters in Minnesota to hold a lock on Minneapolis-St. Paul. All theater profits were lumped together, and split 70 percent for Paramount and 30 percent for RKO. This kept the two giants from spending considerable amounts of money in direct competition. It also created a veritable regional monopoly where independent exhibitors were cut out of the first run, either by relegation to the subsequent run by the Big Eight, or by being forced out of business by the large chains. Even though over 60 percent of all domestic theaters were small independent movie houses, their market share was slim compared to the national chains.

Theater pooling also created a damaging environment for the independent producers. Any regional monopoly or "closed situation" gave theaters the ability to dictate terms to the producers. In classic Hollywood, the theaters did not always share box office proceeds with filmmakers. This was something that the producers needed to negotiate through their distributor. When a theater chain held monopoly control over a region, the theater customarily offered only a flat rental for the film without a share of the ticket sales—while the producers forced to take it or leave it. In a closed situation, it was unlikely for an independent producer to gain a percentage of the box office, and therefore made it impossible for the independents to get what they considered to be full market value of their pictures.

AS THE STUDIOS RECOVERED from the Depression, they knew that the provisional protection of the Roosevelt administration, which supported block booking with misgivings, would end once the NIRA was struck down. It was only a matter of time before the studio system was called into question. When Hollywood increased its production of A-list films in an effort to attract a broader share of audiences in the mid-1930s, the industry hoped that the improvement in overall film quality would make Hollywood less deserving of the government's antitrust indignation.

A couple of years later when a noticeable dearth in topnotch studio releases hit Hollywood, the studios' plans to pacify the government's antitrust concerns were jeopardized. In 1938 the studios dealt with an increasing dissatisfaction from the public and the press complaining about the slump. Carl Laemmle, no longer in control of Universal, told the *New York Times*, "Everywhere I go and everybody I have spoken to during the past year has complained about the same thing—bad pictures."

That September, Joseph M. Schenck at Twentieth Century-Fox commented on a particularly miserable season, "Also, there was a period during the early Summer when there were practically no good new pictures coming along. Three or four weeks of poor pictures had a damaging effect upon business." The perceived decline in film quality came on the heels of the economic recession in late 1937 and early 1938. By the end of the first quarter of 1938, the combined profits of the Big Eight had already dropped 47 percent from the previous year.

Opponents of Hollywood observed, as the independents would have them believe, that the major studios were stagnant and dry of ideas. Out of the hundreds of films in release, there was one stand-out film that received practically universal critical praise, and sur-passed all industry records to become the highest grossing film up to that point with over $8 million at the box office. That block-buster was Walt Disney's *Snow White and the Seven Dwarfs*, not a star-studded studio prestige project but an independently-produced feature animation experiment that embarrassingly outdistanced the studio powerhouses. The majors referred to 1938 as an off season. (And of course, Hollywood's big year was just around the corner). However, at the time, the slump gave ammunition to the detractors of the studio system. An editorial in *Variety* blamed block booking as the culprit: "The wonder is not the scarcity of outstanding, smashing film hits, but that under the present system of industry operation there are any hits at all."

The United States Department of Justice took advantage of the window of opposition to announce its suit against the Hollywood oligopoly on July 20, 1938. The defendants included Hollywood's eight major studios, 25 of their affiliated companies, and 132 exec-utive officers—all accused of monopolization in restraint of trade. According to the 22,600-word, 119-page complaint drafted by Assistant Attorney General Thurman Arnold, the government was reacting to "numerous complaints by independent producers, dis-tributors, and exhibitors and by the theatre-going public." Film attorneys expressed surprise that the lengthy complaint abandoned the use of precise legal phraseology that was standard for almost every petition of its kind. The *Paramount* petition, they said, was written in the non-legal language of the trade.

The Department of Justice sought relief on eleven grounds, and planned to outlaw numerous trade practices that commonly gave the producer-distributors the upper hand over exhibitors.

Frequently the studios designated play dates, mandated clearance, set admission prices, and controlled the practice of double features, giving the Hollywood studio far too much power and monopoly control according to the Justice Department. The suit had two overall objectives: the complete abolishment of block booking, and the end of the theater ownership by the studios.

A large section of the Justice Department complaint was devoted to the history of the motion picture industry, the rise of Paramount, and the discrimination levied against the independent exhibitors. Occasional comments also mentioned the problems of the independent producer. According to the petition, "the independent producer does not have access to a free, open and untrammeled first-run market in metropolitan cities in which to dispose of his pictures. Entrance to this market by an independent producer is only at the sufferance of [the defendants] who control it."

There was no mistaking, however, that the *Paramount* suit was designed primarily to protect the independent exhibitor. The Justice Department complaint stated that the independent exhibitors were being driven out of business by the oligopoly and that "it will only be a question of a short time" before their extinction unless the monopoly power was checked. The small theaters, which had suffered greatly under the NIRA sanctions, dictated the focus of the *Paramount* case early on.

For the most part, the independent producers were still being equated with the major studios. In fact, the entire United Artists management team became defendants along with the rest of the Big Eight company executives. This meant that Mary Pickford, Charles Chaplin, Samuel Goldwyn, and Loyd Wright, who all later founded SIMPP, were charged with monopoly allegations, as newspaper tag-lines trumpeted their names, and linked them to the Hollywood conspiracy. Case in point, when the antitrust announcement made national headlines, the July 21 *New York Times* mentioned only three individual defendants on the front page—Pickford, Fairbanks, and Chaplin—the most recognizable names in the suit, and arguably the most independent-minded of the entire list of defendants.

With so much at stake in the *Paramount* case, the independent producers planned to be active antitrust participants. They could not afford to have their credibility undermined by the misleading press reports. They learned a lesson from the *Famous Players-Lasky* case ten years earlier, and refused to have themselves and their studio United Artists linked to the Hollywood conspiracy. In 1940 Chaplin, Pickford, Goldwyn, and Wright were taken off the list of defendants after they petitioned the Justice Department. (Fairbanks had passed away in 1939.) However, the independents could not convince the government to release United Artists Corporation from the suit. Though UA was the smallest of the majors, the Justice Department considered it part of the Big Eight nevertheless, and upheld the charges of co-conspiracy against the distributor.

BY THE TIME the *Paramount* suit was underway, the major studios had already spent time fortifying. With the block booking controversy intensifying in Congress, the *Paramount* suit was not a surprise to Hollywood; and the studios made sure they were prepared for the Roosevelt administration's anti-monopoly case. One month before the Justice Department announcement, the studios anticipated the suit by forming a committee of film executives to promote industry self-regulation. Sidney Kent, the Twentieth Century-Fox president who also defended block booking at the Senate hearings, served as chairman of the industry conciliation committee, and announced its formation following a June 25 meeting at the White House between President Roosevelt and industry leaders.

On the same day that the Justice Department filed its complaint, the Motion Picture Producers and Distributors of America released its statement from Will Hays, setting the tone for the industry with tact rather than harsh words. He welcomed "judicial clarification" in a language that whispered to those familiar with Hollywood history that the suit would be infested with months, or perhaps years, of conciliatory activity. Undeterred by the government suit, Sidney Kent also reflected the industry attitude "that the most intelligent and satisfactory solution to our problems eventually will be reached through self-regulation rather than through litigation." He assured the press, "We shall continue the work of our committee to that end."

The *Paramount* case defendants were given 20 days following the service of each subpoena to file their answers with the Justice Department. But with the large number of companies and officers to be served, the 20-day limit proved unrealistic. Just as in the *Famous Players-Lasky* case a decade before, the studios were granted extensions which gave the Hollywood conciliation committee time to formulate a compromise deal.

Attorneys predicted a two year trial if the case went to court. Both the studios and the government were eager to avoid such an expense. Widely circulated reports at the end of 1938 suggested that the committee would soon approach the government to settle the suit with a consent decree compromise. The Department of Justice reiterated its stance: after years of experience with Hollywood complacency and studio legal gambits, no deal would be considered unless it achieved all purposes of the suit including the elimination of block booking and complete theater divorcement.

During 1939 the government refined its case as it advanced toward a trial date set the following year. As an indication of the complex nature of the Hollywood antitrust charges, the Justice Department filed suit against several large independent theater chains that acted as regional monopolies. Though not subsidiaries of the studios, these local circuits were accused of acting in collusion with the major Hollywood distributors to destroy competition. The government initiated three antitrust suits, directed at several large theater chains, which also implicated the major studios as co-defendants. The first suit, *United States v. Griffith Amusement Co.*, came in April 1939, followed later that year with *United States v. Schine Chain Theatres* and *United States v. Crescent Amusement Co.*, both in August.

The most famous of these, the *Schine* case, challenged the theater chain headquartered in Gloversville, New York (the suburb of Albany which was coincidentally familiar to film historians as emigrant Sam Goldwyn's adopted home town). Theater owner J. Myer Schine, who held a commanding position in upstate New York, had expanded his chain to 148 theaters in six states. (He later owned a hotel chain scattered from coast to coast which included the Boca Raton Club in Florida and Los Angeles' Ambassador Hotel.) Schine operated without competition in 60 U.S. towns where his companies owned all of the local theaters. The events of the *Schine* case paralleled the *Paramount* suit; it languished for years, and reached the Supreme Court around the same time in 1948.

These separate suits against large unaffiliated theater chains, indicated the complex nature of the film antitrust war that the U.S. government waged on many fronts in the 1930s and 1940s. The Justice Department hoped that each case would help provide momentum for the other. These theater suits also illustrate the exhibitor-based emphasis of the early stages of the *Paramount* case before the independent producers became heavily involved with the formation of SIMPP.

On June 3, 1940, the *Paramount* case went to trial in Federal Court in New York. Wanting to avoid the unpleasant public scrutiny, the studio heads effected an eleventh-hour negotiation that suspended the trial on June 17 after only two weeks of preliminary hearings. Private negotiations took place between the studios and the Justice Department throughout the summer months in the midst of a heatwave-stricken New York City.

Suspicious of the secret meetings, some of the independent producers began to protest the activities of the major studios in an effort to influence the negotiating process. At this point the producers participated only on an individual basis, and even at that, their involvement was sporadic. Samuel Goldwyn hoped to rally the independent movement by attacking one of the industry's irrepressible practices—the multiple bill, better known as the double feature.

The double feature rose to popularity during the early years of the Depression when theater attendance dwindled. To help stimulate business, many theaters chose to show two features, instead of one feature with short subjects. Usually an A-picture, serving as the main attraction, was coupled with a lesser B-picture. Toward the end of the 1930s, multiple features became the standard practice at an estimated 60 percent of all theaters in the country. Some areas, like Chicago, regularly showed three features for the price of one. Independent producers who primarily made A-pictures viewed the double feature as the stepchild of block booking. They complained that their prestige films carried the extra B-film as baggage, and that box office proceeds were disproportionately shared between the films even though many patrons left before the second feature began.

Sam Goldwyn used the double feature as his issue *du jour* to attack the mass-production of the studio system. Certainly the distributors were not entirely at blame for the double feature, as it largely began as an exhibitor innovation. But Goldwyn concluded that major studios actually promulgated the practice by over-producing features with far too many B-films despite the recent efforts of Hollywood to concentrate on more prestige films.

The production of "filler movies" was shortsighted, he claimed. Rather, Goldwyn believed, it was in the best interests of the producers, the distributors, the theaters and the public to have better-produced films with longer theater stays and more successful runs. "Then, I am firmly convinced," he prophesied, "there would come a marked improvement in quality. It stands to reason that better stories can be written and better pictures made when the artists have more time to give them."

That summer during the *Paramount* case deliberations, Goldwyn utilized his promotional expertise to incite public awareness on the antitrust issues. "The double feature is killing the picture industry," he told the *Saturday Evening Post* in a July 1940 article titled "Hollywood Is Sick." He also discussed the problems of block booking, and announced that he had hired George Gallup's sampling group, the American Institute of Public Opinion, to conduct a poll on several controversial industry practices, including block booking and the ever-popular double feature.

The following month the Gallup poll results showed that 57 percent of ticket buyers were against the double feature. Goldwyn continued to publicize the issue with a nationwide radio debate on CBS's "People's Platform" on August 24 to speak out against the multiple bill, hoping that the opinions of the average moviegoer would influence the government negotiations with the Hollywood studios.

Goldwyn also knew that the double feature controversy made for an easy target, as movie audiences on the whole associated double features with the overall cheapening of movie entertainment. Overwhelming public opinion consistently denounced the multiple bill. Unfortunately box office patterns proved quite the opposite— that, despite the public lip service, double-feature presentations regularly outperformed single-film showings. Regardless, Goldwyn knew that agitating mass opinion against the prevailing practice would send a message to the Justice Department negotiators that the public was not in approval of the "old, inefficient distribution system" that promoted quantity over quality.

During that same month in the summer of 1940, David O. Selznick spoke out against another industry abuse that promoted inferior picture-making—blind bidding. Rumor had it that the deliberations between the studios and the Department of Justice included a provision that would outlaw blind bidding. Selznick called a press conference. After the incredible back-to-back performance of *Gone With the Wind* (1939) and *Rebecca* (1940), he reorganized his Selznick International Pictures interests into a new company called David O. Selznick Productions, Inc.; and at the launch of the new production company, Selznick threw his support behind the Justice Department by attacking the "sight unseen" sales policy of the major distributors. Only four years earlier his statements on blind bidding helped the MPPDA defeat the Neely-Pettengill anti-blind bidding bill. This time, he clarified his position on the issue by refusing to allow blind bidding on his films. He declared that his new movies would be sold to exhibitors only after they were completed. "If they are successful in their first test engagements, the price will be pegged accordingly," he affirmed. "If they are unsuccessful, we'll take the rap."

By the end of the summer, newspapers disclosed details of a deal worked out between government and studio attorneys. By all reports the Justice Department had indeed caved on several key issues by allowing the studios to retain their theater chains in exchange for a limitation on block booking. If the studios would comply with several antitrust sanctions, a restrict block booking to packages of no more than five films each, then the government would release the major distributors from all pending antitrust actions. The Big Five studios and the government agreed on a consent decree behind closed doors during a two-day conference in October 1940. The *Paramount* case was called off.

Neither side claimed victory in the Consent Decree of 1940. Compromise was evident on every issue, but the studio system came away from the first phase of the *Paramount* case clearly intact. Block booking, one of the focal points of the antitrust action, was regulated but not eliminated. The consenting studios could continue to sell films in blocks of up to five features. Full-line forcing, or the block booking of short subjects, was prohibited in the arrangement. The Big Five also agreed to outlaw blind bidding in favor of *trade showing*, a plan suggested by the Justice Department, requiring all films to be shown to prospective buyers in each territory ahead of time, much like Selznick had already pledged to do.

In return, the studios were allowed to reactivate the industry's arbitration system. The Consent Decree organized the U.S. into 31 exchange districts, with an appeals board in Rockefeller Center in close proximity to the film business headquarters in New York City. The film boards of trade would be paid for by the studios, and be administered by a new branch of the American Arbitration Association which selected board members with no film ties past or present. The Big Five provided all start-up expenses, each contributing $465,000 for the first year. Despite arbitration costs, this came at a great savings to the studios which were spending upwards of $1 million each on the *Paramount* trial. The studios had always preferred the informal "promptly heard and promptly decided" arbitrations cases, resolved within hours and without court involvement. They had desperately wanted to return to the arbitration system since it was disbanded early on in the Depression. The Consent Decree of 1940 gave them their wish.

Furthermore, Paramount, MGM, Twentieth Century-Fox, Warner Bros., and RKO were allowed to keep their movie theaters. The government would not press the divestiture issue if the vertically integrated majors promised to eradicate past predatory practices and not expand their theater holdings without federal approval.

While acknowledging the improvements brought about by the Consent Decree, the independent exhibitors were generally dissatisfied with the results of the compromise. The independent producers were enraged. The government was accused of backpedaling their antitrust case as, remarkably, neither block booking nor vertical integration was eliminated in the compromise. Granted, blocks of five films each was a considerable change compared with the Zukor block booking heyday. However for independent producers, the improvement was trifling. To the producers, even a double feature was considered intolerable. As far as they were concerned, under such a consent decree, one of their prestige films in a package with four studio B-pictures was effectively the same as before.

However, there was an escape clause included in the Consent Decree when it was signed on November 20 by Federal Judge Henry W. Goddard. Having nothing to gain in the compromise, the Little Three caused a near breakdown in the negotiations the previous July when they backed out of the consent decree agreement. Universal and Columbia, which did not own theaters, relied heavily on block booking. United Artists, which neither owned theaters nor block booked, resented the deal altogether. The Little Three became dissenting parties to the Consent Decree of 1940, and considered themselves exempt from the agreement.

So according to section seven of the Consent Decree, if the three dissenting studios could not be persuaded to adopt the provisions of the decree by June 1, 1942, the Consent Decree itself would expire. The Big Five would be free to resume their earlier activities; and the government would be permitted to reopen the *Paramount* case.

Even though the Big Five presumed that the Little Three would never sign the Consent Decree, they still had much to gain. Not only did the theater-owning studios succeed in a definite postponement of the antitrust case, but also they were permanently removed from pending ancillary cases like the *Schine* case. They were also granted a three year protection on vertical integration beginning November 1940. More importantly, arbitration was given a mandate to continue indefinitely past the expiration of the decree.

Although the Justice Department had laid off the case, the antitrust controversy continued. The Consent Decree went into effect over the protests of the independent exhibitors, on whose behalf the Justice Department initiated the *Paramount* case. The Allied Theatre Owners of the Northwest sponsored a bill in Minnesota that nullified the Consent Decree at the state level when it was passed by an overwhelming vote in April 1941. This legislation precipitating a showdown between the Big Five and the Minnesota exhibitors which the studios eventually won. Meanwhile in the U.S. Congress, only a few weeks after the signing of the Consent Decree, Senator Neely re-offered his anti-block booking bill to try to declare block booking of any kind illegal once and for all.

The well-regarded Hollywood journalist Adela Rogers St. Johns wrote a commentary on the Consent Decree for *Liberty* magazine in November 1941. "Not since the talkies came to Hollywood has there been so poignant a crisis as now embroils the movie industry," she began her article. "Every silver screen theater is being affected by it. Every star and every picture are involved. Already the changes are drastic, and you can see a few of the results if you happen to go to a movie theater. A lot of things had been simmering under the celluloid surface of Hollywood for some time. What brought them all to a boil was that document of a few million words which for brevity's sake people in Hollywood call the 'consent decree'." Despite the dissatisfaction of the independent theater owners, St. Johns predicted that the battle would gradually shift the balance of power to the exhibitors, and ultimately to the public. The article was another notable example of the emphasis given to the exhibitor problems early in the antitrust struggle.

The independent producers, who were still trying to distance themselves from the studios, were regarded as the secondary beneficiaries of the *Paramount* case. The individual efforts of Goldwyn and Selznick reflected this. Their publicity maneuvers had the antitrust flavor that would characterize the activities of the Society of Independent Motion Picture Producers later on. Unfortunately, their separate activities lacked the same effectiveness that would come with the SIMPP unity. At this point, while the independent producers' influence on the case appeared more or less nominal, the industry analysts envisioned the future being lead by exhibitors. The antitrust battle took an unexpected turn as the independent producers commandeered the *Paramount* case, and won reforms that would usher in a new Hollywood built on a foundation of independent filmmaking.

PART II

SIMPP versus
the Hollywood Studio System

5

Unity

HOLLYWOOD'S FIRST YEAR under the Consent Decree became an unexpected bonanza, at least for the major studios. Many of these factors—a resurgence in the national economy, rising movie attendance, a decline in B-film production—were coincidental with, and certainly not attributable to, the decree itself.

As an indication of the health of the studios, the major distributors intentionally created a surplus of unreleased movies. Paramount managers Y. Frank Freeman and Henry Ginsberg (formerly of Selznick International Pictures) implemented the stockpiling as a buffer against possible future catastrophe. If stricken by labor unrest or international crisis, the inventory of completed films could sustain the studio. This practice also gave the distributor the flexibility to capitalize on trends by withholding pictures until the market for the featured stars or the film's subject matter heated up. Soon all Big Five signatories had accumulated a backlog of new features. At RKO for instance, three independent productions awaited trade showing at the same time in 1942—Orson Welles' *The Magnificent Ambersons*, Samuel Goldwyn's *Pride of the Yankees*, and Walt Disney's *Bambi*.

The studios blamed the surplus of features on the consent decree restrictions. Because all of the features had to be trade shown, and none of them could be sold in blocks higher than five films, the Big Five said that the decree created a bottleneck of films. This was not entirely true, since the practice was common in times of prosperity, and in fact Paramount began its current surplus of films in the summer of 1940 before the Consent Decree was worked out. As the evaluation period for the Consent Decree came to a close, Freeman estimated that more than half of Paramount's annual output was in production or awaiting a trade show.

The independent producers claimed that the prosperity of the industry under the Consent Decree reflected the audience's appetite for quality films. The steady decrease in the number of B-films displayed "the inevitable purging of incompetence and triteness heretofore fostered by volume selling of films," Loyd Wright of United Artists explained. Again, this was also due to mitigating circumstances and not simply to the Consent Decree of 1940.

Independent exhibitors, to whom the benefits of the anti-blind bidding were directed, questioned many of the decree provisions including the mandatory trade shows. The exhibitors discovered that they did not have the large amounts of time that trade show attendance demanded. Within a short time, the special industry screenings were poorly attended by the managers and theater owners, and fell into disfavor.

The theaters had other valid complaints. They became increasingly displeased with the arbitration tribunals. As the disputes between exhibitors and studios were decided more and more in favor of the distributors, the exhibitors filed fewer and fewer cases (a virtual repeat of the arbitration circumstances in the 1920s). With studios charging more money for fewer films, the theaters actually wanted relief from the alarming increase in film rentals—which the studios also claimed was a result of the Consent Decree of 1940. Since no independent theaters were party to any consent decree, their only recourse was through petition to the government, leaving the exhibitors to wonder whether the Justice Department had brought any improvement at all to their situation.

The independent theaters wanted to make their own antitrust deal with the major studios, and the Big Five capitalized on the exhibitors' growing dissatisfaction with the Department of Justice. Certain that the Little Three (and especially United Artists) would not agree to the Consent Decree before the deadline, the Motion Picture Producers and Distributors of America decided to draft its own modified consent decree, with the support of the independent theaters.

The MPPDA joined with several exhibitor organizations to form the Motion Picture Industry Conference Committee in December 1941. Together they had a five-point mission to attack several of the industry difficulties such as tax reform and international trade. However the focus of the group was turned to something called the "Unity Plan" which the Conference Committee created as an alternative to the Consent Decree of 1940 to satisfy the Justice Department and avoid the reactivation of the *Paramount* case.

MGM general manager William F. Rogers served as chairman of the organization, and Jack Kirsch, the president of the Allied Theatre Owners of Illinois, headed the drafting committee to revise the Consent Decree. The independent exhibitors agreed to adjust the limit on block booking from five films to 12 films in each block, if the distributors gave the theaters a liberal rejection privilege. Both the distributors and exhibitors seemed pleased with the compromise, and eager to hammer out the fine points of the deal.

Meanwhile the Department of Justice became aware of the Motion Picture Industry Conference Committee's activities, and viewed their decree-amending efforts with circumspection. They sent a telegram to the group during the Motion Picture Industry Conference in January 1942, prompting a meeting of the distributors and exhibitors that lasted into the late night on January 22. Planning to immediately get the Unity Plan off the ground, the committee asked each exhibitor group to contribute $1,000, and every distributor to pledge $7,000. To promote the image of industry solidarity, the group decided to change the name of their organization to the United Motion Picture Industry (UMPI).

Though, in name, UMPI was seen as a unified effort encompassing the entire industry, the conspicuous absence of the independent producers was evident in the deal being worked out between distributors and exhibitors. Trade showing was being cast aside; block booking was on the resurgence. The prospects for the independent producers were devastating. They feared that the so-called United Motion Picture Industry was undermining any headway that had been made since 1938. The spirit of industry compromise in late 1941 and early 1942 provoked the independent producers to announce the formation of the Society of Independent Motion Picture Producers.

IN FACT, THE UNIFICATION of the independent producers had been rumored several times since the advent of the Consent Decree of 1940. Whenever any of the prominent producers were queried about their plans to organize their own trade organization, they admitted only that such an alliance was "under discussion." The Society began to take shape in secrecy throughout 1941.

Early on, the independent producers decided to organize SIMPP much like the other prominent film trade organizations by selecting a non-filmmaker as president and spokesman. The independents chose Loyd Wright, a prominent Los Angeles attorney who was well-known in the independent community. Wright served as Chaplin's lawyer since the 1920s, and even represented Mary Pickford in her divorce from Douglas Fairbanks in the mid 1930s. Other clients of his included D. W. Griffith, David O. Selznick, and Frank Capra. He served on the board of directors for Selznick International Pictures and the United Artists Corporation, among others.

The executive secretary of the early independent society was James Allen, previously the public relations head of the U.S. Department of Justice. He was known for his extensive knowledge and contacts in Washington, D.C., appropriate to the antitrust agenda of the independents. Actually Allen only served a short time with SIMPP before he was released in 1942 to assume an important wartime position as the assistant to the chief of the motion picture bureau of the Office of War Information, Lowell Mellett (the government censorship liaison sarcastically called "the United States Ambassador to Hollywood").

Financial records of the Society indicated that the group was active by at least the summer of 1941. On September 2, Wright paid a $2.00 filing fee to register the name of the Society with the California Secretary of State. Founding member Walter Wanger personally advanced James Allen expenses for the Society beginning September 5, 1941. Walt Disney contributing the first of the Society's dues in the month of November.

Seven producers signed the original articles, Charles Chaplin, Walt Disney, Samuel Goldwyn, Alexander Korda, Mary Pickford, David O. Selznick, and Walter Wanger. The organizational structure and other policies were settled during a weekend lunch-time meeting on December 20 at Perino's, a Hollywood restaurant that became a regular SIMPP meeting place. All of this was done without the general knowledge of the rest of the industry.

Early in 1942 they began to review the membership of other producers. At a meeting on January 20, they considered the invitation of two producer-directors who both seemed agreeable to the Society. The first was young Orson Welles, who had several intriguing follow-up projects to *Citizen Kane* (1941) in the works, making his Mercury Productions one of the most auspicious new independent production companies in the business. The other SIMPP applicant, the veteran filmmaker Frank Lloyd was the modest and well-liked director of *Cavalcade* (1933) and *Mutiny of the Bounty* (1935). He had headed his own production unit at Paramount, but since 1939 acted as a freelance producer. The previous November, Selznick had loaned out his contract director Alfred Hitchcock to Lloyd who produced the espionage thriller *Saboteur* (1942) at Universal. Welles decided to join the organization, but, for unknown reasons, Frank Lloyd never became a part of SIMPP—leaving the Society of Independent Motion Picture Producers with eight founding producer-members.

Not yet incorporated, the Society waited to announce the formation of the group. If they timed it just right, the publicity generated by the novel idea of independents organizing their own trade organization could be used to help derail the Unity Plan and assist the Justice Department in jump-starting the *Paramount* case.

Unfortunately the news of the Society was leaked to the trade press, without the knowledge of Wright or Allen, and published in the *Hollywood Reporter* on January 23, 1942. Taken from an undisclosed source, the article contained misinformation about the unnamed organization, and even gave a list of members which included those who were not affiliated with the group—including Frank Lloyd, Frank Capra who was already committed in wartime service, and Edward Small who would not join SIMPP for another year. Loyd Wright telegraphed the independent producers the same day of the *Reporter* story. He proposed accelerating plans for incorporation, and to have James Allen announce the formation the next week.

When the announcement was made in Hollywood, James Allen released a lengthy statement detailing the reasons why the organization was formed—to "strengthen and protect the role and function of the independent producer of motion pictures." Their primary purpose was to protect freedom of the screen "that the motion picture shall be maintained as a force for good and as an integral part of a democratic society." They vowed to publicize issues that affected the audience members, and put pressure on the Justice Department to step in when necessary. During the press conference, SIMPP discussed some of the ways in which the independents had been disadvantaged in the industry.

To clarify misleading press reports, the SIMPP announcement claimed that the intent was not "to create a minority or opposition group within the industry," but rather "to cooperate with other motion picture groups and through which me may make our own contributions to sound and healthy progress." Nevertheless, SIMPP was the only significant trade organization to oppose UMPI's Unity Plan, and was widely regarded as a potential troublemaker from the start. In an ironic twist, the *Hollywood Reporter* story broke during the Motion Picture Industry Conference, so that when the formation of UMPI made trade headlines on January 23, they shared the front page of the *Reporter* with the headline "Top Indie Producers in Setup, Organize Away From Hays Influence" along with its accompanying story about independent producers rising in collective opposition against the rest of the industry. The Society leaders were originally enraged by the news leak to the trade press, but the fortuitous timing could not have been better planned for the independents as the formation of SIMPP overshadowed the organization of UMPI.

By March 1942 the UMPI committee officially disclosed its plans for a modified block booking arrangement between studios and exhibitors. UMPI would soon try to convince the Department of Justice to accept the plan as an amendment to the Consent Decree of 1940 which was to expire in less than three months. The Unity Plan officially recommended limiting block booking to 12 films or, for the larger studios, up to 25 percent of the annual studio output. Of these dozen films, five would be trade-shown and would not be subject to exhibitor cancellation; the remaining films would be sold blindly but two of the seven could be canceled by theaters. The plan received the support of the major studios and most of the influential exhibitor organizations including the Motion Picture Theatre Owners of America, Allied States Association of Theatre Owners, and the Independent Theatre Owners Association. UMPI's Jack Kirsch explained that copies of the Unity Plan were being mailed to exhibitors throughout the country, urging the theaters to join with the major studios to petition the Department of Justice to accept the proposal as an alternative consent decree.

On the evening of March 30, the Society of Independent Motion Picture Producers reconvened at Perino's "to consider the desirability of taking firm position relative to efforts being made to change [the] system of selling pictures and resorting to block booking." The producers agreed to counteract the UMPI plan with their own statement, addressed to the independent theater owners but directed at the public. Loyd Wright issued the press release on April 13, 1942. It was sent to the leading exhibitor groups, the industry trade publications, and the national press in leading cities. This was SIMPP's first group assault on the Hollywood studio system.

The SIMPP president contended that the improved industry conditions since the Consent Decree went into effect were a direct result of the termination of old-time block booking. He boldly argued for the abolishment "both in spirit and effect, of the out-moded and highly monopolistic practice of blind selling and block booking," SIMPP cautioned the independent theaters not to be tempted by the lure of studio concessions "conceived under the guise of industry unity." The public statement denounced the so-called Unity Plan as contrary to the public interest.

SIMPP timed the press release with another publicity coup aimed against the block booking Hollywood studios. George Gallup's Audience Research Institute had undertaken a new study of block booking, at the impulse of the independent producers. The results, which made the papers on April 15, were released one day after the SIMPP attack on block booking. According to the survey of audience members, 16 percent of those interviewed understood block booking in a broad sense. This indicated that only a fraction of the public were cognizant of the studio practice. But of those who understood its implications, 90 percent were opposed to it.

The UMPI chairman William Rogers refuted the results of the block booking poll as a fractional misrepresentation of the average theatergoer. Rogers claimed that SIMPP could not possibly con-clude that the public stood behind the independent producers when the vast majority of the public was unfamiliar with block booking.

The leading theater organizations backing UMPI accused the independent producers of using their prominence with audiences to generate damaging publicity against the Unity Plan favored by the industry on a whole. "Obviously selfish," Ed Kuykendall president of the powerful Motion Picture Theatre Owners of America called the SIMPP press release. He purported that 80 percent of the exhibitors would benefit by the Unity Plan, contending that the independent producers had no genuine interest in exhibitor prob-lems: "They are trying to protect themselves in their method of sell-ing one picture at a time at exorbitant rentals."

Abram F. Myers of the Allied States Association of Theatre Owners stated that members of his organization never regarded these producers as true independents because all of their "indepen-dent" films were released by the major studios. Myers observed that in recent memory, independent producers such as David O.

Selznick worked against the Neely-Pettengill anti-block booking bills. Myers even accused the producers like Samuel Goldwyn of a not-so-reluctant participation in block booking their own films when it was to their advantage.

Samuel Goldwyn personally responded to the heated comments in an open letter published in the *New York Times* on May 3. Opening his letter with a reiteration of the Gallup poll statistics on block booking, Goldwyn promoted his anti-block booking stance as a service to the public, heralding the decline in inferior films. "The only shortcoming of the system," he said of the Consent Decree, "is that five pictures are too many." Taken aback by the accusations of selfishness, Goldwyn laid blame with the indolent theater owners who wanted to share in Hollywood's profits but none of its losses. "The trouble with the exhibitors," Goldwyn said, "is that they have no interest in the problem of the theatregoer, who wants to be intelligently entertained. Because it is cheaper and easier, because it requires no initiative or showmanship, they are willing to choke their screen with shoddy, trite product." He blamed the exhibitors of lack of foresight, "The thing they forget is that good pictures are made individually, not en masse, and they cannot be sold like sardines, one looking exactly like another in a can which has never been opened." He cautioned the theater owners that the Unity Plan would bring cheap pictures sold in bulk that would continually drive away audiences as it had during the industry slump in 1938.

In the letter, Goldwyn spotlighted one of Myers' insinuations that charged Goldwyn with block booking his own films together. Goldwyn lambasted the false claim, "I challenge Mr. Myers to present evidence of one instance in which a Goldwyn picture has been sold as a part of any package. And I guarantee that they are not going to be sold in packages as long as I make them."

In their attempt to undermine the UMPI proposal favored by the majority of the industry, SIMPP expected the spontaneous and unanimous opposition from the film trade. They also knew that they risked alienating their former allies, the independent exhibitors.

On April 29, SIMPP held a meeting to discuss the problems created by their initial attack on the Unity Plan and to "lay the groundwork for a campaign to thwart the so-called Unity effort and preserve the advantages of an open market for the licensing of films," SIMPP meeting notes indicated. The group was called together in New York by Loyd Wright and John C. Flinn, who would replace James Allen as executive secretary effective May 1. Several key independents sent their east coast representatives to the meeting— Grad Sears (United Artists vice president in charge of distribution), James Mulvey (representing Goldwyn), William B. Levy (for Disney), and Steven Pallos (from Korda's London Films).

"Changed sentiment within the trade, with the exception of a few isolated spots, is not anticipated," the meeting notes reasoned. "The drive must be aimed to reawaken the public groups and the public press to the realities of the proposals." In other words, long experience had shown that the independent producers could not convince the industry itself; they would have to take the issues to the people. SIMPP decided to undertake a national publicity push orchestrated between the eastern and western branches of the Society, as well as the publicity departments of the various producers, to convince the public to continue the pressure on the Department of Justice with a letter writing campaign.

During the first week of May, the Society drafted a petition in the form of an open letter to Assistant Attorney General Thurman Arnold. It was titled "Shall Block Booking of Motion Pictures Be Permitted to Return?" and printed as a special pamphlet to be mailed to film representatives, special civic organizations, and various government bureaus. SIMPP executive secretary John Flinn personally delivered a copy of it to Thurman Arnold, head of the antitrust division of the Justice Department.

The letter was dated June 1, 1942, the same day that the Consent Decree of 1940 expired. The Justice Department had only a short time to make up its mind, whether it would accept an alternate plan, like the Unity Plan, or take the Big Eight back to court.

In the open letter, written by Loyd Wright and John Flinn, the producers were introduced as entrepreneurs in a "unique and highly vulnerable position." They asserted that the independents' existence, and that of their highly articulate films, depended on competition free from monopoly control. "The names of the members of this Society," they said capitalizing on the filmmakers' reputations, "are synonymous with the most courageous, artistic and popular films over a period of years." In the pamphlet SIMPP reaffirmed its complete objection to block booking of any kind. The diatribe contained scathing language ("poisonous influence" and "villainous career") to decry the indulgence of block booking as "the root of all evil in the film industry."

In addition to the names of the Society president and executive secretary, the letter was signed by SIMPP executive committee members Roy Disney, Samuel Goldwyn, David O. Selznick, Walter F. Wanger.

Meanwhile, the UMPI committee presented the Unity Plan to the Department of Justice. Despite the efforts of SIMPP, the industry trades reported that the UMPI proposal would almost surely be accepted. As late as July 9, the industry expected Thurman Arnold to adopt the plan with minor changes: "Speedy Approval Is Seen," one trade headline roared. The major studios were confident; Paramount, Warners and RKO began selling their films in accordance with the plan, as if it had already been accepted. Twentieth Century-Fox, as a sign of good faith, continued with the five-picture block, expecting to make additions to the blocks when the new consent decree finalized. However, the Department of Justice admitted that a recent public opposition to the Unity Plan sparked by the independent producers gave them pause for consideration. Mentioning the SIMPP letter as one of the most significant protests, the Justice Department said it would need to consider the UMPI amendment in the light of these new circumstances. The Society of Independent Motion Picture Producers urged its members to keep the pressure on the government.

Samuel Goldwyn held a press conference in New York on July 20, 1942 to publicly denounce the UMPI plan. As a former salesman, Goldwyn had a natural ability for public relations. He became accustomed to seasonal trips to the east coast to promote his films with the same individual attention with which he had produced each feature back in Hollywood. Goldwyn discovered that his publicity sojourns to the business capital of the industry gave him ample opportunity to use the hoopla surrounding the release of his films to bring attention to various antitrust issues.

That July Goldwyn had been in New York to launch *The Pride of the Yankees* (1942) in one of the most successful film openings of his career. The Lou Gehrig biopic staring Gary Cooper was set to become one of the year's top attractions, and Goldwyn took the opportunity to further attack the Unity Plan, block booking, and the double feature. For a long time, Goldwyn tried to get his distributor RKO to exempt his films from double feature showings. Finally, with *The Pride of the Yankees* they consented to a mandatory single bill policy for Goldwyn's film.

Goldwyn believed that Americans, willing to pay a higher price for a more powerful car, would also be willing to pay higher admission to see his $1.7 million film as opposed to a low-budget B-western. "This is the time to stop all the double talk about single features," he stated in anticipation of wartime shortages and rationing. "There is a war on. We must save time and materials." He advocated the industry continue the trend toward fewer films with more quality in each one, suggesting a voluntary 40 percent reduction in Hollywood's output.

He claimed to have access to the collection of 100,000 letters in the Justice Department files that were sent by movie patrons who supported the views of the independent producers. "Any revision of the consent decree," he said in summation, "which would make it easier for studios to market bad pictures would be a step backward in the advancement of the screen."

The Justice Department indicated that the antitrust division supported this action during the war, to preserve raw film ingredients that were also essential to producing certain kinds of explosives. The antitrust division admitted publicly that they agreed with SIMPP—that to allow the Unity Plan's 12-film blocks would result in the unadvisable trend to more B-films. Seeing the new report from Arnold, John Flinn telegraphed the Society: "AM MORE

ENCOURAGED THAN AT ANY PREVIOUS TIME THAT WE ARE WINNING THIS UMPI FIGHT."

The Unity Plan was indeed toppled by the Department of Justice when Thurman Arnold rejected the proposal on August 17. Thereafter the United Motion Picture Industry faded. William Rogers his work at UMPI, then resigned as general sales manager of MGM to become president of RKO.

Now that the Consent Decree of 1940 had expired and was completely nullified, block booking became a question for the Big Five studios. Technically the major distributors were under no block booking restrictions at all. However, the overwhelming public opinion made cheapie film production unacceptable with large segments of the audience and the government. In a September 1942 Gallup poll, 71 percent of the respondents preferred that double features were outlawed during the war, while an additional 18 percent were undecided. The message was overwhelming: audiences did not want bulk-produced films.

Metro-Goldwyn-Mayer announced that it would modify the five film limitation and adopt a new policy of eight film blocks. The other Big Five distributors continued to sell films in blocks of five as a sign of good faith. All films would continue to be trade shown. Most studios followed the theory that it would be wiser to disappoint the exhibitors (by continuing with the unpopular provisions of the Consent Decree) than to antagonize the government (with reverting to pre-*Paramount* case practices).

For the duration of World War II, the Big Eight control over the American film business actually proved advantageous for the country. With a mature oligopoly in full power, the government could closely monitor the industry without resorting to nationalization. The major producer-distributors proved to be patriotic participants as they complied with the rationing of materials from raw film to movie set construction. In conjunction with the Office of War Information, the content of films was temporarily regulated as well, handled in a manner not unlike the way in which the MPPDA already enforced the production code itself.

Though the oligopoly was a plague on peacetime economic free-
doms, the Hollywood studio system became a powerful asset in the
war effort. The Hollywood monopoly received a stay from the government for the duration, similar to the delay caused by the drastic
circumstances of the Great Depression. However, the Justice
Department would not sanction the anti-competitive practices the
way it had under the National Industrial Recovery Act in 1933.
Officially the antitrust division still claimed the *Paramount* case
was open, but clearly the Roosevelt administration was not interested in upsetting the industry as the country became preoccupied
with World War II.

6

Moving In

THE SOCIETY OF Independent Motion Picture Producers immediately expanded beyond the eight founding producers, as invitations were extended to filmmakers who had gained independence from the studio system. The first new addition to the group came when former MGM producer Hunt Stromberg joined in the spring of 1942.

Stromberg had been one of the key MGM executives for many years. In the 1920s he was one of MGM's "big four" managers along with Louis B. Mayer, Irving Thalberg, and Harry Rapf. Stromberg's stature at the studio increased in 1933 when Mayer suppressed Thalberg's central-producer system to undermine the growing authority of Thalberg and to redistribute creative control at the studio. Thereafter Stromberg became one of the four prestige film producers with his own unit and an uncommonly high degree of freedom at the studio. The other three MGM producers were David Selznick, Walter Wanger, and Irving Thalberg. In 1937 after the exit of Selznick and Wanger and the death of Thalberg, Stromberg was invited into the ultra-rare management circle that received a percentage of Loew's profits—1.5 percent in addition to his $8,000 weekly guarantee. During the depression when Loew's finances consistently landed in the black, the Treasury Department listed Stromberg as one of the ten highest paid executives in the United States. Seeking more creative freedom, he left MGM and formed his own independent production company before joining SIMPP in 1942.

Stromberg, born in Louisville, Kentucky in 1894, had a career as a newspaper reporter and sports writer before making the jump to film. He followed a fellow advertising friend into the motion picture industry, and became publicity director for Goldwyn Pictures. In 1918 the company sent Stromberg to California, where he developed an interest in filmmaking, and served as assistant to Thomas Ince. After writing, producing, and directing his first film in 1921, he resigned from the Ince staff to form Hunt Stromberg Productions.

Stromberg relinquished his ties to the major film companies of the time to establish himself as an independent producer. In February 1922, Stromberg interested Bull Montana, a popular matinee idol and former Fairbanks protégé, in a long-term contract to star in two- and three-reel comedies. He also hired comedy director Mal St. Clair, who had been responsible for several successful shorts with Mack Sennett and Buster Keaton. Soon the publicity helped bring in several distribution offers from Robertson-Cole and W. W. Hodkinson. His independent debut came after Sid Grauman saw a rough cut of Stromberg's *A Ladies' Man* (1922) and immediately booked it for a premiere at his Million Dollar Theater in Los Angeles on April 30, 1922.

After only a few years as a pioneering independent, Stromberg abandoned his own company in 1924 to join the newly merged Metro-Goldwyn-Mayer as an associate. During his distinguished tenure he was responsible for over one hundred features, specializing in dramas and musicals. His $2 million, three hour production of *The Great Ziegfeld* (1936) became the longest Hollywood sound film at the time, MGM's most expensive film since *Ben-Hur* (1925), and one of the studio's biggest hits. Some sources have credited Stromberg as the first MGM supervisor to receive "produced by" credit at a time when the title of "producer" was alien to the film studios.

But Stromberg ended up in a contract dispute with Louis B. Mayer in 1941. On December 13, after 18 years with MGM, Stromberg resigned, walking away from a lucrative contract with three years to go. Mayer finally released him from his obligations, and Stromberg officially left the studio on February 10, 1942. The trade papers expected him to join United Artists in some capacity, perhaps working with Selznick or forming a partnership with former UA executive Murray Silverstone who recently resigned from the studio. Instead Stromberg revived his independent production company exactly 20 years after its first incarnation, and signed his own five-year distribution deal with United Artists.

Stromberg was already well-connected to the independent producers, and many of his employees were important members of the old Selznick International team, including Lowell V. Calvert and Kay Brown. Myron Selznick, who brokered the deal between Stromberg and UA, was one of the primary investors of Hunt Stromberg Productions, Inc. Also, David Selznick's attorney Lester Roth became secretary of the independent production company, and Loyd Wright president of SIMPP served as Stromberg's lawyer.

He launched the company with a project based on Gypsy Rose Lee's *The G-String Murders* which was released as *Lady of Burlesque* (1943) with Barbara Stanwyck. It provided his independent company and UA with an immediate hit that grossed $1.85 million.

THE SIMPP PRODUCERS also welcomed William Cagney into the Society during its first year. As the business manager for his famous older brother James Cagney, William gave up his own acting career in 1934 to serve a similar purpose as Sydney Chaplin had for his younger brother Charlie. After the Cagneys battled against the studio system for years, the brothers organized Cagney Productions in 1942, and joined the independent movement.

James Cagney began his Hollywood career at Warner Bros. in 1930 at the age of 30, and quickly gained a reputation as one of the most difficult and independent-minded of the studio contract actors. He rode the studio's wave of gangster films to achieve near

instant popularity, then fought for years to avoid being typecast in
tough-guy roles by Warner. He complained about his journeyman
salary and the factory-like conditions in the early 1930s, and voluntarily went on suspension in a much-publicized showdown with
the studio, then an unprecedented move by a performer. His weekly salary was doubled to $3,000 when he returned to the studio in
1932.

He then walked out on his contract again that same year in a disagreement largely sparked by block booking. After receiving word
that his films were being used as the primary attraction in Warner
Bros. movie blocks, he sought to punish the studio for profitably
pre-selling his films by walking out on an unfinished picture called
Blessed Event which was subsequently assigned to another Warner
contract actor. Again he was reinstated at Warners, with a higher
salary, and greater creative stipulations.

In 1936, he left the studio again. No major studio would touch
the free-agent actor, and even the independent producers like
Goldwyn and Selznick reportedly were not willing to reward the
highly-paid star and risk encouraging other actors to walk away
from their production commitments. So this time he began to take
his first steps as an independent with his brother William Cagney,
who had taken an active role in the contract disagreements with
Jack Warner.

Grand National Films, one of the independent distributors was
willing deal with the Cagney brothers. Edward L. Alperson, former
Warner sales manager, operated the up-and-coming Poverty Row
studio which had acquired the backlot of the influential Educational
Pictures (the short-subject specialist that released Felix the Cat
silent cartoons in the 1920s and introduced Shirley Temple in
1934). Hoping to follow the path of Columbia Pictures, Alperson
began to seek A-list talent, and agreed to grant Cagney semi-inde-
pendence with complete creative control, $100,000 per film, and
ten percent of the profits. But like many ill-fated independent distributors that tried to make the jump to major status, Grand
National was unable to secure first-run bookings in the era of the
big studios. The debt-ridden company was liquidated in 1940.

Anticipating the demise of Grand National, William Cagney negotiated yet another deal with Warner Bros. The studio offered James Cagney $150,000 per picture, complete script approval, plus profit participation of any film the reached blockbuster level of $1.5 million. William Cagney would oversee quality control as producer, and receive screen credit as associate producer. The Cagneys finished out their contract at Warner's with a series of well-made and highly-regarded films, culminating with *Yankee Doodle Dandy* (1942).

In March 1942 the brothers announced the formation of their own independent company. William Cagney, who continued to show great promise as studio producer, proved himself to be on par with other enterprising independents, acquiring property and talent to expand their organization beyond a mere showcase for his brother Jim. The company was commonly known as Cagney Productions, but its official name was William Cagney Productions Inc.

The Cagneys were courted by United Artists at the same time as Stromberg. Both of these production companies benefitted from UA's new willingness to provide financing in an effort to generate more feature product. In the past independent producers, had to bring their own money to the table, financing their own movies through their own means. But still suffering from the product shortage following Goldwyn's departure in 1940, UA decided to offer partial financing through its own United Artists Productions. To help raise additional funds, James Cagney generated collateral by deferring his own $150,000 salary, as part of his agreement with UA.

THE THIRD IMPORTANT ADDITION to SIMPP in 1942 was industry pioneer Sol Lesser whose experience in all three branches of the film industry made him a unique SIMPP member.

At the age of 17, Lesser inherited his family's San Francisco nickelodeon upon the death of his father in 1907. Following an aggressive expansion into distribution, he became a leading film exchange operator in California. He also ventured into production, and became a vertically-integrated mainstay at First National. In 1920, Lesser founded the West Coast Theatres, in partnership with Abe and Mike Gore, which also rapidly expanded until it became the main first-run theater chain in the Pacific states. With plans of a leisurely retirement, Lesser sold his West Coast interests to a financier in 1926. Shortly thereafter the independent chain fell under the control of William Fox, and became the scourge of the independent producers for many years.

His retirement was short; and boredom prompted his reentry to the film industry as an independent producer with his own company called Principle Pictures. His purchase of a small Los Angeles theater became the start of his Principle Theatres chain. He even formed the Principle Distributing Corporation, and later created his own financing operation, the Principle Securities Corporation.

His friendship with other veteran independents also created strong ties at both United Artists and SIMPP. When Joseph Schenck was at UA, Sol Lesser was closely associated with him in several film and theater ventures. The Lessers were instrumental in bringing Walt Disney to United Artists in the early 1930s, and remained life-long friends of the Disneys.

Lesser's association with Charlie Chaplin went back even further. Back at First National, Lesser claimed that part of his responsibility was to deliver Chaplin his payment upon delivery of his films. In the early 1920s, Lesser began producing pictures with child star Jackie Coogan concurrent with Chaplin's masterpiece *The Kid* (1921). Lesser respected Chaplin's desire to postpone the release of the Lesser-Coogan films until after Chaplin completed his film. By doing so, Lesser not only ensured a friendship with Chaplin that lasted for years, but Lesser also found that his films with Coogan were far more valuable by waiting until after the success of *The Kid*. Chaplin even invested in the Progressive Theatres at a time when Chaplin refused to become a partner in even the United Artists Theatre Circuit. Chaplin held on to the Progressive stock for many years, and during his exile in the 1950s, Lesser visited Chaplin in Switzerland and repurchased the shares of the theater company.

Sol Lesser also produced the Tarzan movies beginning in the 1930s, another excellent example of the urbane business methods of the respected producer. In 1931 when MGM was making the highly-anticipated *Tarzan the Apeman* (1932), Lesser announced that he had previously acquired the film rights to the Tarzan character from another independent producer who had optioned the rights from Edgar Rice Burroughs himself in 1928. The courts upheld Lesser's rights, and Lesser was in a position to put the screws to MGM. Surprisingly, Lesser allowed MGM to continue with its version for a nominal fee. This resulted in a tremendous coup for Lesser. By momentarily stepping aside, just as he had with the Chaplin-Coogan arrangement, *Tarzan the Apeman* became a sensation for MGM in 1932, and left Lesser with the lucrative film rights to future film adaptations. By not alienating the creator of Tarzan, Lesser also entered into a close association with Edgar Rice Burroughs. Lesser released his own Tarzan films through his Principle Distributing Corporation in 1933, and the series became one of the mainstays of his independent operation.

In the fall of 1941, Sol Lesser took an executive producer position at RKO but found it lacking the excitement of independent production. During a management shakeup at RKO shortly after SIMPP was formed, Lesser decided to return to independent filmmaking during this exciting time for the independents. He quit RKO in February 1942, after only six months as an executive, and joined the Society of Independent Motion Picture Producers.

SIMPP ALSO BEGAN to lose the first of its members in 1943 when Alexander Korda left the Society to enter into a short-lived merger between his London Films and MGM-British. Soon, Korda returned to independent production, but he focused his efforts in the British film industry, and never returned to SIMPP.

Nevertheless, SIMPP expansion was steady during its early years when World War II restrictions discouraged new film companies that otherwise would have filled the Society. At the end of its second year, SIMPP consisted of 12 member-producers: Goldwyn, Selznick, Disney, Chaplin, Pickford, Wanger, Welles, Stromberg,

Cagney, Lesser, and two new members Edward Small and Edward A. Golden.

Edward Small had one of the most prolific careers of any independent producer, a longevity to rival even Goldwyn. However unlike Goldwyn, Small shunned publicity, so that even though he was one of the most influential and wealthy Hollywood producers, his low profile left him largely unknown to the public.

Edward Small, whose physical stature befit his name, was a talent agent with production ambitions much like Myron Selznick. At the age of 15, Small organized his own agency in New York, and adopted his life-long slogan: "Personality is a commodity." Beginning in 1917 at age 26, his entrance into production was gradual. He moved his operation, the Edward Small Agency (later the Small Company), to Hollywood and turned to producing full-time in 1924.

He cofounded several memorable independent production companies. In 1932 he formed Reliance Pictures in a three-way partnership with Joseph Schenck and Harry M. Goetz. With his company releasing through United Artists, Small produced *I Cover the Waterfront* (1933), *Palooka* (1934), and *The Count of Monte Cristo* (1934). In 1938 he formed Edward Small Productions where he continued to make some of his high-grade literary projects including *The Man in the Iron Mask* (1939). Small was also a critic of the United Artists management, and threatened to lead a sit-down strike against the studio owners in 1942 when UA failed to meet his terms. Edward Small joined SIMPP in 1943, and became the chairman of the membership committee during the Society's great expansion at the end of World War II.

Edward Golden, called "Doc" by friends, was a dentist practicing in Boston when he entered the film industry around 1912. Allegedly, when Hiram Abrams visited Golden for a tooth extraction, the affluence of the visitor prompted the dentist to look into the film business. Entering at the states rights level, he became established as one of the leading New England franchise distributors following his vigorous promotion of *The Four Horsemen of the Apocalypse* (1921).

Later Golden became an important manager at Monogram Pictures, where he hired Steve Broidy, the individual who became one of the most prominent independent distributors. Golden joined Republic Pictures and then decided to form his own independent production company in 1941. His Poverty Row experience compelled him to invest in low-cost, high-yield productions. His first independent film *No Greater Sin* (1941) cost $42,000, and made $150,000. Next he produced the acclaimed anti-Nazi hit *Hitler's Children* (1942), released through RKO at a negative cost of $200,000 and grossed a phenomenal $3.25 million.

As THE UNITED STATES effort in the World War II turned a corner in 1944, SIMPP membership was aided by the favorable tax shelter set up by the government earlier in the war. Under this tax reform, highly-paid employees were able to reduce their income taxes by forming their own production companies. Most of the Hollywood movie stars and executives payed between 60 and 70 percent of their income in taxes. In the most extreme cases, personal income tax topped out at around 90 percent. By forming a company or partnership, an independent would be subject to only a 25 percent capital gains tax.

Even the established independents had been burdened by the previous tax structure which had subjected the struggling independents to considerable restrictions. For example, David O. Selznick forever lost the residual rights to *Gone With the Wind* (1939) in a tragic business blunder that was caused by the Treasury Department's narrow interpretation of the tax laws at the time that Selznick International Pictures was liquidated in 1941. His loss was the major studios' gain, as the film fell into the hands of Metro-Goldwyn-Mayer. The classic went on to make millions of dollars more for MGM in the years to come.

The new liberating tax inducement provided an influx of independents that helped diversify the Society of Independent Motion Picture Producers. SIMPP began to offer membership to production companies as well as to individuals. The first of these came in 1944—Rainbow Productions, the corporate alter ego of writer-producer-director Leo McCarey.

McCarey, with over 20 years experience directing in Hollywood, was one of the most celebrated filmmakers to emerge from the studio system. He was also one of the many talented alumni from the Hal Roach Studio, the independent company which launched the careers of many other independents-to-be including Harold Lloyd, George Stevens, Tay Garnett, and Frank Capra. McCarey has been widely credited as the mastermind behind the Laurel and Hardy team-up, and the director of some of their best silent two-reelers produced by Hal Roach.

Roach, also famous for the *Our Gang* (a.k.a. Roach's Rascals or *The Little Rascals*), had operated as an independent since 1918 with a Pathé distribution deal. In the 1930s, as his short subjects kingdom was threatened by double features and block booking, he sold his backlog of independently-produced shorts to his distributor MGM in order to convert to feature filmmaking with films like the *Topper* trilogy. In 1938 Roach moved his production company to United Artists, and produced *Of Mice and Men* (1939) and *One Million B.C.* (1940). He joined SIMPP around the same time as Rainbow.

Leo McCarey, who had left the Hal Roach Studio in 1929 to become a freelance director, made films for several independents including Joseph Schenck (*Indiscreet*, 1931) and Sam Goldwyn (*The Kid From Spain*, 1932). McCarey hit pay dirt at Paramount directing the Marx Brothers in *Duck Soup* (1933), and at Columbia with the blockbuster *The Awful Truth* (1937).

One of his greatest box office successes was *Going My Way* (1944) which McCarey made for Paramount. The film was based on McCarey's own original story, which he developed into a Bing Crosby vehicle. McCarey's profit participation as writer-producer-director on *Going My Way* made him the highest paid artist in Hollywood that year earning over $1 million.

But he was not content to remain merely a studio employee. He created a sequel to *Going My Way*, and decided to take it independent. The film, *The Bells of St. Mary's* (1945), was produced by his own company Rainbow Productions and released through RKO.

Once again, McCarey's movie became one of the most popular hits of the year, out-grossing the already-enormous take of *Going My Way*. The success of *The Bells of St. Mary's* also had a trigger effect on the principle actors Bing Crosby and Ingrid Bergman, both of whom went independent shortly thereafter. In 1946 Crosby, then the number one box office star in Hollywood, likewise joined SIMPP.

ANOTHER SIMPP addition in 1944, Benedict Bogeaus, rose out of obscurity to the forefront of the independent movement in only a few short years. A Chicago native born in 1904, Ben Bogeaus began as a real estate investor who ventured into several business enterprises, including radio manufacturing, zipper-making, and eventually film production. He divided his time between America and Europe, claiming to have made and lost several fortunes during his life. He experimented with films in France and Germany, then came to Hollywood in 1940 hoping to find a film-related business opportunity. Following a stint as a manufacturer of a portable film development system ideal for wartime use, he established himself as an ace independent producer with his first four films—*The Bridge of San Luis Rey* (1944), *Dark Waters* (1944), *Captain Kidd* (1945), and *The Diary of a Chambermaid* (1946).

Strictly speaking, his film budgets fell below the A-category, but the features yielded unusually high profits by utilizing name stars and efficient production value to belie the movies' actual costs. "All independent producers go broke sooner or later," Bogeaus later remarked. "It's because they try to make artistic pictures. I make good commercial ones. It pays off."

One of Bogeaus' lasting legacies was as landlord of the General Service Studio in Hollywood which played a key role in the independent movement. The General Service Studio, originally known as Hollywood Studios, Inc., was built in 1919 by a former Chaplin employee John Jasper. General Service neither produced nor distributed; it was simply an open film facility with space for rent to producers who wanted to stay off the major studio backlots. The General Service property was located in Hollywood on Santa

Monica Boulevard on the corner of Las Palmas, just a few blocks east of old United Artists (Samuel Goldwyn) lot. The General Service was a popular production facility even before Bogeaus. Harold Lloyd, who went independent in 1922, made films on the lot before he purchased his own studio situated on a hill overlooking Santa Monica Boulevard. In 1926, Howard Hughes filmed his earliest movies at the General Service lot, which at the time was known as the Metropolitan Studios.

The ownership and the name of the studio lot changed several times in the 1920s and 1930s. In fact, it was not known as the General Service Studio until 1933 when the powerful Western Electric division of AT&T acquired the sound-equipped lot to add to its extensive holdings that dominated early talking films. To avoid antitrust scrutiny, Western Electric transferred the property to another of its subsidiaries known as General Service. The government busted Western Electric's talkie empire, and ordered AT&T to sell General Service in 1941. At the time, Benedict Bogeaus was one of the independent producers leasing space on the lot, along with others like Alexander Korda who made *The Thief of Bagdad* (1940) there.

Bogeaus outbid Edward Small for control of the studio in the spring of 1942 after General Service was put on the market. Actually, Bogeaus underbid Small, acquiring control of the property for $460,000 (and $200,000 of liabilities) by promising to allow the government to use the facility for defense purposes. Under Bogeaus' control, General Service soon became a popular alternative to the more stately Goldwyn lot that usually operated at capacity. By 1945 the General Service Studio housed 21 independent producers, most of whom released their films through United Artists, and many of whom became members of SIMPP.

David L. Loew was one of those producers. In fact, he briefly took control of the General Service Studio in 1943 before the lot reverted back to Bogeaus in March 1946. One of the twin sons of MGM founder Marcus Loew, David was elected to the Loew's Inc. board in 1922 at age 24. He resigned from the studio in 1935 to launch his own production career at Hal Roach. He then became involved with several independent ventures of his own beginning in 1941. He partnered with director Albert Lewin, a friend of his and a former supervisor at MGM under Thalberg, to release *The Moon and Sixpence* (1942) through United Artists. In 1943 with Arthur S. Lyons, Loew organized a company called Producing Artists, Inc. And then, at the end of the war, he formed Enterprise Productions with Charles Einfeld, the former Warner Bros. publicity chief. Some of David Loew's best remembered films were produced at the General Service Studio, including Jean Renoir's *The Southerner* (1945) and the Marx Brothers' *A Night in Casablanca* (1946).

Constance Bennett was another independent producer who made films at General Service, released through United Artists, and maintained a SIMPP membership. Bennett was an industry veteran with experience as an actor that went back to the days of Lewis J. Selznick, the father of Myron and David O. Selznick. She entered films through her father, matinee idol Richard Bennett, who starred in Samuel Goldwyn's first independent production *The Eternal City* (1923). A chance meeting between Sam Goldwyn and Constance lead to her emergence as a Hollywood performer in 1924. She attained stardom in the early talkies period at RKO as the sultry blonde in movies like David O. Selznick's *What Price Hollywood?* (1932). Outspoken and dissident, Bennett had a canny business sense that lead to her desire to become her own producer. She also earned a permanent place at the card table of high-stakes gamblers Goldwyn, Selznick, and Schenck. Later in life she operated her own clothing and cosmetics enterprise with extraordinary success. Her younger sister Joan Bennett married Walter Wanger in 1940, making Constance the sister-in-law of the SIMPP founder.

Another SIMPP producer, Harry Sherman, who was born in 1884, began in the film industry as an exhibitor, and made a killing on *The Birth of a Nation* (1915) states rights in the west, much like Louis B. Mayer had in New England. In 1935 he formed Harry Sherman Productions planning to produce low-budget Westerns. His claim-to-fame—the introduction of the Hopalong Cassidy character—made his films so exceptionally popular that he became one of the few B-film independents that was distributed by major studios (both Paramount and United Artists).

Arnold Pressburger, a Slavic immigrant about the same age as Alexander Korda, spent many years as a producer in Europe before he arrived in Hollywood in 1941. In fact, at the Sascha Film studio in Vienna after World War I, Pressburger served as a production executive when Alexander Korda made films there as a Hungarian refugee. While in Hollywood, Pressburger continued to ally himself with high-profile European expatriate directors. Among his films, which he released through United Artists, were Josef von Sternberg's *The Shanghai Gesture* (1941), Fritz Lang's *Hangmen Also Die* (1943), and René Clair's *It Happened Tomorrow* (1944).

Another cosmopolitan who joined SIMPP toward the end of the war, Seymour Nebenzal, was actually a Jewish native of New York, but entered films in Berlin and was commonly thought of as a European. He founded Nero-Film in the mid-1920s, and produced the classic thriller from Fritz Lang, *M* (1931). Facing Nazi censorship, Nebenzal fled Germany, crossing the boarder with his automobile full of film negative. He changed the true spelling of his name from "Nebenzahl," and came to Hollywood in 1939 where he produced *Summer Storm* (1944), *Whistle Stop* (1946), *Heaven Only Knows* (1947), and *Siren of Atlantis* (1948). Following financial setbacks in the late 1940s, Seymour Nebenzal returned to Germany on a permanent basis in 1950 but remained a SIMPP member essentially up to his death in 1961.

Writer-producer-director Andrew L. Stone was another General Service tenant, UA producer, and SIMPP member who helped influence the independent movement. While working for the major studios in the beginning of his independent career, Stone concentrated on light comedy and musical formats (*Hi, Diddle Diddle*, 1943, *Bedside Manner*, 1945, and *Fun on a Weekend*, 1947). However he is best remembered for his later thrillers and urban melodramas (*The Steel Trap*, 1952, A *Blueprint For Murder*, 1953, and *Cry Terror*, 1958). By utilizing natural street settings and actual locations, he pioneered a portable, flexible production method with a much smaller crew that added a unique flavor of authenticity and permitted the production of quality films on a tight budgets. Stone established himself during the silent era with *The Elegy* (1927), his independently-produced and economically-made two-reel movie that came to the attention of Adolph Zukor. During the 1930s and early 1940s he was a director at Paramount and Twentieth Century-Fox. With his own production company he made the memorable musical *The Girl Said No* (1937) distributed by Grand National.

In 1943 he formed his own independent company called Andrew L. Stone Productions to release through United Artists. His wife Virginia Lively Stone became one of his chief collaborators. When the Stones left United Artists in 1947, they were called "Hollywood's only man-and-wife moviemakers," running their production company from their home. Andrew wrote, produced, and directed; Virginia served as co-producer, film editor, and production manager. For their later crime stories, they became amateur criminologists by keeping in touch with police stations across the country. They drew their source material from their own private files of over 15,000 criminal case histories.

Industry veteran Charles R. Rogers also joined SIMPP at the end of World War II. He entered the film industry as an independent exchange operator, and purchased the New York states rights for the controversial smash hit Elinor Glyn's *Three Weeks* (1924). Rogers served as sales manager at L. J. Selznick's Select Pictures, and then as business partner with Hunt Stromberg before Stromberg went to MGM. In 1928 First National offered him an independent producer contract, and Charles Rogers launched his own company. After moving his operation to the newly-formed RKO, he became temporary head of production during an RKO management crisis in 1931.

When the Laemmles were ousted from Universal in 1935, Charles Rogers was brought in to revive production. He is best remembered for producing Gregory La Cava's *My Man Godfrey* (1936) and for originating the Deanna Durbin series which carried the company through the tail end of the Great Depression. Rogers returned to independent production in 1938, and by 1941 joined

United Artists. He was a well-respected member of SIMPP from 1945 until his fatal car accident in 1957 at age 64.

As THE WAR drew to a close, the Society of Independent Motion Picture Producers had expanded to 25 members. The members each contributed annual dues of $5,000 to help the association meet the growing demands of the independent movement. The funds also allowed the Society to increase its activities, especially since the independent producers decided to jump-started the antitrust movement even before the end of World War II.

7

Halls and Armories

GOING INTO WORLD WAR II, the independents appeared to be in a favorable position for the duration of the conflict. As previously mentioned, the government agreed with the independent producers that the elimination of widespread B-filmmaking made sense from the standpoint of conservation of money, man-hours, and raw materials. This prevailing attitude was borne out by the Justice Department's rejection of the UMPI Unity Plan in August 1942, as well as the visit of the Office of War Information's Lowell Mellett who came to Hollywood later that year with a message intended to inspire the end of the double feature.

Independent production companies, which by nature required a relatively small staff, also escaped many of the problems faced by studios that lost a significant portion of their man-power to wartime activities. In fact, of all the independents, Walt Disney Productions was hit the hardest by the war, since the animation studio required a large number of skilled workers, similar to one of the Hollywood majors.

The wartime was a boom period for the American cinema in general. As most forms of amusement were subject to radical government rationing, the movies became the primary public entertainment, and the film industry claimed a record 25 percent of the country's total recreational dollars. Swing-shift screenings for factory workers kept many urban movie houses showing features at all hours, frequently to crowded theaters. Federal movie admission taxes even made film-going a patriotic activity. "You could run film backward through a projector and people would look at it," went one famous wartime saying in Hollywood.

However, the elimination of the double feature and the focus on quality films with long stays in the theater unexpectedly put the squeeze on independents for several reasons. Even though SIMPP had tenaciously supported these reforms at the outset of the war, the majors turned it into their own benefit. As films took longer to make their way through the city runs, the major studios quickly filled the few open spots with studio-produced features. Often, theaters were booked far in advance, creating a freeze on the first-run and key subsequent-run showings for many movies, which SIMPP claimed was in clear violation of antitrust laws. The SIMPP executive secretary John Flinn reported in 1943, "present conditions are tougher and selling is more difficult for the independent than at any time in the history of the business."

Many of the top independents were also hindered by the continuing reluctance of theater chains to offer producers a percentage of the box office. During World War II when popular films were easy to come by, many exhibitors were not inclined to go out of their way to show an independent movie, only to be badgered by a producer who wanted a cut of the theater proceeds.

Of the independent producers who opposed the theater policy, Goldwyn was the most outspoken and vehement. The problems were two fold, he claimed. To begin with, he blamed the major studios for taking advantage of the box office prosperity by decreasing the number of films without improving film quality. Then he criticized the theaters that refused to pay more money for better films, which discouraged the producers of prestige films.

"The art of showmanship has been forgotten," he said, "and little regard is being shown the public or the future of the business because of the satisfied attitude that anything or everything shows a profit nowadays."

Like many of the independents, Goldwyn actively participated in distribution by appointing his own sales representative to cooperate in the booking and marketing of each of his films. According to his distribution deal with RKO, Goldwyn received the right of final approval of every rental agreement, as he and other producers previously had at United Artists. This meant that Goldwyn could cancel any deal with a theater that offered an unsatisfactory price. In fact, most UA producers were accustomed to this provision to insure that their films realized their commercial potential. Goldwyn decided to exercise this option to take a bold stand against the theater monopolies that existed in territories all over the country.

While the major studios held oligopoly control over the first-run theaters in the major cities, many independent chains monopolized the neighborhood and rural regions. One such closed situation was the Sparks circuit in Florida. The Sparks chain had once been a part of the short-lived Universal theater circuit from 1925 to 1927 until Carl Laemmle, faced with the expense of converting to sound films, voluntarily sold off the theaters. Sparks was an independents chain that had a local monopoly in 14 cities in Florida. It was a small-scale example of some of the other theater chains that maintained a regional monopoly even though they were not affiliates of the Hollywood studios (i.e., the Schine chain in upstate New York and Sudekum theaters in Tennessee).

In early 1942, the Sparks theater circuit denied Goldwyn's demands for a percentage deal on his latest release *The Little Foxes* (1941). Goldwyn withheld the film altogether, knowing that the highly-anticipated movie—then doing record box office in the major cities—would help publicize the squeeze being put on the independent producers. Goldwyn bought large advertisements in Florida newspapers with the headline, "I Regret That You Cannot See 'The Little Foxes' in _____," inserting the name of the respective Sparks-controlled town. In the ads, he explained why he felt the percentage basis was the only fair way for both producers and theaters to profit. "I believe and have always believed that the producer of a motion picture, the man who invests his money in it and exercises his judgement which make it good or bad, should gain or lose in proportion to the favor with which the public receives the picture." Goldwyn also included the location of the nearest theater that would be playing his movie.

Over the next few years, Goldwyn refused to show his films in communities dominated by a theater chain that declined to share the box office. He invoked the same philosophy that W. W. Hodkinson pioneered in the days of the Patents Trust, Goldwyn claiming that giving producers a share of the profits of their films was the only way to insure that producers would continue to make quality movies.

Under the unfavorable conditions for independent producers, SIMPP hoped that the government would reinitiate the *Paramount* case before the end of World War II. As of November 20, 1943, the Department of Justice was legally free of all consent decree restrictions, and could pursue the case at will. Meanwhile, throughout 1943, representatives of the Society of Independent Motion Picture Producers met with Tom C. Clark, the new assistant attorney general who headed the antitrust division. The Justice Department seemed to express an interest in reactivating the *Paramount* case, and welcomed the potential involvement of SIMPP to aid the prosecution. However, months passed with no government action taken.

When Tom C. Clark took over the Hollywood antitrust suit, he told the press that the Justice Department was interested in pursuing the case, but had not yet decided how to approach it. SIMPP executive secretary John Flinn called together three SIMPP east coast representatives, Grad Sears, James Mulvey, and Roy Disney. In a confidential meeting, they proposed that the Society should prepare its own brief to submit to the Department of Justice to avoid any further delays in the *Paramount* suit. They began the first stage of their plans by authorizing the Society to gather a collection of evidence against the monopolies in the film industry to present to the government. The Society encouraged its members to publicize the antitrust issue, and offered its support to any independent producer willing to take part. Sam Goldwyn lead the assault to help SIMPP reach its goal of getting the Justice Department to start the antitrust case back up by the summer of 1944.

Goldwyn prepared his latest release *Up in Arms* (1944) as a showcase for his recent discovery, comedian Danny Kaye. Hoping that Kaye would become a valuable asset for Goldwyn's independent company, the producer spent $2 million on a lavish Technicolor musical to serve as the comedian's film debut. The producer even requisitioned the Walt Disney Studio to create an animated finale for the film's climax. (After great expense, the Disney animation was cut out of *Up in Arms* by Goldwyn, who was accustomed to making last minute—and usually very costly— changes in production while searching for the most suitable final product.)

Sam Goldwyn decided to use the appropriately-titled *Up in Arms* to bring attention to the antitrust struggle. In one the most skillfully-orchestrated promotional stunts of his career, Goldwyn involved the Society of Independent Motion Picture Producers in the marketing of the film. The resulting publicity coup made national news and became part of Hollywood legend.

Goldwyn had announced that all theaters that wanted to show *Up in Arms* would be required to do so on a percentage deal with the producer. Releasing through RKO, Goldwyn believed that *Up in Arms* had enough clout to take on some of the more difficult theater monopolies, and he was content to refuse any theater chain that would not offer him a share of the box office.

In the spring of 1944, he took on Balaban & Katz, the massive Paramount subsidiary that controlled the troublesome Chicago area. In the past when the Balaban & Katz chain had agreed to pay for Goldwyn films on a modified percentage deal, the films were given undesirable play dates and showings on off-hours. Goldwyn believed his films in the Chicago area were earning one-eighth of what they would in an open situation.

Carrying out his long-promised threat to take his films and exhibit them himself, Goldwyn rented the Woods theater, a small independent movie house, to show *Up in Arms* in the Chicago area. Goldwyn's feature played successfully throughout the summer, and netted him over $175,000, a fantastic take for a theater of limited means, and far in excess of the $30,000 he usually received from the Paramount circuit.

The most significant *Up in Arms* battle came later that year when Goldwyn and SIMPP took on a subsidiary of the notorious Fox West Coast theater monopoly. SIMPP helped Goldwyn single out Reno, Nevada as one of the areas where the Fox theaters operated without competition, and decided to make a stand there. The showdown became one of the defining moments in the independent struggle.

All theaters within 35 miles of Reno were controlled by T. & D. Junior Enterprises, Inc., a Twentieth Century-Fox affiliate also one-quarter owned by Fox West Coast. The T. & D. subsidiary itself was a complex, multi-structured company that operated over 100 theaters in Nevada and northern California under several corporate identities. The chain was accustomed to dictating terms in the regions where its theaters dominated. The monopoly refused to grant any film, including *Up in Arms*, anything but a flat film rental. Goldwyn, on the other hand, not only insisted on a percentage of the gross profits, but demanded a sliding scale that increased the producer's percentage as the box office increased. The negotiations between the exhibitor and the producer began in June 1944, and lingered for weeks. For over two months, Goldwyn was represented by John C. Flinn of SIMPP; and when T. & D. rejected Goldwyn's terms (as expected), the Society was ready to back the renegade producer as he fought one of the largest movie monopolies in the country.

In a closed situation there were few options for Goldwyn to exhibit his own film. The State Auditorium in Reno, the only facility that had seating large enough to accommodate the crowds that Goldwyn expected, became off-limits when local officials declined to rent it to the flamboyant outsider. Desperate to locate a venue, Goldwyn decided to build his own theater by shipping projection equipment from San Francisco. But his idea for a massive canvas tent was condemned as a safety hazzard. Finally he found a location on the outskirts of Reno next to the railroad tracks—the El Patio ballroom, which Goldwyn converted into a makeshift theater at his own expense and over tremendous local opposition.

T. & D. Theatres played into the independent producer's plans by creating opposition that helped to generate publicity. The theater chain took out newspaper ads that ridiculed Goldwyn's so-called theater of folding chairs nailed to a temporary wooden floor, showing his film within earshot of the Southern Pacific railroad. At first the negative press seemed to turn public sentiment against the independent producer. SIMPP recruited other independents to participate in the preparations for the August 22, 1944 opening night. Mary Pickford agreed to attend the premiere in person. Walt Disney, Orson Welles, and the Cagney brothers all contributed public statements concerning the incident.

While media attention intensified, so did local hostility, until Goldwyn outmaneuvered the powerful Reno syndicate and won over local officials by donating the opening night box office to the Camp and Hospital Service Committee, the Reno chapter of the Red Cross. This turned his show-of-defiance into a charity event, and guaranteed a strong attendance. The press came to Reno for the media event which was carried over live radio. Goldwyn and Pickford had their pictures taken as they ceremoniously hammered the four-hundredth wooden chair to the floor of the former night-club.

Pickford, a great supporter of both the independent fight and of the Red Cross, brought her own prepared speech and the endorsements from the other SIMPP members. She had personally and bitterly clashed with Goldwyn at several times over the previous decades, but had always publicly declared her admiration for the incorrigible producer. She effortlessly concealed any animosity toward the man who had created frustrating conditions for her while they were together at Famous Players-Lasky, United Artists, and later at SIMPP. The following is a complete transcript of Pickford's radio address given before the showing of *Up in Arms*:

> Good evening I am proud to be here tonight to represent two most worthwhile causes, first, the benefits for the camp and hospital service committee of Reno, secondly, to take my stand for

independence and freedom from the dictates of a picture theatre monopoly. When Mr. Samuel Goldwyn telephoned me I dropped my personal business for the time being in order to be here tonight, well knowing the vital importance of this issue of monopoly, an issue not only vital to Mr. Goldwyn and all independent producers but to the future advancement of the American motion picture industry itself.

I have known Samuel Goldwyn the better part of my life as a man of high purpose, of great courage, a producer of artistic integrity. It is such men as Samuel Goldwyn whose vision, courage and inspiration has led and emanated the motion picture from the obscurity of the Nickelodeon era up to the great and dignified medium of entertainment which it is today. To produce the film *Up In Arms* Mr. Goldwyn spent a whole year of intensive work and two and a half million dollars of his own; that is a lot of time and very great deal of money but to what avail? Only to be told upon the completion of a year's work and expenditure of two and one-half million dollars that he shall not be permitted to show his picture but dictated by a theater monopoly. I would prefer and in this I am assured you would agree to sit on a wooden chair, a wooden bench, or even on the floor to see a fine film than to rest upon plush covered opera chairs and to be forced to witness a dull, stupid film in the most elaborate movie palace in the country. No, my friends all the grandeur of the finest theater does not make nor mar a great film. Bricks, mortar, plush and soft lights are empty things without fine entertainment which commemorates the very living soul of the theater.

We are making history here tonight, you, Mr. Goldwyn and I, for we are taking our stand from our inalienable rights for free enterprise and a free America to see to it that no man, group, combine nor monopoly shall dictate where, when or how we shall show our picture.

Our boys, American boys, this very night on the four corners of the earth are fighting and dying in order to protect Democracy and the American way of life. Shall we here at home fail them? Shall we permit the American way of life to perish here in the United States while our men are fighting for that same God given right in every part of the world? Certainly not, so I say it is not merely whether this one or a dozen of Mr. Goldwyn's pictures do, or do not play in Reno or for that matter in the entire state of Nevada. It is rather the question whether he and I or other Americans are to be given an opportunity to carry on our lives and our business openly, honestly and fairly.

There are a number of wires that have come to us, too numerous to read here, so I shall read just this one from an author whom you all know, respect and love. It is Walt Disney, one of the outstanding independent producers of the motion picture industry. It is an indication of how the creative workers of Hollywood feel about monopoly and I quote, 'Samuel Goldwyn, Riverside Hotel, Reno, Nevada, I heartily endorse your efforts to carry directly to the people of Reno and indirectly to the American public the question whether the motion picture industry as an industry should continue to exist under American competition principles or be throttled by monopolistic restrictions and limitations. When the channels of motion picture reach the public are restricted or blocked it behooves all of us who are charged with responsibility to the public for the industry to break down these barriers. Impending world competition which will be based on low cost and fostered by forming governmental endowment franchise and tariffs make it imperative that our American products at least in our own country be permitted to operate without artificial obstacles being thrown in its path by selfish interest. The American picture must continue to receive returns, commensurate with the large costs and the better living standards of the people who make them. Our government has recognized the importance of American films as political and commercial assets in foreign relations for America, to lose its leadership in motion pictures would be a blow to all American industry and to our public relations. The motion picture industry and in time the American public will acknowledge and appreciate yours, Sam, your courage and foresight, regards, Walt Disney.' This is Mary Pickford, good night and thank you.

Following Pickford's speech, Samuel Goldwyn introduced *Up in Arms*, and also commented on the significance of the battle being waged for economic control of the movie industry. He closed his address by declaring that he and the SIMPP producers were prepared to hire halls and auditoriums in other cities in order to break down prevailing inequities.

These threats by independent producers of showing their own movies were not new. Back in 1930 when the United Artists struggle with Fox West Coast erupted, Goldwyn warned the theater chain that he would form his own makeshift exhibition enterprise before he would ever give in to the unsatisfactory terms of the Fox monopoly. Many of the independent producers were accustomed to road showing their films, and persistently threatened to exhibit their movies whenever they felt an overwhelming urge to buck industry trends. In 1940, when Charlie Chaplin met resistance to his anti-war film *The Great Dictator*, he became more determined "even if I had to hire halls myself to show it." When theater chains repudiated Orson Welles' explosive *Citizen Kane* (1941), Wells exclaimed, "I'll show it in a ball park with four screens, in auditoriums, at fairs, in circus tents, if necessary." In fact, Fox West Coast actually bought the regional exhibition rights to *Citizen Kane*, but refused to show it, in order to suppress the movie. The move so incensed Welles that he became a willing participant during the Goldwyn showdown against the Fox affiliate in Reno.

Some of the producers made further inroads into exhibition. Within a year after the Reno incident, the Samuel Goldwyn Company entered into a joint theater venture with David Selznick's Vanguard Films to secure a first-run foothold in New York City. They become long-term renters of the Astor Theatre, an impressive 1100 seat movie house on Broadway. There they controlled all of the theaters bookings, and each took turns premiering their new movies. The arrangement essentially gave either producer a guaranteed outlet to run a road show debut that could last for several months before demand slackened. Among the most important films that debuted at the Astor when it was controlled by the independents were Selznick's *Spellbound* (1945) and Goldwyn's *The Best Years of Our Lives* (1946). After two years, around the time that Selznick formed his own distribution company, they allowed the lease to expire.

DUE IN PART to *Up in Arms*, the government case against the Hollywood studios heated up. Goldwyn had anticipated the debacle in Nevada and alerted Thomas O. Craven, United States Attorney at Reno, to the situation. Goldwyn filed a complaint as a member of the Society of Independent Motion Picture Producers in which he alleged that T. & D. Junior Enterprises had taken an active part in discriminating against independent films including *Up in Arms*. Craven received clearance from the office of the Attorney General on August 17, a few days before the Reno film opening. The Justice Department also involved the FBI in an investigation that lasted into October.

T. & D. defended itself by attacking the independents. "The reason the picture is not shown in the T. & D. theatres is not that we refused to buy the picture," the district manager N. Dow Thompson said on behalf of the chain, "but rather because Mr. Goldwyn's sales organization refused to sell it for a showing in Reno unless we bought the picture for all of our situations, in some of which Mr. Goldwyn's terms were exorbitant. . . ." Nevertheless the FBI report blamed the T. & D. chain for manipulating local officials and conspiring to maintain a monopoly in an effort to suppress the independent film.

While Goldwyn and the other SIMPP members were fighting exhibitors, the Society executive committee continued its petition of the Department of Justice. Tom C. Clark remained in contact with SIMPP president Loyd Wright, who intervened on behalf of SIMPP when the Big Five submitted a new consent decree in which the studios proposed that they keep their theaters. That August, the Attorney General rejected the latest distributor consent decree, and filed a motion in Federal Court demanding theater divorcement within three years. Government attorneys were busy readying their case when the FBI report on *Up In Arms* recommended that the Justice Department intercede on behalf of the independent producers.

"As long as the independents have to deal with the big five for theaters it seems there will be trouble," the Justice Department declared in a press release that month that commented on the *Up in Arms* incident. "If all the theaters they now have continue to be controlled by the big five companies, the independent producers will find it difficult to get screens for the product."

Unlike the Balaban & Katz fight, Goldwyn expected to lose money in the Fox West Coast showdown in Reno. The El Patio ballroom had cost Goldwyn between $25,000 and $30,000 to convert into a theater, while the out-of-the-way ballroom only brought in about $1,000 each week. However, in terms of publicity value, the figures were impossible to calculate monetarily. For helping to accelerate the *Paramount* case, it was money well-spent. After the Reno event, SIMPP celebrated as the Justice Department took the major studios back to Federal Court in New York City late in August 1944. Both the government and the independent producers prepared for the District Court hearing of *United States v. Paramount Pictures, Inc. et al*—the phase of the antitrust case which the press commonly referred to as the New York Equity Suit.

8

Of Merit Instead of Power

THOUGH THE ANTITRUST movement served as the focal point of the Society of Independent Motion Picture Producers, the group was also involved in negotiating better terms for the producers on many other industry issues. The independents had long considered themselves ideologically separate from the studio system, but even they would admit that their ties to the industry were still undeniable. Four of the eight SIMPP founders—Disney, Goldwyn, Selznick, and Wanger—retained their memberships in the Motion Picture Producers and Distributors of America during the early years of SIMPP. The MPPDA was still considered the instrument of the major studios, but at this point many of independents considered it to their advantage to keep their voice in the industry association. The independent producers took the offensive against many of the industry practices that were administered by the MPPDA and that were unfavorable to the independents.

For example, since 1925 the MPPDA maintained the Title Registration Bureau which allowed the member companies the ability to reserve specific film titles, whether or not the company had any intention on making a movie by such name. Since titles and names were not subject to copyright protection, the title registration division of the Hays Office helped protect its members with self-enforced rules that avoided the duplication of titles and kept the more devious filmmakers from intentionally creating confusion in the marketplace. Unfortunately for the independents, the rule disadvantaged newcomers who effectively found most of the intuitive-sounding titles already reserved by the large studios.

On occasion the title registration created problems even for more established independents. When Chaplin received the copyright for his forthcoming picture titled "The Dictator" in November 1938, he then discovered that Paramount owned the MPPDA title registration. Rather than pay the $25,000 that Paramount asked in order to transfer the rights to the Chaplin studio, Chaplin decided to alter his title to *The Great Dictator* (1940) instead.

Even though each company was limited to 250 name registrations, the studios were able to tie up thousands of titles using their many subsidiary companies as registrars. On the other hand, the studios claimed it was not fair for an independent producer who released only one or two films a year to be afforded the same registration limit as a studio that released as many of 50 features annually.

In 1943 SIMPP asked for title registration reform. Will Hays told the Society that he was entertaining a substitute plan that would incorporate a sliding scale that allowed larger companies to reserve more titles. However SIMPP felt such a plan would be a deterrent to new producers. Instead the MPPDA agreed to limit the number of feature titles to 100 feature names per company. The self-regulated title registration system, with slight modification, is still in effect in Hollywood to this day.

Another issue that commanded a significant amount of SIMPP effort was the international situation that would have long-range effects on the economics of Hollywood after World War II. The end of the war had suddenly opened up several foreign territories that were previously unavailable during the conflict. All of the studios were eager to exploit their older films to these overseas markets.

However, these foreign countries inevitably sought to limit the number of U.S. films by stiffening restrictions and quotas that had been in place before the war. Each country enforced the restrictions to help strengthen their own domestic film industries. Meanwhile the Hollywood distributors were jockeying for position in a foreign free-for-all that threatened to lock out the small companies and independent producers.

Samuel Goldwyn urged the Truman administration to adopt freedom of film as its policy both at home and abroad. Goldwyn considered it an unavoidable follow-up to preserving democracy overseas, as well as an outgrowth of his domestic struggle against the Hollywood monopoly. The independent producer proposed "that the matter of a free screen, unshackled by Government controls, monopolies or quotas be taken under consideration by the United Nations Conference." The entire SIMPP philosophy had been based on the premise that the film market should be dictated by the individual merit of each film, and not by the size of the distributing company. Although the antitrust efforts were bringing reform to the United States, the heady foreign situation was threatening to cancel out the independents worldwide.

One indication of the importance of the international negotiations was evident from a telegram the SIMPP executive secretary sent to Mary Pickford in 1944. Before the end of the war, United Artists and its producers decided to defect from the MPPDA in order to distance the distributor from the other Big Eight majors being brought under antitrust fire. Loyd Wright and John Flinn at first agreed that SIMPP could more appropriately represent the studio, but later they reported back to Pickford in anticipation of the international export problem, that the severity of the quota situation would demand that United Artists deal closely with the MPPDA for the time being. So instead of resigning from the Hays Office, UA remained in the Hays organization, but also increased its activity in SIMPP. United Artists Productions, Inc. (the UA-owned production company formed in 1941 out of the old Walter Wanger studio) and its vice president George Bagnall joined as official SIMPP members in 1945. Over the next few years, the United Artists Corporation's membership in the MPPDA remained shaky as the distributor continually threatened to withdraw.

When Loyd Wright originally became SIMPP president in 1941, he considered his role in the Society temporary until a permanent full-time leader emerged. At the end of the war, he believed that what SIMPP really needed was its own Will Hays—a strong executive and political insider who would help the group achieve its international aims as well as its domestic antitrust goals.

Loyd Wright selected a committee of six SIMPP members to choose the new president. The committee consisted of Samuel Goldwyn, Walt Disney, Walter Wanger, Sol Lesser, Edward Small, and the committee chairman David O. Selznick. In less than ten days of negotiations in early June 1945, the Selznick committee invited former chairman of the War Production Board Donald M. Nelson to become the new president of SIMPP. He accepted the position, and the $50,000 annual salary, at the June 12 meeting of the committee, and Selznick announced the news at a press conference that same day.

An executive at Sears, Roebuck and Co. from 1939 to 1942, Nelson's background was in business, which the SIMPP committee welcomed as a suitable direction for the Society to take in the postwar atmosphere. Furthermore, Donald Nelson also had experience in international negotiations as Roosevelt's presidential emissary to China. The new president came to SIMPP with a deal of political clout as well. While head of the War Production Board, Nelson was one of the government officials who set priorities for national resources, holding the lifeline of Hollywood during World War II through the supply of raw film stock. Nelson said he was attracted to SIMPP by the challenges of the foreign market as the war subsided. He also proposed an aggressive antitrust agenda. He announced that a legislative branch would be maintained in Washington, D.C., in addition to SIMPP's offices in Los Angeles and New York. Loyd Wright stayed on as general counsel for the Society of Independent Motion Picture Producers.

The executive secretary John Flinn was put in charge of a newly-expanded Hollywood base of operations. Unfortunately Flinn died unexpectedly in 1946, leaving his duties to be filled by several emerging figures in the Society. Flinn's actual position was occupied by a new secretary Marvin L. Faris. However, many of the executive responsibilities were assumed by representatives of the leading producers—specifically two key delegates: James Mulvey, president of Samuel Goldwyn, Inc., and Gunther Lessing, vice president of Walt Disney Productions.

James A. Mulvey had been with Sam Goldwyn from the inception of his independent production company in the early 1920s, and over the years became Goldwyn's most trusted business confidant. Before Goldwyn, Mulvey worked for the old Boston & Westchester Railroad in New York, then moved to Price-Waterhouse where he served as an accountant to movie client Sam Goldwyn. When Goldwyn went independent in 1922, he hired Mulvey to run his New York office to enable the producer to became a hands-on filmmaker on the west coast. Mulvey preferred anonymity, and rejected generous offers to become a high-ranking executive at several major studios. He remained as president of Samuel Goldwyn Productions (later Samuel Goldwyn, Inc.) for over four decades. In what was essentially a privately-held company, Goldwyn took exception to his rule of never taking on partners, and gave Mulvey a five and a fraction percentage ownership of his independent studio. James Mulvey, who specialized in distribution, was frequently consulted by his colleagues on complex industry issues, making him ideally suited for the collaborative interests of SIMPP.

Gunther R. Lessing, one of the most colorful and controversial Disney figures, has usually been overlooked or over-exaggerated by historians. He headed Disney's legal department for many years before the Disney brothers promoted him to vice president and general counsel of Walt Disney Productions. At the Disney studio, known for its laid back atmosphere where everyone was addressed by their first name, it was Gunther Lessing who Walt referred to when he said, "The only Mister we have at the studio is our lawyer, Mr. Lessing."

Lessing earned his law degree from Yale, and spent his early career in Mexico where, most Disney biographies say, he briefly acted as council for Pancho Villa. According to historian Kevin Brownlow, Lessing arranged the strange 1913 deal between Villa and the Mutual Film Corporation to create a silent movie based on the outlaw. He came in contact with the Disney studio during the early Mickey Mouse years, when the Disneys battled with their states-rights distributor Patrick A. Powers—a former partner of Carl Laemmle's and a consummate example of a former two-fisted independent outlaw who graduated to film-baron status only to torment other independents. The Disney brothers hired Gunther Lessing to represent them in late 1929 and early 1930 to protect their rights to their cartoons from the predatory Pat Powers. Lessing stayed at the studio for 35 years.

Lessing's influence on the Disney enterprise has been difficult to determine due to the sinister spin most Disney chroniclers give to his career at the studio. On a positive note, one Disney studio production manager has credited Lessing with the monumental suggestion that Walt Disney turn his own name into a trademark to serve as a brand upon which to build his company. Yet over the years, a great deal of the studio dirty-work fell to Lessing as the Disneys empowered him with many key responsibilities. When Walt and Roy Disney went to Europe on an extended stay in the spring and summer of 1935, the administrative duties of the company fell to Lessing who communicated with the brothers in lengthy memos. In the early 1940s, Lessing became the subject of scorn as the conservative leader of the anti-unionization effort to shield the Disney studio from organized labor. Lessing was also a member of the Short Subjects Committee for the Office of the Coordinator of Inter-American Affairs, and arranged to have Walt Disney taken out of the country on a good-will tour of South America in 1941 while Lessing and Roy Disney handled the labor negotiations. Ultimately the infamous strike was settled in Walt Disney's absence and—largely to his disappointment—in favor of the unions, despite Lessing's hardball tactics.

At least one Disney employee later suggested that the disastrous resolution to the strike undermined Lessing's authority at the studio. Subsequent biographers characterized the aging attorney as a sympathy case, kept on at the studio due to the loyalty the Disneys customarily showed to longtime employees who were no longer necessarily of use to the company. However, this characterization of Lessing as a "broken-hearted old man" contrasted with the continued responsibility placed on Gunther Lessing. After he was kicked upstairs to serve as vice president, he remained as spokesperson on most of the studio's important legal matters. He presided at the Disney studio board meetings which Walt Disney, the chairman of the board, infrequently attended, and which Lessing always headed even when Disney's presence was requested. Lessing was also thrust in the firing lines to tackle difficult situations such as the House Un-American Activities Committee in the late 1940s where he served as Walt Disney's close advisor. The Disneys were willing to engage their trusted legal counsel in potentially confrontational film activities, and found the Society of Independent Motion Picture Producers to be an appropriate match for Lessing.

Both James Mulvey and Gunther Lessing became important leaders of the Society. Mulvey would demonstrate his resourcefulness as a negotiator representing the independent producers in many of the foreign territorial disputes over quotas, while on the legal front, Lessing would stimulate the Society's antitrust agenda. As Mulvey and Lessing's influence grew, it also illustrated the prominence of the two most important SIMPP members, Goldwyn and Disney.

OPERATING AS a non-profit organization from its inception, SIMPP realized that in order to increase its court activity, it would need to increase its financial resources. The $5,000 annual dues discouraged some prospective members, but if the dues were lowered, SIMPP's financial resources, already tight, would be further inhibited. So effective July 1, 1945, a new structure was implemented in the bylaws of SIMPP which encouraged new membership but also collected additional funds from the more successful producers. Annual dues were lowed to $2,500 with each member contributing three-eighths of one percent of the domestic box office gross of each new release.

By the end of 1946, the Society increased its financial surplus, operating with an annual budget of $181,000. Despite the new restrictions, the organization continued to attract most of the new independent producers. In addition to those previously discussed, new members included William Goetz, Jesse L. Lasky, Jules Levy, Jack Skirball, and Preston Sturges. For the year 1945, SIMPP producers accounted for an impressive $40 million of annual production expenditures, or roughly equal the size of the largest Hollywood studios. The newspapers reported that SIMPP was the first organization that could really rival the MPPDA in scope and intent.

At the time, the Motion Picture Producers and Distributors of America faced its own set of challenges as the Hays administration weakened. The temporary difficulties were signified by the defection of Warner Bros. in 1944. Previously protesting the Hays handling of the labor unions, the cantankerous studio decided to resign from the united industry defense as the antitrust case headed to trial, preferring to defend itself alone rather than be subject to the compromises being handled by the industry organization whose power and influence appeared to be eroding. As the *Paramount* case headed to trial in 1945, the Warner Bros. studio vowed to protect its vertical integration as intensely as the government had sought to break it down. The Warner resignation from the MPPDA, and the perpetual United Artists threats to leave, further indicated the divisions that existed in the industry following the war.

After two monumental decades at the head of the MPPDA, Will Hays retired; and the organization followed the lead of SIMPP by hiring a businessman as its new leader. In September 1945, the MPPDA elected Eric Johnston, formerly with the U.S. Chamber of Commerce, to serve as president with an annual salary of $150,000. As part of a revitalization of the MPPDA, Johnston consolidated the New York and Hollywood offices, brought Warner Bros. back into the association, and changed the name of the MPPDA to the Motion Picture Association of America (MPAA).

BY THE TIME of the reorganization of the MPAA, the second phase of the *Paramount* case, the New York Equity Suit, was under way. On October 8, 1945 the Big Eight and the Justice Department were back in Federal Court, and the prognosis did not look favorable for the integrated studios, due in part to an anti-monopoly decision handed down in the *Crescent* theater case.

The *Crescent* trial (also known as the *Sudekum* case named after the large Tennessee defendant) was the first of the three great exhibitor suits filed in 1939 to make it to the Supreme Court. Even though the Consent Decree of 1940 had exempted the studios from the *Crescent* case in 1940, the theater chain trial was widely viewed as a measure of government predisposition to legal intervention in the film business. In fact, the SIMPP executive committee hastily involved the Society in the case by attempting to file an *amicus curiae* brief with the Supreme Court in 1944. Spending over $10,000 to unsuccessfully file the brief, SIMPP leaders later admitted that they did not give the Society enough time to complete the approval process. Nevertheless the incident helped enhance the reputation of SIMPP as a trustbusting organization, and the expensive misstep helped bring about the financial restructuring of the Society the following year. More significantly, "while the Supreme Court did not permit the filing of a brief," the SIMPP leaders reported to their members, "it is felt that the government's position was strengthened by our request to file and the publicity resulting therefrom."

The industry carefully took note as the Supreme Court decided against the Crescent theater monopoly, and condemned its anti-competitive practices. With a hint of the problems in store for the major Hollywood studios, the language of the *Crescent* decision seemed ominous for the Big Eight as the Supreme Court claimed that "somewhere in the background a greater conspiracy from which flow consequences more serious than we have here. . . ."

In the New York Equity Suit, the *Paramount* case defendants used many of the same arguments as before the war, pitching block booking and vertical integration as an economic necessity. Following the incredible war-time box office windfall, the Big Eight could no longer shelter their businesses practices behind the guise of industry hardship that had postponed previous government interaction during the Great Depression and early in World War II. The entire industry, lead by Paramount Pictures, was riding an unprecedented profit growth as theater attendance peaked to its all time record in 1946. The massive Paramount theater holdings, which had nearly brought the studio to ruin in the Depression, now allowed the company revenue to skyrocket. Paramount reported an unheard-of $39 million profit for the year 1945-46, more than twice that of the second place studio Twentieth Century-Fox.

Even with the booming conditions, the studios complained about the instability of the current foreign situation, and argued that the Hollywood majors could not afford to be toppled from their position of strength at home just at the time when more leverage was needed to overcome international quotas and restrictions.

Interestingly Hollywood faced an even larger threat, one which was not yet identified as a significant enough menace to provide for convincing argument in the *Paramount* case but, nevertheless, a challenge that brought widespread changes that would help undermine the studio power-base. This, of course, was the rise of television as a popular medium. As discussed more in chapter 14, this new influence from television coincided with—and helped fuel— the independent film movement that was changing the way Hollywood made movies.

For the opening arguments in the *Paramount* trial in New York, the Justice Department began by presenting charts ("scrap paper" its was referred to on several occasions by the studio attorneys) to demonstrate the Big Five stranglehold on the first-run theater markets with additional evidence that claimed that the Little Three acted in collusion with the theater-owning majors.

Legal counsel for Warner Bros., which at the time was not yet reconciled with the MPAA, said, "These theatres provide a sure outlet and make it possible to spend these millions on pictures. Strike down that quality and this industry is sunk." RKO, the smallest of the Big Five, defended itself by deflecting the accusations. "To say it has created a monopoly is incredible," the RKO attorney declared. United Artists still innocently claimed that its did not know why UA was part of the antitrust suit.

Two weeks into the trial, Adolph Zukor testified, retelling the history of the Paramount studio to show that he was literally forced into vertical integration by the predatory exhibitor organizations like First National. He denied all conspiracy charges, including the allegation that his studio used block booking in order to eliminate competition and maintain their dominant position in the first-run theater market.

The trial wrapped in January 1946, and the industry awaited the decision to be handed down by the three New York City judges Henry W. Goddard, Augustus N. Hand, and John Bright. The New York Equity ruling came in June 1946 as something of a surprise to both sides.

The Hollywood studios, including the Little Three, were found guilty of conspiracy in restraint of trade with charges that focused on block booking. The court put an interesting interpretation on block booking, indicating that the copyright ownership of any film was, in actuality, a limited monopoly protected by the U.S. Constitution. Based on the precedent from other recent patent antitrust cases, the court declared that the combination of two separate copyrights threatened free trade and was considered illegal. Also theater pooling, where two competing theater chains combine for mutual advantage, was also outlawed.

However the court permitted the Big Five studios to retain their own theater chains. Vertical integration was not declared illegal per se; pooling was considered the culprit. So instead, the court ordered the major studios to eliminate all theater pools, and allowed the Big Five keep their large circuits.

"We cannot concede to the prayer of the plaintiff," the ruling indicated, "that the major defendants should be divested of their theatres in order that no distributor of motion pictures shall be an exhibitor." The court claimed that to divorce the theaters from the studios would not solve the monopoly problem, but supplant the experienced Hollywood owners with new owners who may render worse public service and perpetuate territorial monopolies. The court's solution was competitive bidding, a controversial concept of sorts, where studios would be forced to accept the auction price of "the highest responsible bidder." The distributors were forbidden to discriminate against any theater, and had to sell each film without the semblance of block booking. To aid in this, the court also protected the studio practice of run-zone-clearance (if executed in a "reasonable" manner), and also upheld the film arbitration system.

At the end of 1946, an appeal was heard by the Statutory Court, and a new ruling was issued which upheld most of the provisions of the District Court ruling. However, the new decision placed additional restrictions on run-zone-clearance, and called arbitration into question.

None of the participants were satisfied with the result of the New York Equity Suit. The Department of Justice, which considered theater divestiture the only proper remedy, refuted the mandatory court-directed competitive bidding as unexpected and unwanted. The Big Five were disappointed with the Statutory Court departure from the long-dead Consent Decree of 1940. While the Big Five agreed to comply with the ban on theater pooling (which they in fact did by July 1, 1947), they protested the elimination of block booking. Universal and Columbia, who felt like they were dragged into the suit, were devastated by the block booking ban.

Though SIMPP was not entirely pleased with the outcome, the independents had many things to celebrate. The SIMPP public relations department said that "there can be no question that the verdict is not entirely satisfactory because it did not result in complete divorcement of theater ownership." However, for the first time since the FTC investigations in the 1920s, "the majors have been publicly pronounced guilty of monopolistic practices which the American people regard as abhorrent and inimical to their best interests, while the independents have aligned themselves on the traditional American side of fair play and freedom of the individual to do business on a basis of merit instead of power."

The Society's public relations director congratulated the independent members for helping to spur the government into action: "It can safely be said that without the intervention of the Society the motion picture industry might be forced to operate to this day and in the foreseeable future under another consent decree." Furthermore, the trial generated more exposure for SIMPP—"publicity space worth thousands upon thousands of dollars, and goodwill and prestige for which there is no material yardstick."

Both the government and the major studios submitted appeals that would send the *Paramount* case to the Supreme Court. The independent producers welcomed the Statutory decision as an appropriate preamble to the real fight ahead.

9

New Blood

S AM GOLDWYN ARRIVED in New York in November 1946 for the world premiere of *The Best Years of Our Lives,* his new independently-produced film that would go on to become the year's box office champ and Oscar frontrunner. As usual he looked for an industry issue to rail against as he warmed up the New York press for his promotional blitz. For his publicity angle he drew attention to a contradiction that he experienced while on the east coast. Even though film attendance was at a record high, people complained about the abundance of disappointing features from Hollywood. He claimed that audience members peppered him with the same questions all week: "What's the matter with Hollywood? Why have the pictures been so poor this year?" He called a press conference on November 18, 1946, three days before the opening of his film, to lay blame at the feet of the Hollywood studio system.

During the gathering at the Samuel Goldwyn offices, the producer emphasized several familiar points: that Hollywood paid too much attention on star value and not enough on entertainment value; that a good story was the most essential ingredient in the making of a good film; and that Hollywood simply made too many films, period. "There are not enough good writers with a real story to tell, to write 400 or 500 pictures a year. I have always felt that on the writer hinges the true quality of any picture, no matter who the producer, the director or the stars. Stars are made by good stories, killed by bad ones."

Walter Wanger, then in New York on a return trip from Europe, joined up with Goldwyn. Wanger addressed the press corp on the same day, and had a similar message as Goldwyn. They both claimed that Hollywood was rich, lazy, and complacent. Also they said that Hollywood suffered from the same thing that plagues any creative entity that no longer needs to struggle and fight for its ideas—rapid and unavoidable stagnation.

"Hollywood has long needed the stimulus of outside competition," Goldwyn declared, conveying the crux of his message. To stir Hollywood out of its "fat-cat complacency" had been the mission of many of the SIMPP producers who aspired to cinematic excellence. Goldwyn welcomed competition, and said that the industry was badly in need of "new blood."

The independent movement survived the challenging war years, and found that the box office explosion that spilled over into the immediate postwar period helped fuel an independent production boom. World War II had instilled a general feeling of independence in Hollywood's roster of former contract talent. Many actors, directors, and in-house producers returned from war service with a reluctance to rejoin the studio system. The favorable tax situation that allowed independents to pay capital gains instead of sky-high income tax also contributed to the attractiveness of independent set-ups. As *Harper's* magazine commented in 1946, the maverick artists were making the shift to independent production "clutching the banner of freedom in one hand and an income tax blanket in the other."

The studio system also seemed to be in regress as the courts issued the New York Equity decisions that declared block booking, blind selling, and other practices in violation of antitrust laws. The time was ripe for the independent movement to take off.

Unfortunately when Hollywood was hit by the industry recession in the late 1940s, the independents on the whole suffered more in general than the major studios which were built to weather economic downswings. The most important producer-directors that had gone independent at this time, such as Frank Capra, John Ford, Preston Sturges and Alfred Hitchcock, were forced to scale-back or temporarily abandon their independent plans.

A two-fold challenge for SIMPP developed. The most obvious problem was trying to sustain the growth in the Society during this time when many new companies were solvent for only a short time. At the end of 1946, the Society's two dozen members had made 33 films, spending over $45 million in production costs. SIMPP made trade headlines by announcing the ambitious plans of its members in 1947—57 features costing an estimated $88 million. While many in the industry predicted recession, SIMPP president Donald Nelson impetuously recommended more feature production on heavier budgets. The decline in attendance was already taking place, and many independents did not survive. By 1948 SIMPP membership temporarily declined to 17 producers before it picked up again.

The other challenge SIMPP faced was trying to find ways to attract the new wave of producer-directors who were going independent at a rapid rate. Many of these directors, though their independent operations were modeled after those of the SIMPP founders, were less inclined to feel kinship in the producer-centric organization. Also, the producer-directors were some of the most fiercely maverick filmmakers. Directors like John Ford and Howard Hawks were so extremely individualistic that they saw little immediate gain in paying the dues to an organization to advance the independent movement. This self-seeking temperament plagued all independents, not just the producer-directors. It had characterized the independent movement from the silent days forward, and would later bring SIMPP to a standstill in the late 1950s.

Three new companies, formed just prior to the end of the war—Liberty Films, International Pictures, and California Pictures—typified this period of the independent movement, and helped inspire the explosion in independent production. Two of them joined SIMPP, and all three lasted only a short time as independent production companies.

LIBERTY FILMS, PROBABLY THE MOST heralded postwar independent production outfit, was the brainchild of Frank Capra who entered into a partnership with two other producer-directors, William Wyler and George Stevens.

Frank Capra had developed close associations with the founders of SIMPP through his independent production efforts before World War II. In the spring of 1937 Capra visited Alexander Korda at the Denham Studios during a vacation to England. The trip began a nine month exile from Columbia Pictures as Capra plotted his own freedom from the studio system and unsuccessfully tried to form his own company. When he and Robert Riskin founded Frank Capra Productions in 1939, David O. Selznick rented them office space at Selznick International. Loyd Wright, who filed Capra's incorporation papers, encouraged a distribution deal with United Artists. Despite the support of Mary Pickford, the negotiations broke down after delays caused by Chaplin's reluctance. Later in May 1941, Korda, Selznick, and Capra formed a three-way entente in an attempt to take control of United Artists, but the partners struggled with the logistics of the takeover. While Korda and Selznick argued over the details, Capra considered distribution deals with other studios. Frank Capra nearly became the ninth founding member of SIMPP, but instead put his career on hold when he liquidated his production company in December 1941 and joined the Signal Corps, one month before the organization of SIMPP.

Toward the end of the war, Capra renewed his independent aspirations. According to Leo McCarey, he and Capra originally planned to go independent together, but "couldn't see eye to eye." Instead Frank Capra discussed his new independent production plans with Sam Briskin, the former Columbia production executive who had a long friendship with the director. As World War II ended, they decided to form an independent production company, announced as Liberty Films on January 29, 1945 and incorporated in April 1945.

Capra envisioned the future of the industry dominated by producing directors, with Liberty providing a financial and creative umbrella. They convinced others to join, including William Wyler in July, and George Stevens toward the end of the year. Liberty arranged for distribution through RKO, which offered to finance three films from each of the directors—a combined production deal that totaled over $15 million.

Throughout 1946 the large amount of publicity generated by Liberty ignited the independent production market. "Undoubtedly there will always be big studios. . . ." Capra wrote in anticipation of the emergence of the independent filmmakers, "but we hope they will be divided by the individual creative efforts of the independents, of which, fortunately, I happen now to be one together with Producer-Directors William Wyler and George Stevens, and production executive Samuel J. Briskin, under the emblem, Liberty Films."

Unfortunately Liberty's ambitions were curtailed during the difficult start-up period. Wyler had to fulfill his prior production commitment with Sam Goldwyn by directing one more feature from a prewar contract. Stevens still awaited military discharge for months after the war's long end. So the initial film from Liberty was from Frank Capra. He produced and directed his masterpiece *It's A Wonderful Life* (1946), starring James Stewart who also returned from the war reluctant to resume his former position as MGM contract player. The $2.3 million film was the most expensive of Capra's career, and although it was well-received, the movie was not the unqualified Capra blockbuster that they had hoped would inaugurate the new company.

On the other hand, the Wyler-directed Goldwyn film, *Best Years of Our Lives* (1946) grossed $11.3 million and became the highest grossing film behind the champion *Gone With the Wind* (1939). *It's a Wonderful Life* also suffered from direct competition with *Best Years of Our Lives* in key markets. Thus Wyler unexpectedly contributed to the declining fortunes of Liberty before ever making a film for the company.

Unable to overcome the negative cash-flow, Capra and Wyler decided to avoid an unpleasant takeover by offering Liberty and its director contracts to the highest bidding studio. MGM and Paramount offered to purchase the company, and the latter studio landed the prestigious deal. Stevens protested the sale, unwilling to relinquish his independent status. He withdrew from Liberty to join Leo McCarey at Rainbow Productions. When Stevens realized that McCarey was also having second thoughts as an independent, and would soon sell his production company to Paramount Pictures, Stevens returned to Liberty to finalize a deal with the major studio in May 1947.

Liberty became a subsidiary of the Hollywood giant for $3.1 million in Paramount stock. Capra, Wyler, and Stevens were given producer-director status at the studio, and Sam Briskin became a Paramount executive. Though the major studio promised autonomy for the filmmakers, Paramount demanded approval of script and budget, prompting Wyler to remark, "I guess there is no such thing as complete independence unless you put up your own money."

Capra recalled the sale of Liberty—his final gasp as an independent—with great regret. He later admitted that it was a mistake to give up, but that at the time he had felt strongly that he needed to handle it the way he did. Liberty Films remained a working division at Paramount until the subsidiary was terminated in a joint agreement with Frank Capra in March 1951.

Liberty Films was never a member of the Society of Independent Motion Picture Producers or United Artists. The actual reason is unknown. One Capra biographer wrote that UA denied Liberty a distribution deal, an indication of the atrophy of Capra's commercial credibility during the war. But this claim seemed far-fetched given the perpetual product deficiency at UA and the unanimous trade adulation Liberty received from its inception.

The reasons Liberty did not join SIMPP are also speculative. Possibly the Liberty partners decided to wait until the company got on its feet (which it never did). More likely, Liberty never joined because the three owners espoused the same attitude of other independent directors who were typically not as inclined to enter into a fellowship with the other independent producers. Given Capra's expansive master plan of Liberty as a home for independent directors, Liberty was essentially envisioned as a society unto itself. It is also reasonable, given the organization of Liberty where all company decisions were made collectively, that if at least one of the partners were disinterested in SIMPP that Liberty would never join.

INTERNATIONAL PICTURES, FOUNDED BY producer William Goetz and RKO executive Leo Spitz, had a brief history that echoed Twentieth Century Pictures from the decade before. In both cases, the independent owners quickly turned their outfit into one of the most auspicious producers in Hollywood, only to merge with a major studio to command more leverage in the industry. In fact, Goetz was a producer at Twentieth Century and worked under Darryl Zanuck for many years before going independent on his own. Goetz, married to Louis B. Mayer's daughter Edith, also shared much in common with Mayer's other son-in-law David O. Selznick; both were producer-executives who rose though the studio ranks with dreams of running their own company.

Goetz, vice president of Twentieth Century-Fox, became temporary head of the studio when Darryl Zanuck joined the war effort in an extended service overseas in 1942. The new responsibilities for Goetz were effective only during the hiatus, but Zanuck received reports from the studio that Goetz's behavior appeared overly ambitious. When Zanuck returned to Twentieth Century-Fox in 1943, Goetz faced an uncomfortable confrontation with the studio head. Goetz resigned.

In late 1943, William Goetz decided to form his own independent company with Leo Spitz, a former lawyer who worked as a movie company advisor. In January 1944 Spitz helped secure distribution through RKO, and together they organized International Pictures.

Both International principals had independent connections. Spitz acted as an advisor on the Selznick International liquidation in December 1940. They decided to establish a high-profile reputation by attracting other independent or quasi-independent filmmakers like Fritz Lang, Sam Spiegel, and Orson Welles. SIMPP welcomed International Pictures into the organization, and viewed the company as one of the most promising recent additions to the Society. But International was actually less interested in independence, and more keen to accumulating clout in the industry. As Goetz looked for additional ways to distinguish the International label, his company became closely associated with Universal, where he sensed that the shifting tides might provide opportunity.

The largest shareholder of Universal at the end of World War II was British film magnate J. Arthur Rank. The vertically integrated industrialist Rank controlled a massive production-distribution-exhibition film company in England, and was seen as the largest foreign threat to Hollywood's worldwide dominance. Like Korda in the 1930s, Rank had aspirations of extending his empire to America, but had difficulty acclimating American audiences to his British films. Rank became intrigued with SIMPP, observing the independent movement as an opportunity to gain a foothold among the major Hollywood players. He intended on combining the resources of his own company with that of International and Universal to form United World Pictures, using block booking to compel exhibitors to accept his British films.

Some of the independents made alliances with the J. Arthur Rank Organization. Walter Wanger and Edward Small released films through Rank's distributor Eagle-Lion; and David O. Selznick formed Selznick International Pictures of England with Rank backing. However in the public arena, many of the outspoken SIMPP members shared the views of the general industry that targeted Rank as a threatening outsider. His image was not improved by the Anglo-American film trade difficulties in the late 1940s which made producers on both sides of the Atlantic more hostile.

Unable to get the United World block-booking scheme off the ground, Rank helped bring about a merger between Universal and International. The International management team was brought in to head the reorganized studio called Universal-International with William Goetz as president and overseer of production and Leo Spitz as chairman of the board. Rank nearly became a major partner in the deal, but was unable to expand into a controlling interest and was forced to back out.

The merger was announced on July 30, 1946, as Universal profits were showing steady growth. Universal had gravitated away from the B-movie focus that had been the studio's bread-and-butter; and the new management team continued to make deals with independent producers like Diana Productions—the production company formed by Wanger, his wife Joan Bennett, director-producer Fritz Lang, and screenwriter Dudley Nichols. However, in the following year, the Universal fortunes began to plummet rapidly as recession enveloped the industry. Following several years of financial losses, Universal-International was acquired by Decca late in 1951. The record company took control of Universal, and ousted Goetz and Spitz as the company headed toward conglomeration.

The relatively short careers of Liberty and International Pictures in the mid-1940s made the fleeting stability of independent producers appear even more bleak. The major studio, it seemed, was the unavoidable destination of production companies both successful and unsuccessful. Not only had SIMPP lost one of its most powerful members in the Universal-International merger of 1946, but the inability of the International management to weather the large-scale transformations taking place at the close of the studio era shed uncertainty over the direction of Hollywood's future.

THE INDEPENDENT HOWARD HUGHES entered the film industry in a unique and enviable position: unwilling to be dictated to by any Hollywood studio, and in a position to bankroll himself. He was an influential figure in the Hollywood progression toward independent filmmaking, as well as a memorable participant in the *Paramount* antitrust case. California Pictures, formed in partnership with writer-producer-director Preston Sturges, was one of Hughes many independent stints in Hollywood, as well as his final independent production venture before he took over RKO in 1948. California Pictures was also one of the new postwar production companies that typified the rise and retrenchment of the independent producers in the late 1940s.

Howard Hughes started his film career in 1926 at the age of 20, two years after inheriting his deceased parent's tool fortune. Hughes formed Caddo Productions, and hired A-class talent like director Lewis Milestone, screenwriter Ben Hecht, and Pickford director Marshall Neilan. By 1928, he signed a distribution deal with United Artists, and moved from the Metropolitan (General Service) Studios to the United Artists lot, where he headquartered his film operation through the years, even after his RKO purchase.

Hughes produced three monumental films in the early 1930s— the ambitious aeronautical feature *Hell's Angels* (1930), the seminal newspaper film *The Front Page* (1931), and the potent gangster movie *Scarface* (1932). These features gained Hughes a reputation not only as a successful film producer, but as a rebel whose eccentric use of wealth and whose disregard for industry convention was despised by the studio moguls. In 1932 the 26 year old Hughes announced, to the relief of the Hollywood establishment, that he was retiring from the movie business to devote his time to aviation. He formed the Hughes Aircraft Company that same year, and became a popular media figure with several speed records and around-the-world flights.

Hughes reentered Hollywood in late 1939, finding his brand of prestige independent production in vogue. Motivated by the successful opening of *Gone With the Wind*, Hughes decided to make a Western feature to be called "Billy the Kid" which, after running into title-registration conflict with MGM, was eventually filmed as *The Outlaw* (1943). Hughes expected the film to become the quintessential Western, as his earlier films had in their respective genres. Instead the film is remembered for the prolonged censorship opposition from the Hays office, and the lingering advertising campaign that was far more lascivious than the movie itself.

During this return to independent production, Hughes reinvented his image. Although he kept his demanding disposition and his disrespect for the studio system, he shed the tuxedo-clad bachelor style of his youth in favor of the rumpled suits and vagabond look that would become his trademark. At the same time, his famous eccentricities gradually became more pronounced, especially after his 1946 near-fatal test flight in which Hughes crash-landed his experimental XF-11 in Beverly Hills, next door to the home of Joseph Schenck.

During 1943 Howard Hughes and Preston Sturges began discussing the joint venture that would evolve into California Pictures. Continually finding himself sidetracked by his aircraft commitments, Hughes needed a capable filmmaker who could also shoulder the production responsibilities of the film company. Hughes was drawn to Sturges who shared a similar background with the wealthy renegade. Like Hughes, Sturges was a successful entrepreneur—operating his own engineering company and restaurant-nightclub—all on the side of a brilliant film career. Hughes frequented Sturges' restaurant called The Players, and established a friendship with Sturges during Hughes' early years in Hollywood. Hughes became the unofficial model for the hero in Preston Sturges' *Sullivan's Travels* (1942), featuring the exploits of a Hollywood playboy who goes slumming to experience the life of the common man.

Sturges rose to prominence as a screenwriter for the major studios in the 1930s. During a successful tenure at Paramount, he became a director, and then producer-director, who was also accustomed to contributing his own stories and screenplays. Acknowledged as one of the Hollywood studio-era artists with a recognizable body of work, Sturges decided to take his production unit independent. He left Paramount one month before the tremendously successful release of *The Miracle of Morgan's Creek* in January 1944. The film put Sturges in hot demand, but he turned down several generous studio contracts to become his own boss as an independent producer.

In February 1944, Sturges agreed to join in partnership with Howard Hughes. Taking a hefty pay-cut to secure his creative autonomy, Sturges became one of the few independent writer-producer-directors in the postwar era. Though Sturges held a majority interest in California Pictures, the Hughes Tool Company financed the operation, and held an option to reclaim Sturges' stock should disagreement arise between the partners. In August 1944 contracts were signed, and the California Pictures Corporation was organized. Later that year they entered into a distribution deal with United Artists, and joined SIMPP.

For his first independent film *The Sin of Harold Diddlebock* (1947), Sturges coaxed comedian Harold Lloyd from retirement to star in a sequel of sorts to Lloyd's silent comedy masterpiece *The Freshman* (1925). With a lavish $2 million budget, Sturges suffered from the same extravagance that tainted other studio filmmakers who became independent. Hughes had pledged not to intercede during production, even as the film exceeded its budget and went way over schedule. However, Hughes was disappointed with the final movie, and stepped in after the film was poorly received in early previews. Hughes delayed the final release of the film so that it could be reedited and rereleased at a later date.

"I became an independent producer to get away from supervision," Sturges said of the incident, from which his career never fully recovered. "When Mr. Hughes made suggestions with which I disagreed, as he had a perfect right to do, I rejected them. When I rejected the last one, he remembered he had an option to take control of the company and he took over. So I left." Hughes assumed control of the California Picture Corporation, and forced the resignation of Sturges in October 1946, leaving behind a second unfinished film, *Vendetta*.

Howard Hughes complained about the large amounts of money consumed by the two independent prestige films. Even years after the end of California Pictures, during a visit the home of William Cagney, Hughes fussed over the expense—$5 million, he claimed, in a story humorously retold in the autobiography of Preston Sturges.

Having been burned in his latest independent venture, Howard Hughes decided to broaden his film interests by taking over a major Hollywood studio. In early 1948 the trade papers reported that Hughes was in discussions with Floyd Odlum's Atlas Corporation, the holding company in charge of RKO. Back in the Depression, Odlum had helped reorganize Paramount, and purchased

Paramount debentures at their basement price in 1933. He sold his Paramount holdings at a profit, and used the proceeds to acquire the troubled RKO studio from David Sarnoff and RCA. RKO emerged from receivership in January 1940, in part by maintaining profitable and prestigious relations with independent producers like Disney and Goldwyn. But following the film recession of the late 1940s, Odlum was apprehensive about divorcement and the looming television threat. As RKO profits and stock prices began to dip, Odlum became interested in selling out.

In May 1948 Hughes agreed to purchase the Atlas stock in RKO for $8.8 million. J. Arthur Rank had also been interest in RKO, but Odlum reportedly took no competing bids in order to preserve the relationship between the Atlas aircraft company and Hughes' TWA. The price for Hughes also seemed far less considerable compared to Hughes recent expenditures with California. Howard Hughes, one of Hollywood's most detested independent producers, became the dictator of a Big Five film company.

10

The Independent Directory

MANY OF THE DIRECTORS who decided to go independent followed a similar pattern as Liberty Films and the other independent producer-director operations. John Ford, Howard Hawks, and Alfred Hitchcock worked within the studio system, and each of them had also directed pictures for some of the independents like Wanger, Goldwyn, and Selznick. When they went independent, all of the directors emulated to some extent, the Capra-Briskin or Sturges-Hughes corporate structure by partnering with a more business-minded counterpart. Like many of the independent producers in the late 1940s, the producer-directors apparently overextended with extravagant initial productions, then spent years trying to keep their production companies afloat, usually by taking side jobs directing for the major studios. Each director's respective company—Argosy Productions, Montgomery Productions, and Transatlantic Pictures—had a notable role in the independent movement, but none of the three joined with SIMPP.

Before going independent, John Ford was one of the most acclaimed directors of classic studio era. He shared the rebelliousness of the independent producers, and had a reputation for mistreating the producers he worked with in Hollywood. He began making inroads to independent production in the 1930s.

King Kong (1933) producer Merian C. Cooper left RKO in 1934 to form Pioneer Pictures to specialize in the experimental Technicolor film process, and convinced Ford to join the new independent company. Ford used his own money to purchase stories and acquire properties that later become important films for him, including two magazine stories "The Quiet Man" and "Stage to Lordsberg."

Pioneer Pictures was merged into the newly-formed Selznick International Pictures in 1936, and Ford faced opposition from David O. Selznick, who was not interested in producing Ford's A-movie Western film "Stage to Lordsberg." Ford shopped his project to other producers, and even tried to form his own independent company in June 1937 called Renowned Artists in collaboration with producer-director Tay Garnett and actor Ronald Coleman. Before Ford's independent plans could materialize, Walter Wanger agreed to produce Ford's film, offering the director 20 percent of the profits. The project, renamed *Stagecoach* became one of the most acclaimed films and successful blockbusters of 1939.

Following the success of *Stagecoach*, John Ford and Merian C. Cooper formed the first incarnation of Argosy Pictures. But Ford hedged his bet by also signing with Twentieth Century-Fox as a director under Zanuck. Meanwhile Wanger agreed to sponsor the first Argosy film *The Long Voyage Home* (1940), which turned out to be the only critical and commercial failure from Ford during this extraordinarily prolific period.

At the end of World War II, Ford and Cooper decided to turn Argosy into a full-fledged independent production company, and the director turned down a lucrative contract renewal with Zanuck. Argosy Productions was reorganized in March 1946 with $500,000 in capital and a multi-picture distribution deal with RKO. Merian Cooper was president. John Ford became chairman of the board.

Finally free of the brow-beating bosses, Ford decided to make an expensive adaption of a Graham Greene novel about a priest in an atheistic Latin American country. Ford's unconventional feature, known as known as *The Fugitive* (1947), became a costly fiasco for the producer-director unaccustomed to the lack of mooring that brought down many other independents like him. Some historians have speculated that Ford's previous fights with the studio system had actually served as one of the dynamics of his filmmaking, and that many of the director's independent films were lacking in comparison with his own studio pictures that were born out of a creative struggle with the system.

In an effort to strengthen Argosy's finances, Ford returned to his signature genre with *Fort Apache* (1948) and *She Wore a Yellow Ribbon* (1949). But he also had to make outside pictures for studios like Twentieth Century-Fox to keep his independent company solvent. Regardless, Argosy was dropped by RKO, so Ford and Cooper released their next films through Republic Pictures. The independent distributor was eager to establish an A-picture reputation, and offered Argosy a deal with a favorable 15 percent distribution fee and 50 percent of the profits.

Ford made his long time pet project *The Quiet Man* (1952), but despite the enormous popularity of the film, it became the final Argosy production as Ford entered into a legal dispute over the notorious bookkeeping of the Poverty Row studio. Subsequently Ford had a falling-out with Merian C. Cooper when Cooper left Argosy in May 1952 to become the head of the Cinerama Corporation. Cooper left a financial void that was difficult for Ford to fill. Argosy was eventually dissolved in January 1956.

HOWARD W. HAWKS MAINTAINED tight artistic control of his films, and was known to walk off the set when the studio or its producers interfered. Like many of the independent producers, Hawks viewed himself as a hit-maker, creating films that pleased himself, but were designed to entertain the masses. He could not consider himself a success unless his tastes were in synchronization with the public. By carefully selecting his own projects, and methodically reworking them on the set, Hawks naturally gravitated toward a position where he could be his own boss.

Hawks had become close friends with Charles K. Feldman, a talent agent since 1932 who had film production ambitions. Feldman negotiated on behalf of Hawks to direct *Sergeant York* (1941), the Jesse L. Lasky independent production that became a box office smash. During World War II, Hawks and Feldman organized H-F Productions an independent company that acted more like a liaison with the studios to provide the director more creative leverage. H-F acquired talent and story properties, developed material, and then sold each project as a package to a studio, usually with Hawks as producer-director. Two Hawks successes at Warner Bros. originated in this manner, *To Have and Have Not* (1944) and *The Big Sleep* (1946).

Hawks and Feldman formed their independent company Monterey Productions in 1945. Hawks and his wife held a majority share of the company, while Feldman received the coveted title of executive producer. They were assisted by another agent-turned-producer Edward Small who arranged a distribution deal for Montgomery at United Artists. Small and his investors syndicate also financed the first Montgomery project *Red River* (1948). Unfortunately out-of-control spending pushed the budget sky-high. Originally estimated at $1.7 million, *Red River* suffered from severe cost overages that exceeded the budget by an astronomical $1 million. Production stalled while Hawks refinanced the film. In the process he ceded most of his interests in the film to Small.

After spending $2.8 million, and with Monterey's share going to creditors, Hawks renegotiated with United Artists for better percentage terms, and threatened to take the film to another distributor if they would not give in. Deadlock ensued when UA refused to cancel Monterey's contract. Meanwhile, Small threatened to foreclose if the delay continued.

Monterey was forced to move out of its headquarters on the Samuel Goldwyn lot, and disbanded in 1947 while the fate of *Red River* was still being fought over. Though the film became a smash hit when it was released the following year, Hawks was unable to keep his independent company alive. Hawks was already raising revenue by directing for Sam Goldwyn. He then accepted an offer from Darryl Zanuck to make films at Twentieth Century-Fox.

ALFRED HITCHCOCK CAME to Hollywood under long-term contract with David O. Selznick. Although the association with Selznick provided the director a high-profile entrance into the industry and a degree of artistic freedom, Hitchcock found Selznick's creative vision unavoidably obtrusive. He also resented the producer's loan out deals that sent the director to various studios, at a significant profit to Selznick. Most of Hitchcock's early American films were made on loan to other producers and studios, expanding the director's exposure to the industry, and laying the seeds of his own independent desires.

While still working off his Selznick contract, Alfred Hitchcock formed an independent company with an old associate of his, British distributor and exhibitor Sidney Bernstein. At the end of World War II, they founded Transatlantic Pictures to produce films intermittently in Hollywood and London. The partners arranged for distribution through Warner Bros. and financing through the Bankers Trust Company. The company shared the London headquarters of Bernstein's Granada theaters, and awaited the fulfillment of Hitchcock's Selznick obligations in 1947.

Hitchcock made ambitious long-range plans, typical of the other first-time independents. He even adopted an experimental cinematic style in an effort to elaborate on his own thriller narrative formula. Unfortunately after the disappointing returns from his two independent films, *The Rope* (1948) and *Under Capricorn* (1949), Hitchcock folded Transatlantic Pictures. In 1949 Hitchcock signed a four-picture contract as producer-director at Warner Bros. trying to revive his artistic and commercial career.

Eventually, Ford, Hawks, and Hitchcock all returned to independent production with more caution the next time around. After Argosy, Ford organized John Ford Productions, and continued to direct memorable films into the 1960s. Howard W. Hawks formed his own company Winchester Productions through which he produced the science-fiction classic *The Thing from Another World* (1951).

Alfred Hitchcock had the most amazing comeback from both an artistic and an independent production standpoint. When Paramount offered him a profit-sharing contract in 1953, Hitchcock's agent Lew Wasserman negotiated a provision for the filmmaker to retain the rights to his movies including *Rear Window* (1954), *The Man Who Knew Too Much* (1956), *Vertigo* (1958), and *Psycho* (1960). A further indication of Hitchcock and Wasserman's business astuteness came at the inception of the *Alfred Hitchcock Presents* television series in 1955 when CBS relinquished all program rights after first broadcast to Hitchcock's own company Shamley Productions. Later on, Hitchcock sold the rights of many of these properties to Universal in exchange for a sizable interest that made him one of the largest stockholders in the studio.

TWO NEW MEMBERS of SIMPP during the postwar period survived the independent production shakedown to show that the independent movement and the Society itself were still viable. Sam Spiegel and Stanley Kramer represented the generation of independent producers who received their apprenticeships during the tail end of the studio system, and then came into their own as independent producers in the post-*Paramount* film industry.

Sam Spiegel, in the words of historian Kevin Brownlow, was "perhaps the last authentic movie tycoon" who arrived in Hollywood a generation too late. He was an illegal Polish immigrant who acquired a criminal record and was deported in 1929, only to return to the United States ten years later. While hiding from the immigration department, he adopted the pseudonym S. P. Eagle, and teamed with former Paramount producer and musical director Boris Morros to make *Tales of Manhattan* (1942) for Twentieth Century-Fox.

Morros and Spiegel went separate independent ways after World War II. Morros partnered with Paramount executive William Le Baron to form Federal Films, a SIMPP member company from 1946 to 1957. Spiegel went to International Pictures to make *The Stranger* (1946) which he was to produce, John Huston to direct, and Orson Welles to star in. Instead of Huston, Welles became attached to the project as actor-director, and Spiegel convinced Huston to form an independent partnership together called Horizon Pictures. Horizon Pictures was formed in 1948 by Spiegel and Huston, along with Jules Buck, an associate producer who made films with Huston during the war.

Their first independent picture *We Were Strangers* (1949) was a financial disaster. Huston borrowed money from MGM; in exchange, the director was required to make two films there—*The Asphalt Jungle* (1950) and *The Red Badge of Courage* (1951). Meanwhile Spiegel set out to revive Horizon by arranging the financing for *The African Queen* (1951) with the company's limited means.

Sam Spiegel attracted a top-flight cast with profit participation and salary deferments. Humphrey Bogart received 25 percent of the profits, and Katherine Hepburn took 10 percent. Huston, as director and partner of Horizon received 50 percent of profits. Financing came from a British distributor Romulus Films, Ltd. which put up production costs in exchange for the exclusive rights to distribution in the eastern hemisphere. In so doing, Spiegel pioneered a production method that has become commonplace for Hollywood independent producers to this day—financing domestic films by pre-selling foreign distribution rights.

The African Queen was released in the U.S. and Canada by United Artists, and became a huge success. John Huston left Horizon after a falling out with Spiegel. But the company continued, with Spiegel firmly in control, and Horizon maintaining its SIMPP membership throughout the existence of the Society.

Spiegel independently produced *On the Waterfront* (1954), the Elia Kazan-Budd Schulberg project that was rejected by several major studios. Spiegel finally abandoned the screen name S. P. Eagle when his film was released by Columbia. *On the Waterfront* broke box office records and won a best picture Oscar for Spiegel.

Spiegel also set up a Horizon branch office in England, believing that British co-productions would be the wave of the future. He acquired the rights to two old Alexander Korda projects *The Bridge on the River Kwai* and the D. H. Lawrence autobiography *The Seven Pillars of Wisdom*, the latter which Lawrence himself had sold to Korda in 1935. Spiegel hired one of Korda's former associates David Lean to direct Horizon's production of *The Bridge on the River Kwai* (1957). The film resulted in one of the biggest hits of the decade, and Spiegel and Lean made a follow-up epic out of *The Seven Pillars of Wisdom,* which was retitled *Lawrence of Arabia* (1962). After three best-picture Oscars, Sam Spiegel became the fifth SIMPP member to win the Irving G. Thalberg Memorial Award (the others were David O. Selznick, Walt Disney, Samuel Goldwyn, and Stanley Kramer).

Along with Spiegel, the later independent movement was bolstered by Stanley Kramer, the fiercely independent filmmaker who continued to produce successful films well into the television era. His experience with the major studios reached back to 1933, and he was something of a lower-budget operator before he joined SIMPP in 1948. But lacking the same immersion in the Hollywood business establishment as the SIMPP veterans, his entrance into the independent community was refreshing. Kramer broke through the Hollywood blacklist by freely hiring many artists subpoenaed by the HUAC. He championed a unique brand of social consciousness in order "to use film," he stated, "as a real weapon against discrimination, hatred, prejudice, and excessive power."

Stanley Kramer went independent at the end of World War II, in a joint venture with Armand S. Deutsch, one of the heirs to the Sears, Roebuck fortune. The partnership was short-lived as Deutsch decided to buy out his partner and form an independent production company with Hal Horne. (The Horne-Deutsch production company called Story Productions Inc. joined SIMPP in 1946.) Kramer took his proceeds from the sale, and started his own independent company Screen Plays Inc. in May 1947.

In contrast to the high-budget prestige films of the other independents, Kramer produced the acclaimed anti-boxing melodrama *Champion* (1949) on a 23-day schedule for $590,000. He launched Stanley Kramer Productions Inc., and became involved in the Krim and Benjamin reorganization of United Artists. He produced *Cyrano de Bergerac* (1950), acquiring the film rights from Korda, and debuted the film through a successful road-show release under the aegis of his own production company. His next independent production was the Fred Zinnemann-directed hit *High Noon* (1952) which grossed an astounding $12 million worldwide.

Experiencing many of the same financing problems as other postwar independents, Kramer moved his company to Columbia Pictures to become an in-house independent under a five-year, 30-picture deal. As his budgets increased, so did his tremendous range of filmmaking—from Dr. Seuss' off-beat surrealist fantasy *The 5,000 Fingers of Dr. T* (1953) to the Marlon Brando motorcycle movie *The Wild One* (1954). His most successful production at Columbia was *The Caine Mutiny* (1954) which became one of the highest grossing films of the year.

In 1954 Kramer set up a new production company, the Stanley Kramer Picture Corporation, which released through United Artists. He reduced his film production schedule in order to become an independent producer-director, entering another phase of his career with several groundbreaking movies that were highly-regarded in the industry. His films tackled issues like racism (*The Defiant Ones*, 1958), nuclear holocaust (*On the Beach*, 1959), evolution (*Inherit the Wind*, 1960) and genocide (*Judgment at Nuremberg*, 1961). Kramer remained an active SIMPP member until the Society folded in the late 1950s.

MEANWHILE IN THE LATE 1940S, SIMPP members struggled through the difficult boom and bust of the postwar period. Even the more established producers were hit-or-miss during this time.

Independent producer David Loew had only a brief stay with SIMPP. He had formed Enterprise Productions, designed as an aggressive advocate of profit sharing with production talent. In 1946 he convinced Ingrid Bergman to join Enterprise to make *Arch of Triumph* (1948), her first film after fulfilling her contract with Selznick. The highly-anticipated movie was troubled in production, and had its release delayed in a disagreement with United Artists. *Arch of Triumph* cost over $4 million to make, and lost an estimated $2 million at the box office—"probably the greatest commercial failure in the history of motion pictures," said UA's Grad Sears. Loew left SIMPP, grew tired of film production, and in the early 1950s turned his back on his movie career to become a painter.

Harry Sherman also planned to take advantage of the postwar prosperity until it went sour. He had turned over the production of the Hopalong Cassidy series to the star William Boyd, so that Sherman could concentrate on moving into the A-picture market. However, the independent veteran was plagued by financial problems brought on by the film recession in the late 1940s. Sherman was forced to drop out of SIMPP, but a few years later he renewed his membership with the Society as he tried to jump-start his career. Just as he was getting back into production in 1952, Harry Sherman died.

Other independents including Constance Bennett, the Cagneys, and Hunt Stromberg also had to curtail their production operations after high-cost independent films failed to replicate the successes of their earlier pictures. Though *Arch of Triumph* was perhaps the costliest independent disaster, the most disappointing was Walter Wanger's *Joan of Arc* (1948). The movie was produced by Sierra Pictures, a company formed by Wanger, working in partnership with director Victor Fleming and in conjunction with Ingrid Bergman's En Corporation. Sierra received the largest single-film loan ever, $3.5 million, for *Joan of Arc*—which eventually became the most expensive movie ever made, $4.5 million. Though the gross receipts were far from disastrous, the exorbitant costs resulted in a sizable net loss, which provoked Wanger to say, "It should never have been made by an independent."

SIMPP members insisted that the difficulties in the industry were seasonal, and that the rise and fall of ticket sales did not eliminate the need for quality A-pictures. Donald Nelson defended the independent production movement in an article written for the *Annals of the American Academy of Political and Social Science* for a special issue in November 1947 that was devoted to the motion picture industry. Nelson, then president of SIMPP said that even though the independents represented a fractional portion of the entire industry, they were responsible for an inordinately high amount of the industry's innovative films, including six of the ten all-time box-office champions: *The Birth of a Nation* (1915), *Gone With the Wind* (1939), *The Best Years of Our Lives* (1946), *Duel in the Sun* (1946), *The Bells of St. Mary's* (1945), and *Snow White and the Seven Dwarfs* (1937).

"If there are risks in independent production, there are also advantages," the SIMPP president wrote. "The independent producer is far more flexible than the major studio. It is this factor of adaptability which ensures his survival against odds that often appear impossible. It is not unusual to see every box-office drop accompanied by a flurry of rumors that the independent producer is finished and running for the cover of the major studios. There is no doubt, of course, that in times of any severe recession the number of independents is reduced. This is true of small business anywhere. But through all the box-office cycles of Hollywood history, the independent producer has not only survived, but prospered."

Nelson was vigorously preparing the Society to participate in the *Paramount* case which reached the Supreme Court in late 1947, ironically, during one of the bleakest times for the independent movement. "On the decision of the Supreme Court," Nelson remarked, "hinges much of the future of the independent producer and, therefore, of the American motion picture."

Though the independents were confident about the *Paramount* case and of the new outlook the ruling would bring, SIMPP and the independent movement faced many impediments, including the government repeal of the capital gains tax break and the increasing troubles with overseas quotas and restrictions. Indeed the setbacks proved momentary, however, the decline in movie ticket sales was not. The film recession of the late 1940s was actually the beginning of the long downward swing of theatrical motion picture attendance that would forever be altered by television.

Despite the enthusiasm of the Society of Independent Motion Picture Producers, rumors persisted in Hollywood that the unraveling of so many independent production companies was taking its toll on the activities of SIMPP. Society president Donald Nelson was plagued with personal problems, including his well-publicized multiple divorces that made him the subject of gossip columns. Also his health deteriorated, and on July 21, 1947 Nelson was hospitalized with "a transient spasm of a blood vessel" which the trade papers exaggerated as a debilitating coronary thrombosis. He would eventually die from a stroke in 1959 during a party given by Veronique, the wife of actor Gregory Peck.

On December 9, 1947 Nelson announced his resignation from SIMPP. The press speculated that it was due to the uncertainties of independent film production. But in his moving letter of resignation, Nelson drew upon the resilience of the independents, confident that the difficulties faced by SIMPP were momentary, and that his resignation was coincidental with his interests in projects outside the organization. His main caution was the Society's overhead expenses, of which, the president's salary was the biggest single item. "If the Society can survive and remain intact for the present— and I believe it can, possibly under temporary leadership from within its own ranks—I am confident that forces which are now at work will reshape the whole structure of film marketing to the great encouragement and benefit of independent production."

After a dip in SIMPP membership, the size of the Society steadily increased and rapidly expanded in the wake of the antitrust rulings of the late 1940s. Thereafter the growth continued throughout the existence of the organization. The Society viewed the difficulties of the late 1940s as a weeding-out of less resilient independents. Some independents had been ill-prepared for the recession; others were reckless. In 1947 the government repealed the capital gains tax shelter upon which many of the hit-and-run independents had based their businesses. This bad news for all independents made the survivors even stronger, as the Society of Independent Motion Picture Producers poised itself to make independent production the new standard of filmmaking as the studio system waned.

11

Independent's Day

The Society of Independent Motion Picture Producers was at its best dealing with antitrust issues, and despite the independent meltdown in the late 1940s, SIMPP's participation in the *Paramount* case was not impeded.

Previously SIMPP had preferred to submitted court briefs on short notice, in order to coordinate the Society's publicity efforts with the events of the case. These had been hurried efforts, working late into the night, usually over the course of a weekend, and submitted at just the right time for dramatic effect. For the Supreme Court brief, Donald Nelson, prior to his resignation in December 1947, authorized an extensive research program before executing the independent produces' defense strategy. "Great care should be taken on the Society's brief to the court," SIMPP attorney Morris L. Ernst recommended to the president, "because it not only speaks to the court, it speaks to the rest of the industry."

Part of SIMPP's preparations involved question-and-answer sessions with Robert L. Wright, the chief prosecutor for the government in the *Paramount* case. Wright (incidentally the son of architect Frank Lloyd Wright) had worked on the case since its inception in 1938, and delivered the opening arguments in the New York Equity Suit in 1945. At the invitation of Nelson, Robert

Wright visited Los Angeles in April 1947 as guest of the Society. In a series of meetings, the SIMPP members, and then the SIMPP attorneys, discussed the case as it made its way to the Supreme Court trial calendar for early the following year. The members happily discovered the objectives of the Justice Department in nearly complete harmony with their own desires, and the independents agreed to support the case as needed.

SIMPP's antitrust investigation went into full-swing in the latter part of 1947. To lead the research team, SIMPP selected Robert J. Rubin who joined SIMPP officially as assistant to the president, and soon became general counsel for the Society. Before this, Rubin was a legal expert for the government, and headed all Justice Department antitrust actions on the west coast. Robert J. Rubin (not to be confused with prominent MGM executive J. Robert Rubin) became the antitrust spokesperson for SIMPP, and attended the Supreme Court hearings to speak on behalf of the independent producers.

After months of prearranging their friend-of-the-court status, the Society of Independent Motion Picture Producers completed the *amicus curiae* brief without the approval of the *Paramount* defendants, and officially joined sides with the Department of Justice to restore free competition to the industry.

The SIMPP *amicus curiae* made several demands. First of all, the Society asked that the Supreme Court uphold the ban on block booking so that the dreaded practice finally be declared illegal. The independents also petitioned the Supreme Court to reverse part of the Statutory Court ruling by requiring the majors to dispose of all their theater holdings. "As the only creative force competitive to the defendants," SIMPP declared, the independent producers "continue to operate under a constant burden so long as the defendants continue to own and run their own theatres."

SIMPP also wanted to reverse some of the competitive bidding provisions which would have outlawed road show film selling. If the New York Equity Suit mandate went into effect, the producers would not have been allowed to select prestige theaters that charged premium admission prices—for this would be interpreted as exhibitor discrimination. Road show premieres would be impossible to arrange, and the way in which independents launched their movies would be called into question. SIMPP asked for judicial clarification to declare the independent producers free to market their films in this manner.

The friend-of-the-court petition, filed in Washington by Morris Ernst on December 2, 1947, was one of Donald Nelson's final actions in his executive role with SIMPP. Slightly delayed from its January 12 court date, the Supreme Court trial began on February 9, 1948, nearly one year after the government appealed the Statutory Court ruling.

Attorney General Tom C. Clark opened the government arguments, confident that the wealth of information would prove that divorcement was necessary to end studio domination of the motion picture industry. The counsel said that of the 92 U.S. cities with a population of 100,000 or greater, the studio-owned theater chains held domination over all but four. Over one-third of the cities had no independent theaters at all.

For the major studios, the legal defense included several heavy-hitters, including former Secretary of State James F. Byrnes and 1924 Democratic Presidential candidate John W. Davis. Again, the primary argument was that the *Paramount* case, which would bring an end to the studio system, would cause a disservice to the public.

The case was rapidly tried, and the ruling was handed down by the Supreme Court on May 4, 1948. The decision favored the independent producers on practically every point. The Supreme Court affirmed the Statutory ruling that declared the studios guilty of violating antitrust laws. Once and for all the Supreme Court abolished block booking—ending over 30 years of controversy—by requiring all films henceforth to be sold on an individual basis.

Also the Supreme Court reversed the lower court mandate for competitive bidding, and stated that such an involved legal restriction would involve the government too deeply in the day-to-day business of the industry. Disagreeing with the Statutory decision, the new ruling considered studio disintegration to be the ultimate solution to the problems faced by the independents. The Supreme

Court remanded the decision back to the lower courts with the rec-
ommendation that competitive bidding be nullified and that
divorcement be reconsidered.

The independent producers' years of struggle finally resulted in
a Supreme Court ruling in favor of theater divestiture from the
major studios and the end of block booking. A SIMPP statement
released by Gunther Lessing of Walt Disney Productions called the
decision a "declaration of independence as far as independent
motion picture producers are concerned." Samuel Goldwyn called
the decision "a distinct victory toward restoring free enterprise in
the motion-picture industry."

But skeptics considered the ten-year-old fight far from over. The
case was sent back to the Federal District Court for the final ruling,
in what seemed to many as a never-ending postponement of the
divorcement decree sought by the government.   For instance,
Joseph Schenck interpreted the Supreme Court ruling in more
vague terms, indicating that the high court never actually condemned theater ownership by the studios, but instead had sent the
case back to court. "I think the ruling means the end of the divestiture threat," Schenck declared, in far more optimistic terms than the
grim outlook would indicate.

The delay also gave the major studios time to counteract the
Supreme Court decision with an attempt at another consent decree.
Throughout that summer, the press reported activities of the Big
Five trying to enact a compromise deal with the Justice
Department. In 1948 however, the studios had to deal with something that was not around during the 1940 compromise: a united
independent producer movement, which stood in opposition to any
unfavorable deal, and was willing to take the case to the people
when the studios tried to protect their monopoly.

SIMPP sent a telegram of protest to Attorney General Clark,
which Gunther R. Lessing also forwarded to President Truman on
September 10, 1948 and then disclosed it to the press the following
week. Lessing, who signed the telegram and probably wrote it himself, was acting as vice president and chairman of the SIMPP executive committee.

We are informed that negotiations are in progress whereby the major motion picture company defendants in the anti-trust case (United States vs Paramount, et al) who have been found guilty by the federal district court of the United States Supreme Court of long-continued violations of the law are now attempting to avoid the full effect of the decision of the Supreme Court by procuring the government's agreement to a so-called "consent decree." The members of the Society of Independent Motion Picture Producers unanimously protest any such agreement by the government with these defendants who, in the words of the Supreme Court, "Have shown marked proclivity for unlawful conduct."

The Society of Independent Motion Picture Producers believes that any softening of the application of the law as laid down by the Supreme Court would result in a continuation of monopolistic practices and prevent restoration of a free and competitive screen.

This case has been in the courts for over ten years. One consent decree has already been entered which completely failed to make any correction in the monopolistic stranglehold of these defendants on motion picture exhibition in the United States. The case has been exhaustively tried before the District Court and heard by the Supreme Court, and the Supreme Court has given clear directions to the District Court as to what is to be done to remedy the "bald efforts to substitute monopoly for competition and to strengthen the hold of the exhibitor- defendants on the industry."

It remains only for the District Court to take the final step of putting into effect the Supreme Court's decision in order that the monopolistic grip of these defendants on motion picture exhibition may be loosened. There is absolutely no reason for the Government of the United States to make any deal with these law violators who, again in the words of the Supreme Court, "had the genius to conceive the present conspiracy and execute it with the subtlety which this record reveals."

Such a deal could be regarded only as a betrayal of the interests of the American public which has a vital stake in the maintenance of an open competitive system of decent free enterprise. We cannot conceive that you will agree to any such deal. We urge you, as the chief law enforcement officer of this nation, to see to it that the order of the United States Supreme Court is vigorously enforced and that the full resources of the government are thrown behind the completion of this case in open court and not behind closed doors.

SIMPP feared that another secret negotiation would lead to a devastating compromise, as had happened in 1940 when an antitrust misstep resulted in years of delay. The government, which had first-hand experience with the shiftiness of the Hollywood studios, agreed with SIMPP, and planned the negotiations around the recent Supreme Court victory.

On October 1 the Justice Department sent notice to the attorneys of the Big Five that the government would indeed encourage a consent decree from any company that wished to opt out of the trial, so long as the corporation agreed to a divorcement decree that separated exhibition from production-distribution. The Hollywood majors remained aloof, and they resolved to go back to court to fight divorcement to the end.

"Opinion in trade circles," the *New York Times* reported, "was that the case was back to its beginning in July 1938, since divorcement was the crux of the Government's action. However, it was felt that the Supreme Court's dissatisfaction with these particulars tended to strengthen the stand of the Justice Department." Industry analysts said that it looked as if real change was still uncertain, and perhaps still a long ways away. Then in October 1948 a remarkable turn of events brought the beginning of the end of Hollywood vertical integration.

Howard Hughes, the independent-producer-turned-movie-czar, announced that RKO would immediately comply with the Supreme Court decision by spinning off its theater chain from the studio operations. The move typified his spontaneous behavior, and reverberated from his independent roots as a enemy of the studio establishment. Hughes also had much to gain by forcing a divorcement decree. RKO, by far the weakest of the Hollywood theater owners, would be brought on equal ground if divestiture was successfully enacted across the industry.

Hughes' decision to break ranks with the other major theater owners was one of the singular events in the antitrust case, leading the way for the disintegration of the vertical Hollywood majors. RKO promised divorcement within one year, creating two companies for Hughes to choose one to keep a controlling interest in. With obvious plans to remain a film producer, Hughes kept the RKO Pictures Corporation and sold the RKO Theatres Corporation. The RKO consent decree was signed on November 8, 1948, signaling the finale of the studio epoch.

With RKO proving the precedent for a feasible divorcement, the trial of the remaining four theater-owning studios was set for the following April. Anticipating a costly battle, the mighty Paramount Pictures became the second studio to submit to the divorcement demands. The studio felt the burden on impending legislation looming over the company fortunes, and decided to voluntarily divest their theater chain rather than submit to a court-directed liquidation. Paramount entered into a divorcement decree with the Justice Department on February 25, 1949.

One of the key reasons Paramount capitulated was due to its interests in the new television market where the Paramount studio was establishing itself as a leader. In 1938 Paramount had invested $400,000 in the DuMont Corporation to gain a foothold in television manufacturing. But rather than home television, the studio believed there might be some use for broadcasts into their movie theaters, providing live showings of remote news events, for instance. Also in the early 1940s Paramount bought into several television stations. The studio owned four of the nine operating stations in the U.S., and established the first TV stations in Chicago and Los Angeles. However, according to the Communications Act of 1934, the Federal Communications Commission was authorized to refuse broadcast licenses to any company convicted of monopolistic practices. During the New York Equity Suit, Twentieth Century-Fox and RKO had each unsuccessfully applied for television licences, as the FCC took a wait-and-see attitude until the antitrust case was settled. *United States v. Paramount* also delayed Paramount's plans for television expansion, and the studio could not afford to risk an adverse ruling that would jeopardize its sprawling television duchy.

Paramount would be protected by its consent decree, but the terms were severe and specific. In addition to total separation of the studio from all domestic theaters, the Justice Department restricted the spin-off exhibition company to a maximum of 600 theaters. The Paramount circuit was then 1,450 strong, of which over 1000 were still partially-owned Paramount affiliates. So Paramount decided to negotiate leeway to be able to acquire the controlling interests in several of its affiliates, while selling off its less-desirable theaters. The Justice Department stipulated—so long as Paramount created a free market with no local Paramount monopoly.

Paramount president Barney Balaban, always the diplomat, called the divorcement decree "constructive," and optimistically predicted a solid future for the theater chain: "It will leave the new theatre company with a large, well-selected and thoroughly sound theatre circuit." Though his personal roots were in exhibition, Balaban remained as president at the producing-distributing end of the divestiture. Leonard H. Goldenson, a Harvard graduate who joined Paramount in 1933, presided over the new theater company. However the new Paramount studio, minus its U.S. theater chain, would keep its dominant Canadian circuit of 370 theaters, as well as its important overseas screens. The studio was given three years to comply, but Paramount Pictures, eager to inaugurate a new decade with the divorcement behind them, completed the reorganization on New Year's Eve 1949. Adolph Zukor joined in the media event that heralded a new era of filmmaking.

The other three Hollywood theater-owners resisted the Justice Department demands. "We will not give up our theaters without a court fight," Harry M. Warner announced within a few hours of the Paramount capitulation of February 25, 1949. "We have taken years to accumulate the company assets we have, and we will fight to hold them." Celebrating the twenty-fifth anniversary of the formation of Metro-Goldwyn-Mayer, Loew's told its stockholders that the company bitterly opposed theater divestiture. The Loew's circuit refused to sell off MGM, and reminded the Department of

Justice that the Supreme Court may have outlawed block booking, but it never declared vertical integration illegal per se. Twentieth Century-Fox also protested disintegration. It offered to eliminate some of its more notorious regional exhibition monopolies, if the attorney general would regulate but not force the studio to sell its entire chain. The government rebuffed all proposals, and agreed to see the studios back in court where, by this time, divorcement was virtually assured. The decisive blow came with the Federal Statutory Court decision on July 25, 1949—eleven years and one week after the *Paramount* case was filed.

Though the Society of Independent Motion Picture Producers reached a plateau with the decision in the *Paramount* suit, the Society considered the case as one step toward their ultimate goal of complete freedom of the screen. As Sam Goldwyn cautioned, "it will be necessary to see that divorcement means more than just a transfer of circuit control from one set of hands to another." SIMPP decided to continue the battle against select movie companies in private suits to see that predatory practices were stopped, and, in some cases, damages collected. They were also positioning themselves to fill the void left by the studio system. When Paramount, for years the scourge of the independent producers, finally broke up its vertical monopoly, the producers found themselves in agreement with Paramount's Barney Balaban who said "this consent decree marks the end of the old, and the beginning of the new."

PART III

SIMPP in the Independent Era

12

Diplomacy

HAVING PROVEN ITS staying power toward the end of the 1940s, the Society of Independent Motion Picture Producers enjoyed the recognition of being the leading industry voice for the independent producer movement at a time when the paradigm shift toward independent production was imminent. The year 1948 became one of the Society's most memorable. In addition to the success in the Supreme Court *Paramount* case and the commencement of their own civil antitrust suit (see chapter 13), SIMPP became increasingly involved with industry matters—both as collaborator with and chief rival to the Motion Picture Association of America.

SIMPP continued to assist the independent producers in establishing a position of strength. In May 1947, SIMPP and the MPAA agreed to make information concerning contract talent communal between the major studios and the independents. The agreement was actually between SIMPP and the Association of Motion Picture Producers (AMPP), the MPAA's exclusive casting arm previously known as the West Coast Association formed in 1924. Finally the availability of talent became declassified in an joint resolution that not only indicated the new presence of the independents but also the erosion of the talent lock previously held by the major studios.

SIMPP also to increased its power and recognition during the international negotiations that troubled Hollywood following World War II. In Great Britain, Hollywood's most important overseas market, the new Labour government imposed a mandatory 75 percent tax on all film imports effective August 1947. The tax, levied against each film's "expected earnings," was untenable to the Hollywood studios which accused the British Parliament of selfishly eliminating free speech by being overprotective of its own film industry. Many insiders considered the actions at least in part inspired by the irascible producer J. Arthur Rank as a retaliatory maneuver to punish the Hollywood studios for their unwillingness to receive his British films.

The United States answered with a boycott. All Hollywood distributors withheld their films from England until the tax was lifted. The major studios predicting that England needed American films more than Hollywood needed the revenue generated by the British territories. For months the embargo remained in effect, leaving producers like Alexander Korda caught in the middle. The following year Parliament repealed the tax but replaced it with a quota law that required British exhibitors to show no less than 45 percent British-made films. Parliament also tightened the restrictions on frozen funds by limiting the amount of money that American film companies could remove from Great Britain. The intent was to coerce the Hollywood studios into spending their British-earned frozen money actually in England.

Two representatives from the United States film industry were sent to negotiate the overseas conflict in 1948—Eric Johnston representing the MPAA and James Mulvey for SIMPP. Not only did SIMPP receive equal attention at the London conferences, but the negotiating ability of Mulvey, who was already known as a fair and resourceful arbitrator, brought SIMPP to the fore. Even Johnston, president of the MPAA, acknowledged the indispensability of Mulvey's skill in July 1948 in helping to reach an accord with Great Britain.

But to the astonishment of the independent producers, while the Johnston-Mulvey party was preoccupied in England, the major studios were hastily pressuring the United States Ambassador into making a deal with the French government that would disadvantage the independents. The agreement with France would limit only ten American production companies to legally import films into the French territory. While Hollywood was still dominated by a the majors, the independent producers would be forced into a bitter struggle for the few remaining permits.

Roy Disney sent a lengthy and forceful telegram to Secretary of State George C. Marshall denouncing the arrangement as "highly discriminatory and unfair to the Disney company and others like it." Disney predicted that the deal would result in foreign control by the majors with the likelihood that permits would be hoarded by the studios or, worse, scalped at inflated prices. The telegram urged Marshall not to enter into any international film agreements before conferring with the growing independent segment of the film industry.

Roy Disney asked SIMPP executive secretary Marvin Faris to call a meeting together for August 17, 1948 to discuss the impact of the French situation. At the SIMPP meeting, the independent producers unanimously decided to protest the French agreement by withdrawing James Mulvey from the British negotiation. After a long discussion, the members decided that if the Society continued its participation with the MPAA in the final phase of the British conferences, the independents would jeopardize their standing and risk placing themselves at the mercy of the major studios. The last-minute decision to pull Mulvey came shortly before the diplomatic party left New York to return to England at the end of August.

Mulvey's exit put Eric Johnston in an uncomfortable position. The image of Hollywood solidarity that the MPAA wanted to instill in overseas delegates was being undermined by a disgruntled faction at home. Leaving New York without the independent contingent, Johnston attempted to preserve the credibility of the mission by blaming Mulvey's absence on disagreements within the SIMPP organization. "Walter Wanger, David O. Selznick and Samuel Goldwyn agreed with me that he should go," Johnston told the *New York Times*. "I don't know why they [the other independents] don't want him to." The MPAA chief declared SIMPP divided, which was ludicrous after the Society voted unanimously on two occasions the previous week to boycott the trip.

The Society fumed following Johnston's misstatement, explaining to the press that such arrogance on the part of the major studios was exactly why the independents found its impossible to stand united with the MPAA. In a sharp rebuttal, Goldwyn denied any split in the ranks of the producers, "on the contrary, there is complete unity among us," he explained. "The Society operates on the principle that each member, no matter how small, has an equal voice in Society matters with every other member, no matter how large. My company joined in the unanimous decision made at the Society membership meetings not to send a representative to England at this time, and I have never had any intention of departing from that action of the Society."

When Johnston returned from England, he sought to heal the tense situation between the MPAA and SIMPP with an offer to restore the independent producers' voice in all international negotiations. The Society gave serious consideration to the proposal, and replied in November 1948 that independent group could return to the negotiations only if Johnston promised to consult with SIMPP before making any deal abroad that would impact the industry as a whole. Johnston deflected the demand by telling SIMPP, which had been acting without a president since Nelson's resignation in 1947, that the MPAA did not know from day to day which SIMPP executive was responsible for the official position of the independent organization.

Since the beginning of 1948, the administration of SIMPP had been handled by the executive committee consisting of Sol Lesser, Roy Disney, Edward Small, Marvin A. Ezzell (of Samuel Goldwyn Productions), Daniel T. O'Shea (representing Selznick's Vanguard), Earl Rettig (from Rainbow Productions), and George Bagnall (the vice president of United Artists). Bagnall was the original chairman of the committee, and acted on behalf of Donald Nelson during the president's health absences. When Gunther Lessing became the chairman of the executive committee, he became the Society's chief executive. However, James Mulvey was clearly SIMPP's ultimate international spokesman, as Robert J. Rubin was the Society's voice on antitrust matters. All of this resulted in a confusing division of responsibilities.

Spurned by the lack of a fully-empowered SIMPP authority, Mulvey traveled by plane from New York the weekend after having the leadership issue thrown in his face by Johnston. Mulvey arrived in Hollywood on November 15 for a week-long conference with Sam Goldwyn, where the two of them prepared to convince the independent members to take swift action in electing a new president.

During that same time, they sent Robert Rubin to Georgia on official SIMPP business. In Georgia there was a potential candidate for the SIMPP presidency—a young, progressive leader who gained a reputation as a great trustbuster as state attorney general and as governor. Rubin had just spent five weeks in Washington, D.C. representing SIMPP in the *Paramount* case, and witnessed the harbinger of studio disintegration, the RKO divorcement decree, in October. More certain about the end of the studio system, SIMPP believed that a monopoly-busting Society president would help their antitrust ambitions gain momentum. On Rubin's trip to the south, he was instructed to gage the interest of the secret SIMPP candidate whose experience seemed fitting for the independent film movement.

At a SIMPP meeting in Hollywood on November 18, attended by the big three SIMPP producers David O. Selznick, Samuel Goldwyn, and Walt Disney, the SIMPP executive committee issued a public statement that the Society of Independent Motion Picture Producers was interested in enlisting the services of Ellis Gibbs Arnall, the former governor of Georgia, in an unspecified capacity that would take advantage of his "wide experience in antitrust prosecution."

ELLIS ARNALL WAS A self-proclaimed "practical idealist" who attracted attention as a progressive reformer in Georgia. In 1940 he served as director of President Roosevelt's reelection campaign in the south. In turn, Roosevelt threw his support behind Arnall's decisive gubernatorial primary (in a Democrat-dominated state where the party primary effectively secured the eventual winner). As one of the youngest governors ever elected, at age 35, Arnall opposed graft and corruption in a state dominated by special interests. Attacking many of the regional monopolies, he guided successful antitrust suits against the railroad and highway cartels to the Supreme Court [e. g., *Georgia v. Pennsylvania Railroad Co.*, 324 U.S. 439 (1945)]. Against great opposition, he imposed voting reform that increased black voter franchise, and made Georgia the first state to extended the vote those who were 18 years old.

He also championed prison reform by overhauling the notorious chain gang penal system that had subjected his state to so much nationwide criticism. He attacked political favoritism by voluntarily surrendering the much-abused governor power to grant pardons. Arnall nevertheless took exception in the case of Robert Elliot Burns. Burns had been a praiseworthy figure in the chain gang controversy, and a two-time prison escapee allegedly imprisoned without due process. While running from the law, Burns rehabilitated himself and pseudonymously gave an account of his misadventures in a book that became the basis for the classic Warner Bros. film *I Am a Fugitive from a Chain Gang* (1932). Despite overwhelming public sympathy, the state of Georgia still considered Burns a fugitive. Arnall, who was inspired by the film years before his own political career, decided to inaugurate his administrations's prison reform efforts by pardoning Robert Burns.

The Burns incident also convinced Arnall of the influence of the movie industry on the shaping of public attitudes. In order to enhance its ability to work for the public good, Arnall believed in total freedom of the motion picture marketplace. He therefore found the cause of the independent producers to be compatible with his personal beliefs. Arnall publically called trustbusting "a lot of fun," and maintained that "the survival of democracy and the capitalistic system is dependent on winning the war against monopolies."

Ellis Arnall also brought to SIMPP his organizational ability. The Governor was charismatic, as Donald Nelson was deliberate. Sought after for his renowned speaking ability, Arnall was continually on lecture tour. During his tenure as governor, he drafted a new Georgia constitution and spearheaded a state-wide campaign to rally support for it. SIMPP believed that such enthusiasm was ideal for the continuing attack on film monopolies that the Society would wage in various parts of the country.

Paradoxically, the ratification of the new Georgia constitution, which prohibited more than one successive term of office, brought an end to his popular governorship, and lead to one of the most bizarre elections in United States history. In November 1946 the voters chose Arnall's conservative arch-rival Eugene Talmadge as the new governor. But when Talmadge died one month after the election and before being sworn in, the dispute degenerated into a power-struggle between three potential governors—the governor-elect's son Herman Talmadge, Lieutenant Governor M. E. Thompson, and Arnall who refused to surrender his position. After being locked out of the governor's office in the capital building in Atlanta, Arnall took over the information booth at the capital gates, and ran his administration from the kiosk. His demonstration helped secure the recognition of the Lieutenant Governor as his successor, but in a special election in 1948, the Talmadge regime was voted into power.

SIMPP contacted Ellis Arnall following the three-governor controversy to consult with him on the enduring motion picture monopolies, and perhaps to invite him to join the independent producers as president of the Society of Independent Motion Picture Producers. The members were impressed with Arnall's ability to reverse Georgia's declining fortunes during the war. They saw a parallel with the declining film industry in the late 1940s, and hoped that Arnall would be able to enact a proactive agenda during a time of retrenchment.

Arnall arrived in Los Angeles on December 12, 1948 to attend a SIMPP dinner meeting at Perino's restaurant that evening. Mary Pickford, Edward Small, Walt Disney, Samuel Goldwyn, Charles

R. Rogers, Benedict Bogeaus, George Bagnall, Dan O'Shea, William Cagney, and Marvin Ezzell were among those in attendance at the meeting where Arnall was unanimously elected as the new SIMPP president. The executive committee formed a welcome wagon consisting of Sam Goldwyn, David Selznick, and Walt Disney to personally extend the offer to Arnall.

At a press conference the following day, Ellis Arnall called the Hollywood antitrust fight "the greatest fight raging in this country today." He echoed the SIMPP message from the past few years that after a victory in world war, it would be a tragedy to allow studio monopolies to dictate what movies the American public would see.

"Hollywood has a certain amount of glamour," Arnall admitted to the SIMPP members, "and through that we can take the fight to the public so they can understand it. When the public understands monopolies are holding up better products, monopolies are going to have real resistance from the Government and the people."

THE HOLLYWOOD BLACKLIST in the late 1940s illustrated the complexities that SIMPP faced as the group walked the narrow line between independent production and the industry mainstream. While keeping distance between itself and the House Un-American Activities Committee, SIMPP unavoidably became embroiled in the controversy. However, the diversity of political views of the independent producers made SIMPP's participation in the industry's anti-Communist activities somewhat uneven.

Back in 1944, Walter Wanger lead the liberal Free World Association as it antagonized the Motion Picture Alliance for the Preservation of American Ideals, the anti-Communist group cofounded by Walt Disney. Interestingly, not only was Wanger a partner with Disney on the polo field and at SIMPP, but Wanger also revered Disney as a filmmaking demigod in numerous articles and public addresses. However, during World War II, Wanger demoralized the Disney-supported Motion Picture Alliance. Wanger claimed that the right-wing political group had "linked throughout the nation the words 'Hollywood' and 'Red' and without proof"—to which the Alliance replied that the Communist influences in Hollywood had done a perfectly able job of that without their association's aid. The Motion Picture Alliance included other independents such as Leo McCarey, while the Free World Association claimed Orson Welles and James Cagney.

McCarey and Disney both appeared before the House Un-American Activities Committee during the first week of the October 1947 anti-Communist hearings. Charlie Chaplin, his public image then mired in political trouble, was subpoenaed, but after several postponements was never officially called to testify. The unpredictable Sam Goldwyn, who was subpoenaed as a friendly witness, likewise never testified. "The most un-American activity," Goldwyn told the press even before the blacklist, "which I have observed in connection with the hearings has been the activity of the Committee itself."

After a month of combative testimony before the Congressional hearings, ten "unfriendly" witnesses—including two directors, seven writers, and one producer—with alleged Communist associations evoked their Fifth Amendment rights to avoid incriminating themselves and their colleagues. The industry expected that in the prevailing political climate the House would vote to hold in-contempt the Hollywood Ten, as they were called, to be subjected to fine and/or imprisonment. The heads of the major film companies rushed to New York City on November 24 for a two-day conference to come to a unified consensus.

Originally the Hollywood executives had intimated their support for the Ten, denouncing the HUAC as a politically-motivated smear campaign. But by the time the industry leaders gathered at the Waldorf-Astoria Hotel, the studios had caved to pressure, largely from the investment community, to take a more mainstream stand in opposition to Communism. The Waldorf agreement denounced the behavior of the Hollywood Ten, and pledged that they, the signatory Hollywood executives and producers, would not knowingly hire a member of any politically subversive group. Thus began the Communist blacklist in Hollywood.

The three main groups present at the conference were the MPAA, AMPP, and SIMPP. At the time, SIMPP was considered the representative organization of a significant segment of Hollywood, and had been building important bridges with other leading industry groups like the Association of Motion Picture Producers. Among those independents present at the legendary meeting were Donald M. Nelson (SIMPP president at the time), Samuel Goldwyn, James Mulvey, and Walter Wanger.

At the Waldorf conference, supposedly only three producers objected to the blacklist agreement—Sam Goldwyn, Walter Wanger, and Dore Schary—in events that have been famously retold by Schary and others. However, despite the vocal objections of these producers, all attending industry representatives became signers of the Waldorf agreement in a "unanimous" consensus. In fact, during the conference, Wanger was selected for what was called the Committee of Five that would go to Hollywood to present the declaration to the actors, directors, and writers guilds. Wanger and Schary visited the unions and invited their cooperation in the blacklist, much to the confusion of the industry talent who had counted the two producers among Hollywood's most ardent liberals. Later Wanger became Los Angeles chairman of the anti-Communist group Crusade for Freedom, and in 1950 made amends with the Motion Picture Alliance for the Preservation of American Ideals. He publicly acknowledged a previous "error in judgement" on his part, and hoped "to bury old disagreements and unite to face the common enemy."

The blacklist grew to include writer-producer Sidney Buchman, the most direct SIMPP casualty from the HUAC era. Buchman was once the golden boy at Columbia Pictures, and a close friend of Harry Cohn. While a card-carrying Communist in 1938, Buchman wrote *Mr. Smith Goes to Washington*, the freedom-touting Capra film. At the end of World War II, Buchman resigned from the Communist Party, became an independent producer, and joined SIMPP in 1946. Held in contempt for refusing to name names, he avoided jail sentence on a technicality.

Even though Goldwyn, Wanger, and other independents had signed the Waldorf agreement, SIMPP reserved for its members the right to decide on their own. "The matter of determination of who is a Communist in respect to present and future employment," Nelson told the members, "is left entirely in the hands of each individual producer and studio." Regardless it was an uneasy situation for the Society to be associated so affirmatively with the conference. (Years later Goldwyn, writing to Wanger, recommended against hiring one of the Hollywood Ten. Even though neither of them harbored any personal animosity against the victimized former Communists, Goldwyn reminded Wanger that both the producers' signatures were still on the Waldorf agreement.)

Furthermore, SIMPP had to distance itself from the industry when the blacklist came under fire. In June 1948—evidently after the less-than-successful persuasive efforts of the Committee of Five—the Screen Writers Guild protested the Waldorf agreement in an antitrust lawsuit, denouncing the blacklist as a conspiracy between the three main motion picture trade associations: AMPP, MPAA, and SIMPP.

That same year, a $65 million damage suit enacted by the Hollywood Ten listed SIMPP as a principal defendant. On December 13, 1948, the day that Ellis Arnall became the new SIMPP president, the Society made a break to forever disassociate itself with the blacklist. In a surprise disclosure, SIMPP denied that the Society itself had ever been a party to the blacklist, and sought dismissal from the suit. Not the least of the surprises was that the statement was delivered by Gunther Lessing, the arch-conservative legal presence of Walt Disney Productions. "SIMPP has at no time entered into any of the alleged conspiracies set forth, nor is this organization adhering to any such conspiracy," SIMPP's statement also claimed. "Nor has it created a blacklist. Whether any individual member of the Society chooses to employ or not employ any person is, as it has always been, entirely up to him."

After the press release, the counsel for the Hollywood Ten removed SIMPP from the lawsuit. The blacklisted artists applauded the move as a decisive split in the united industry front. Their attorneys declared that Hollywood's blacklisting days would soon come to an end, but the prophesy proved premature.

WITH ELLIS ARNALL as its new president, the Society of Independent Motion Picture Producers also reevaluated the international situation. To subvert the MPAA deal that favored the major distributors, SIMPP adopted the official position that neither the Motion Picture Association of America nor the major studios had the authority to negotiate any international agreement that benefitted only a part of the industry.

"It is the State Department's duty to see that American pix are played abroad," Arnall declared in New York the same week he joined SIMPP. "Any negotiations with a foreign government should be carried out on government levels." On the other hand, the MPAA claimed that it operated internationally under the Webb-Pomerone Act that permitted companies to band together for certain operations overseas that would be illegal under United States antitrust laws.

Fortunately for the independent producers, the new president of SIMPP brought his political leverage which was further enhanced by the Democratic victory in the presidential election one month earlier in November 1948. While in New York, Arnall was the key speaker at a dinner for vice president elect Alben Barkley. Arnall, the progressive Democrat, also had an audience with President Truman.

Ignoring SIMPP and its new president, the major studios continued their diplomatic efforts with Great Britain. In March 1949, film industry leaders, representing private companies on both sides of the Atlantic, tried to negotiate an international pact by sidestepping the government level. The American film industry was represented by Eric Johnston, Barney Balaban, and Nicholas Schenck. The British triumvirate consisted of J. Arthur Rank, Alexander Korda, and Sir Henry French. Arnall deplored the MPAA for arrogantly attempting such a deal, making it clear that SIMPP refused to recognize any such agreement, nor would the independents be bound by the so-called Anglo-American Film Council.

In mid-April, the SIMPP president met with both President Truman and Secretary of State Dean Acheson. Arnall conveyed to the President of the United States the idea of the American motion picture being the most effective salesman of democracy, a high-profile ambassador of good will, and the best trade developer available to the government. Truman agreed that with millions of dollars sent overseas to rebuild economies, the motion picture medium should also be employed to its fullest.

Ellis Arnall filed a complaint with the U.S. Attorney General Tom Clark which claimed that the Anglo-American deal constituted a monopoly. The MPAA said that the independents could deal with the British territories only if it joined with the MPAA and its international arm, the Motion Picture Export Association (MPEA). Arnall said that the move was typical of the major studios; now that the studio power-base was withering away domestically via divorcement decree, the MPEA was a deliberate attempt to dominate the international market.

"In spite of the fact that Eric Johnston has repeatedly contended that he too has desired the State Department to conduct such negotiations," James Mulvey said, "when it actually came down to practice, the Motion Picture Association has seemingly done everything in its power to usurp that function, apparently in the belief that they were gaining certain advantages for many of their members. We know too from experience that the independents were at a total disadvantage in practically all such deals."

The authority of the Anglo-American Film Council was undermined by Secretary of State Acheson who agreed with Ellis Arnall, and committed the State Department to dealing with foreign governments on behalf of the American film industry. During a two-hour meeting on June 3, 1949, Eric Johnston came to terms with Ellis Arnall in an effort to salvage the Anglo-American deal without having to cede control to government authorities. The MPAA offered SIMPP an equal hand in the international negotiations without having to join the MPEA. However, Arnall refused to attend the London conference, stating in protest of the MPEA that the State Department alone had the power to make such a deal. On June 9, 1949 Gunther Lessing told the SIMPP members that the recent efforts of the Society and its new president "have stopped one of the biggest deals of recent years which would have affected many independents ruinously."

Having succeeded in an important part of their international objective, the members of the Society of Independent Motion Picture Producers also worked on the frozen money situation that was enforced in countries such as Great Britain and France. Only a limited amount of money could be removed from foreign territories by the producer of a film made in the United States. The diverse corporate holdings of a major studio were far better suited to taking advantage of the frozen funds, as some of the majors already had studios in operation in various European cities. However, the independent producers were far more inhibited by the restrictions on foreign money—and usually could not generate enough foreign money to justify an overseas operation. In the meantime the frozen money, called "wallpaper" by the producers, accumulated until it was spent somehow. This encouraged some of the largest independents like Selznick and Disney to make films in England. In the late 1940s, Chaplin also planned to use the British funds to make his next film in his native homeland—a first for him, oddly enough.

Arnall attacked the policy of foreign remittances, "Any system that requires American producers to make their pictures in foreign countries instead of utilizing American human and physical resources for that purpose, is a foolish and absurd policy that will ultimately spell ruin for those depending upon American production for a livelihood. . . . This is the type of thing that our government should concern itself about to the end that conditions may be again made favorable for producing American pictures in America."

Though the remittance ceiling was changed in 1950 to allow independent producers to unfreeze a larger portion of the foreign money, Arnall was not entirely pleased. In the meantime, he encouraged the SIMPP members to make the most of the situation, and helped locate international connections that might be to the producers' advantage. The Israel Motion Picture Studios, Ltd. contacted the Society concerning a legal outlet for their frozen funds by investing in a studio-laboratory near Tel Aviv. The Society also assisted the members in connecting with foreign industries that would be willing to trade goods for the frozen money. For instance a Mediterranean shipbuilding company was interested in obtaining the independent producers frozen Italian lira in a monetary exchange arranged through by a Swiss bank.

In speaking about the foreign difficulties, Roy Disney said, "It would be suicide to be in business today as an independent and not have our Society to thwart some of the machinations of these international monopolists."

James Mulvey also expressed his appreciation of Ellis Arnall, "He has grasped our problems better than any man I've even known who has been in this business such a short time. Now that he knows the problems as they arise, his fearlessness and aggressiveness have brought the results that we have been seeking for years."

The Society of Independent Motion Picture Producers reelected Arnall as president on June 22, 1949. At this meeting, a new position was created—chairman of the board—which was filled by Gunther R. Lessing, an indication of the increasing prominence of Walt Disney Productions at the forefront of the independent movement. Marvin Faris remained the executive secretary.

The producers also decided to modify the Society membership structure to accommodate more producers in the organization. Two categories of members were outlined. Regular members or "Active Members" included the current producers of SIMPP or new independent producers with a proven track record. The designation "Associate Member" was for any new producer or production company not yet actively involved in production, or an established member who suspended regular film work. This proved to be an advantage to all members since any producer would be moved to associate status after 12 months of inactivity. This addressed the complaints of many members who spent long periods of time without a film in release, but still incurred sizable membership fees. Associates still had all privileges of regular members, except voting. When Arnall began at the Society in the height of the industry recession, SIMPP had shrunk to only 17 members. In his two first years as independent production exploded, the Society doubled to

36 member-producers.

Samuel Goldwyn was so pleased with the new momentum of SIMPP that he left the MPAA in 1949 to throw his full support behind SIMPP as the balance of power in the industry shifted to independent production. Back in 1922 he had helped found the major-studio organization when it was called the Motion Picture Producers and Distributors of America, but in the late 1940s he abandoned the MPAA altogether.

"I find myself unable to agree conscientiously with many of the policies formulated by the Association and feel that they do not represent the interest of the independent producers," Goldwyn told the press upon his resignation from the MPAA. "The fight of the independent producer for an open market is a fight for survival, not only for themselves and their employees but also for the continuance of the independent creative efforts which contributed so much to the vitality and progress of the screen. The future of good motion pictures is completely bound up with the efforts of the Society of Independent Motion Picture Producers."

13

The Little Paramount Case

As triumphant as the *Paramount* suit had been for the independent producers, in many ways SIMPP viewed the verdict as a
beginning rather than a finale in their efforts to end monopolistic
control of the industry. Even though the studios were forced to part
with their theaters, the individual divorcement decrees were allowing the massive theater chains to remain largely intact, albeit under
government regulation. As discussed previously, there were already
many large independent theater circuits that wielded monopoly
power without being attached to any Hollywood studio at all; therefore SIMPP continued to monitor the situation even after the studios appeared to capitulate.

At the announcement of the government victory in the Supreme
Court in May 1948, Goldwyn cautioned, "it will be necessary to see
that divorcement means more than just a transfer of circuit control
from one set of hands to another."

When Arnall joined with SIMPP, his antitrust experience sound-
ed-off similar concerns. He remembered his own antitrust case
against the Pullman railroad company. After he succeeded in having the company split in two halves, "one-half set up business on
the other side of the street under a new name." Arnall warned that
in an industry town soaking in nepotism the consent decrees were

allowing the studios to dispose of their theaters to "relatives and friends." For example, disintegrating Twentieth Century-Fox would still leave Spyros Skouras president of the studio, his brother Charles Skouras head its divested chain of National and West Coast Theatres, and his other brother George Skouras president of the United Artists Theatre Circuit.

"Divorcement is a step forward," the president of SIMPP declared following the Paramount divestiture agreement. "The fight against the greedy and arrogant monopolies within the motion picture industry must go on. If the business is to thrive it is essential that fair competition be maintained within it." The independent producers feared that without a proper follow-through the effects of the successful *Paramount* case would be undermined. In its efforts to oppose any manner of film monopoly, the Society began to file civil suits against anti-competitive remnants left over as the studio system collapsed. The first of these was targeted at a subsidiary of Paramount Pictures.

Even before the arrival of Ellis Arnall, during the period when the Society operated without a president, the independent producers already boosted their private antitrust activity. According to a deposition given by David O. Selznick, the SIMPP vendetta began when he was called over to Samuel Goldwyn's house for a meeting one night probably early in 1948.

Goldwyn, aggravated by many of the theater monopolies, wanted to discuss some of the problems with Selznick, Edward Small, and Roy Disney. ("It might have been Walt Disney," Selznick later said, concerning who was present that meeting, "or it might have been Guenther [sic] Lessing, but I think it was Roy Disney.") Goldwyn spoke about "a particularly menacing and reprehensible situation in Detroit" where a Paramount-affiliated theater chain had antagonized the independent producers for years by dominating the first-run market in eastern Michigan. The producers tentatively agreed to investigate the monopoly, and decided to involve SIMPP.

Robert J. Rubin spent several weeks putting together a preliminary report on various "tight" situations across the nation where a potential theater monopoly acted to the detriment of the independent producers. Hiring a special economist to assist in the study, Rubin surveyed all over the country, locating areas where the independent producers' films, on the whole, suffered from depressed rentals. One of these places was eastern Michigan, where the key runs were dominated by the United Detroit Theatres Corporation controlled by Paramount Pictures, Inc. The Rubin report uncovered evidence that would make Detroit an obvious target for SIMPP's first civil antitrust suit, particularly while Paramount still owned the theater chain. At the end of April 1948, just days before the Supreme Court *Paramount* decision, Rubin reported his findings to the SIMPP Eastern Distribution Committee.

The independent producers alleged that a monopoly was maintained in the Michigan territory by the United Detroit Theatres, 75 percent owned by Paramount Pictures, Inc., working in concert with the Cooperative Theatres of Michigan, Inc., a booking organization which negotiated film rentals for its various exhibitor member-stockholders. On paper, United Detroit controlled only four of the seven first-run movie houses in the city. Yet two of the remaining three were operated by the closely related, though separate, H. & E. Balaban corporation. And not only were the United Detroit movie houses the highest revenue-generating theatres in the region, but the collusion between United Detroit and Cooperative Theatres gave Paramount control of 90 percent of all subsequent-run revenue in the area.

The Detroit monopoly had a policy of denying *percentage engagement* deals with the independent producers. In other areas producers were accustomed to share with the exhibitors in a profit-sharing box office bonanza for their popular movies. The independents attributed the overall deflated returns in eastern Michigan to the parsimonious *flat deal* given by the high-handed Paramount affiliate on a take-it-or-leave-it basis.

The Society of Independent Motion Picture Producers decided to start their own private antitrust case to recover damages of lost revenue from United Detroit Theatres and the Cooperative Theatres of Michigan. All legal costs would be covered by SIMPP, and reimbursed to the Society out of the settlement. They queried the producer-members, and found eight independents willing to take part in the lawsuit to recover losses on specific films. The participants were Samuel Goldwyn, Walt Disney, David O. Selznick, Walter Wanger, William Cagney, Edward Small, Benedict Bogeaus, Hunt Stromberg, and Seymour Nebenzal.

The suit was announced at three simultaneous press conferences in New York, Detroit, and Hollywood on August 24, 1948. In coast-to-coast coverage, the Society announced that war had been declared by the independent producers against monopoly control in the industry. James Mulvey presided at the New York City press conference handing out a "pound or two of mimeographed material" to reporters gathered at the Blue Room of the posh Essex House hotel. In Detroit Robert J. Rubin answered questions shortly after he filed the case in Federal Court there. And in Hollywood Gunther R. Lessing announced at SIMPP's Beverly Hills headquarters that the case—independent producers suing exhibitors—was "without precedent in motion picture history."

SIMPP claimed $2,917,272 in combined damages for the independent films listed in the suit. However the treble damage clause of the Clayton Antitrust Act multiplied the compensation three-fold to over $8.7 million plus attorney fees. Goldwyn's $1.5 million share was the largest, and included films like *The Pride of the Yankees* (1942), *Up in Arms* (1944), and *The Best Years of Our Lives* (1946). The next largest was Walt Disney who claimed $974,000 for a film lot that contained all of his golden age full-length features from *Snow White and the Seven Dwarfs* (1937) to *Bambi* (1942). Selznick featured many of his most important 1940s films that United Artists distributed, such as Hitchcock's *Rebecca* (1940), *Spellbound* (1945), and *Since You Went Away* (1944).

The day after the case was filed, Goldwyn and Disney held a joint press conference to confirm their trustbusting position. "The antitrust suit is the opening gun in the fight of independent producers for freedom of the screen. This is the first, but not the last action," Sam Goldwyn declared, as he vowed that the independents would never rest until a free market existed for all of their movies. "We do not intend to let theatre chains turn the silver screen into an iron curtain between the public and our pictures."

Immediately after Goldwyn, Walt Disney spoke. He iterated his intentions to always make high-quality groundbreaking films, and that his purpose of insisting on a greater share of the profits was not to accumulate wealth but to stay in business to make better films. He said that if SIMPP failed in its attempt to return a free market for the independent filmmakers, the public would be subject to "routine entertainment turned out on a veritable assembly line." He characterized the independents as reluctant participants who were drawn into the battle, "We now feel we can no longer afford to tolerate this situation and are obliged to take legal action."

The basic legal precedent for the SIMPP lawsuit was the 1946 *Jackson Park* Supreme Court case that dealt with the monopoly problems in the Chicago territory. The small, independent Jackson Park theater, which had been in operation since 1916, accused the Balaban & Katz exhibitor monopoly of an aggressive double-feature policy, unreasonable clearance, and conspiracy with the major studios. The independent exhibitor had originally sued for $120,000, but as the case made its way through the courts, the small theater was awarded nearly $1 million. SIMPP noted that of particular interest in the case was, firstly, the courts' use of the Balaban & Katz gross ticket admissions as the basis for the award and, secondly, the restraining orders issued against the Paramount theater circuit in that region. SIMPP believed that the independents could easily prove the discriminatory practices in the Detroit area by highlighting the prosperous box office of the Paramount theaters there.

SIMPP's demands were not entirely monetary either. The lawsuit sought injunctions against further monopolistic practice. SIMPP demanded the forced sale of the United Detroit theater holdings and the dissolution of the Cooperative. This was in harmony with the Society's longstanding belief that monopoly control in the industry was not just vertical, but was epidemic on many levels. If they could command a swift and absolute victory against the notorious Detroit situation, the lawsuit—SIMPP hoped—would establish a pattern that would bring other regional monopolies into capitulation, and encourage the government as it followed through with the *Paramount* case. Immediately SIMPP began to identify other regions of the country that would serve as the next legal battlefront once the Detroit case was ended. Unfortunately *SIMPP v. United Detroit* encountered unexpected problems that made the open-and-shut-case a far more involved and drawn-out ordeal.

THE HISTORY OF THE Detroit monopoly went back to the Zukor theater-buying spree of the 1920s. Before Paramount invaded eastern Michigan, a film exchange known as the Cooperative Booking Office controlled most of important theaters in Detroit. This Michigan cooperative was one of the great examples of the booking agencies that sprang up in various parts of the country, created by neighborhood theaters to protect their interests from the rise of the distributor-owned circuits.

Four of the first-run theaters in Detroit were owned by Cooperative members John H. Kunsky (a.k.a. John King) and George W. Trendle. Kunsky, the proprietor of Detroit's first movie house, also pioneered quality exhibition by opening an elaborate Detroit movie theater in 1911 while most of the country was still reacting to the nickelodeon boom.

During 1929 and 1930 Zukor engaged Paramount in its last important wave of theater acquisition. Prompted by the failed Paramount-Warner merger in September 1929, Zukor added another 500 screens to his film empire in various parts of the country. In Michigan he took over the theaters belonging to the Cooperative Booking Office. He ruthlessly demanded the Cooperative's complete withdrawal from the motion picture industry, and later forced Kunsky and Trendle to enter into a covenant never to reenter the movie business in Detroit. Zukor transferred the theaters to a Paramount subsidiary named United Detroit Theatres. The two former Detroit exhibitors decided to concentrate on the radio business, and formed the Kunsky-Trendle Broadcasting Company whose flagship station WXYZ introduced the Lone Ranger in 1933.

The remnants of the old theater cooperative were acquired by another midwestern exchange in February 1930. Remaining independent of all Hollywood studios, the organization was briefly known as the Midstates Theatres, Inc. before it was reorganized into the Cooperative Theatres of Michigan in June 1934. After a short period of direct competition with United Paramount, the Cooperative decided to collaborate with the Paramount circuit instead.

Because of its dominant regional monopoly, the massive chain secured the right of first refusal from all major Hollywood distributors, except Fox, which owned the only other first-run theater in the region. However even the Fox theater adhered to the rigid booking procedure in the region due to Paramount's exhibition power in Michigan. (Ironically, the Fox theater had formerly been a United Artists house back before Twentieth Century-Fox absorbed the UA chain.) Acting as a massive buying combine, the size of the Cooperative Theatres fluctuated over the years. At the time of the SIMPP lawsuit, the organization controlled over 100 theaters in the Detroit area, and another 24 in outlying areas.

The independent producers ridiculed the "highly artificial and restrictive system of picture runs" and stringent booking procedure—first run, second run, pre-key run, key run, sub-key run, third-week run, etc. Paramount had even implemented a bizarre and extreme method of block booking where different theaters ended up showing the same films at the same time. The Society claimed that the Detroit situation represented a movie monopoly in its most advanced form.

SIMPP attracted national media attention when the Detroit suit was filed. In typical independent fashion, they took advantage of their own publicity to encouraging more government antitrust involvement. Within a few days of the beginning of *SIMPP v. United Detroit*, the U.S. House of Representatives Small Business Committee opened an investigation of the Detroit theaters. The events were highly reminiscent of the Reno incident in 1944 when the terse statements of the independent producers against Fox West Coast brought a government examination of the alleged monopolistic situation.

The announcement of the SIMPP lawsuit, the initiation of the congressional investigation of Detroit, the SIMPP removal of

Mulvey in protest of the British negotiations, and the Roy Disney telegram denouncing the France situation all took place around the same time. "Indies War on Majors," blared the front page *Daily Variety* headline on August 27, 1948 that summarized the events of that week.

At the beginning of the *United Detroit* suit, SIMPP reports from the Detroit area were extremely encouraging. Three attorneys represented SIMPP in the case—Robert Rubin, General Counsel for SIMPP, Joseph L. Alioto of San Francisco, and A. Stewart Kerr of Detroit. "The Society is certain to win this litigation. It is in the hands of able attorneys," Arnall said in praise of the Detroit case, "and the aggressive prosecution of this case to a successful conclusion can make a tremendous contribution toward opening up channels of free and competitive distribution for independently produced pictures."

In anticipation of other lawsuits, SIMPP continued to protest the studios that still operated monopolistic theater chains. The Society of Independent Motion Picture Producers filed a formal complaint with the Attorney General attacking the Fox West Coast Theatres in California. Requesting a Justice Department probe of the chain, SIMPP furnished the government with a list of 82 situations in which Fox West Coast and its 234 theaters operated with no competition. Even more incriminating was the "competition" to the Fox West Coast chain, which consisted of circuits like the National Theatres, another Fox-controlled subsidiary with 345 additional theaters.

DIVESTITURE OF THE studio-owned theaters was assured while SIMPP was in Detroit. The Big Five were finally ordered to sell their theater holdings in July 1949. SIMPP was demonstrating with the Detroit case that even though the United Detroit chain no longer belonged to a major studio, the lawsuit was still very much in full swing. As the remaining studios sold their theater circuits, SIMPP looked forward to more legal action. The Society had its eye on the Fox West Coast monopoly; and once the United Detroit case proved a success, they would go after the former Fox monopoly in

California to reclaim lost damages.

In the SIMPP Detroit case another dynamic was present, an undercurrent that symbolized the long-standing rivalry between the two branches of the industry that existed on opposite ends of the industry spectrum: the filmmakers and the theaters. Though SIMPP claimed that the Detroit suit itself was unprecedented, the ongoing feud between producers and exhibitors had been a staple of the industry, harkening back even before the Adolph Zukor battles with First National for industry domination. The animosity has remained intact to at least some extent in the modern motion picture industry as well.

The theaters, which depend on the distributors to provide sure-fire hits, complained about the continual lack of quality and the infrequency of blockbuster-caliber features. The producers and distributors accused the theaters of lacking showmanship and being devoid of any real interest in improving conditions in the industry as a whole.

In fact, the Big Five repeatedly argued that vertical integration was the only suitable solution to the divisive schism in the industry. Early on in the *Paramount* case, Joseph M. Schenck at Twentieth Century-Fox declared that divorcement was a mistake. "Long experience has proved," Schenck said in 1938, "that the producer-owned circuits work out better than the independent [theaters]. That is largely because the independents do not have the vision or the capital to promote themselves to the fullest advantage."

Each side fought to gain the best terms possible. The exhibitors usually insisted on a buffer to protect themselves from a box office dud. In most cases, the theater was guaranteed first dollar on its admissions to cover theater overhead before the profit split with distributors took effect (sometimes called a "house nut" deal). The producers and distributors often complained that, under such an arrangement, the exhibitor rarely lost any money even with a bomb—while the producer suffered tremendous losses. The exhibitors said that this was done because the theater owners could not ultimately control the quality of the films they showed. In many ways, the position of the movie exhibitor was analogous to that of a restaurant which could not prepare its own food. Therefore, the theaters felt that they should not bear the brunt of a bad film.

"I thought that the exhibitors should share the risk with the producer, that no one came down from Mount Sinai with a tablet saying that the exhibitors had to make money on every picture," David O. Selznick said during the suit in Detroit. "I see no reason why exhibitors should make a profit while we stand to lose."

14

Conflicting Interests

SIMPP V. UNITED DETROIT suffered from difficulties only a short time after the suit was filed. The defendant had inherited the stalling tactics of its parent studio, and brought about years of delay similar to the *Paramount* case itself. Paramount Pictures paid the retainer for the United Detroit attorney Rockwell T. Gust, a lawyer with more than 25 years of experience representing motion picture clients. He was hired by Paramount as much for his familiarity with distribution and exhibition, as for his notorious conduct on par with the studio legal staff at its most dubious.

The original complaint filed by the Society of Independent Motion Picture Producers permitted 20 days for the official response from the four main defendants—the United Detroit Theatres Corporation, the Cooperative Theatres of Michigan, Inc., Earl J. Hudson, president of United Detroit, and James F. Sharkey, general manager of Cooperative Theatres. Rockwell Gust asked—and received court permission—for an extensive discovery phase of the trial that would give the defendants the first of many extensions before being required to file a response to the SIMPP complaint.

The defense requested that all of the SIMPP producers who had films involved in the case be ordered to appear for a deposition in

Detroit. Until then, Gust claimed, no response could be filed; therefore no trial could yet take place.

Interpreting the action as a delay, SIMPP at first tried to get the motion vacated. SIMPP council Robert Rubin protested that such an unreasonable demand "simply does not warrant disrupting the production schedules of virtually every major producer in Hollywood for the purposes of attending depositions 2000 miles from their residences and workshops" to speak on the intricacies of distribution and exhibition which, *as producers*, they had only cursory knowledge.

Gunther Lessing submitted a brief for Walt Disney, "Should Mr. Walt Disney be compelled to come to Detroit, it would appear to be a total waste of not only his time, but of defendants' counsel as well." Lessing stressed the need for Disney's undivided attention in Hollywood with the "radical reorganization" of Walt Disney Productions "forced in part by economic factors common to the motion picture industry as a whole."

District Judge Arthur A. Koscinski denied SIMPP, and required the producers to appear for their depositions in Detroit. The court permitted a reasonable time for each independent producer to find an appropriate break in their production schedules to travel to Detroit. United-Paramount stated that they were in no particular hurry. They received the first of many 90-day extensions that would eventually delay the SIMPP trial for three years.

The Society immediately implored each producer that was party to the lawsuit to made the trip as soon as possible so that the case could proceed. Walt Disney was the first to appear for his deposition in Detroit on January 31, 1949. But by the time the 90-day extension expired, only one other SIMPP representative Marvin L. Faris had appeared. As expected, each of the SIMPP producers were involved with various projects that postponed their depositions. So Gust moved for another extension, which was granted without dispute.

SIMPP attorney A. Stewart Kerr, in a letter to Robert Rubin, reminded the Society of the predicament created by the failure of the producers to appear in Detroit. "It is embarrassing me with

Judge Koscinski and has caused comment by fellow lawyers and by the defense." Kerr explained that they risked the case being dismissed.

Upon the urging of the Society leaders, additional members made their appearances, beginning with Hunt Stromberg in April 1949 and then David O. Selznick later that month. Each of the producers went to Detroit, spending the day explaining to the defense that they had no intimate first-hand information that would be pertinent to the Michigan case. Selznick, who for instance had never before been to Detroit, also had not even recently attended any formal SIMPP meeting, delegating many of his administrative responsibilities to Dan O'Shea and other trusted employees. Selznick gave a summary of his life as a producer, recited film costs and grosses from memory, and even gave a ranking of his favorite productions. But as expected, they were of minimal value to the defense attorneys who looked for more detailed exhibition information. Nevertheless, the deposition requirement proved to be an effective delay tactic. Parenthetically, the depositions have provided historians with interesting, though not always accurate, career profiles of the producers in their own words.

Another six months passed until the next producers appeared— William Cagney and Samuel Goldwyn in October. The producers had various reasons for their delay. Some were more recalcitrant than others. Walter Wanger was having difficulty overcoming the lackluster domestic box office of the big budget *Joan of Arc* (1948). The producer's accountant explained why Wanger hesitated in getting to Detroit: "the only picture that we have under this claim is *Lost Moment* (1947), which did such bad business that the train fare would probably exceed anything we might recover." Wanger nevertheless was a strong supporter of the unified independent movement and one of SIMPP's longest active members. After making plans to go to Detroit in May 1949, his trip was put off by retakes on a costly project called "The Blank Wall" (released in 1949 as *The Reckless Moment*), and then stalled by a lengthy trip to Europe to set up overseas financing.

Roy Disney became personally involved in the case by relaying his strong feelings to the members of SIMPP who were delaying their Detroit appearance. "The defense was lucky enough to get away with this," he said in a pressing letter to Wanger. "I think that now is the time for us to put on pressure from every possible angle to keep this whole thing rolling with respect to making free markets possible in every situation. Our case up there is certainly a very important one in that regard and should be aggressively prosecuted to a conclusion."

The United Detroit Theatres and the Cooperative Theatres of Michigan filed for additional extensions as no SIMPP producer was able to make it to Detroit for well over a year. Finally Judge Koscinski rewarded the defense with an extension that indefinitely postponed the trial until at least 30 days after the end of the discovery period. SIMPP objected to the open-ended order, but was overruled.

Walter Wanger finally gave his deposition on January 30, 1951, followed by Benedict Bogeaus two days later. On April 26, 1951, Edward Small became the last SIMPP deponent to appear. It had been two and a half years since SIMPP made headlines with the announcement of the Detroit trial. And the Paramount spin-off succeeded in getting the case bogged down in procedure before even the pre-trial proceedings could begin.

SIMPP's Robert Rubin, who had wanted to pursue a film career outside the Society, resigned from the case in 1950 but decided to remain as a consultant to the independent producers. Then in February 1951, while the Detroit case was wavering, the trade papers announced that Rubin, the former SIMPP general council, would be joining Paramount Pictures as the assistant to Barney Balaban.

The move was more of an ironic twist than it was any sort of deterrent for the case. By this time, Paramount Pictures, the Hollywood film studio, had nothing to do with the SIMPP Detroit lawsuit. Divorcement had already been completed, United Detroit became the subsidiary of the United Paramount Theatres, and SIMPP continued with the case full force. However, the *United*

Detroit suit took a strange turn as the United Paramount company entered television and underwent a transformation that would have a profound effect on the independent film movement.

BACK IN APRIL 1949 when the Paramount stockholders agreed to spin off the theater chain, both the Paramount studio parent and the theater corporation had an interest in broadcasting and the future of television. So when the motion picture holdings were divvied between the corporations, the Paramount television interests were split under the divorcement terms as well.

Paramount Pictures retained the Los Angeles TV station KTLA and the stock in the DuMont network. United Paramount Theatres controlled the Balaban & Katz broadcast division that owned the Chicago television station WBKB and various radio interests. As mentioned previously, Paramount experimented with theater television by furnishing movie houses with broadcast reception capability designed for "instantaneous newsreels" of major news and sporting events. In 1951 United Paramount planned to have 27 such communal television theaters—until the costliness of the project, launched in 1949, was overtaken by home television.

In a surprise move Leonard H. Goldenson, the ambitious president of United Paramount, entered into merger negotiations with the struggling network upstart, the American Broadcasting Company. ABC was then only eight years old, having been created out of the old NBC Blue Network during the war. ABC had expanded its television franchise into New York, Los Angeles, Detroit, San Francisco, and Chicago, but had difficultly competing with the CBS and NBC broadcast powerhouses.

Goldenson believed that the cash-rich United Paramount theater circuit could provide the under-financed network with the working capital—not to mention the industry connections brought by the veteran Hollywood exhibitors—to transform ABC into a major broadcaster. United Paramount, then worth about $119 million agreed to acquire the $25 million, 14-station ABC network pending FCC approval. The proposed merger made front page news when it was announced in May 1951, right around the same time that

SIMPP fulfilled the Detroit deposition requirement and prepared for trial against the United Detroit subsidiary.

The FCC took more than a year to approve the merger, citing Paramount's notorious track record which involved over 180 antitrust actions since the Zukor years. Regardless, Leonard Goldenson planned the future of the company as if the merger had already taken place. His adjustments also brought changes to the SIMPP Detroit case.

Interestingly, back in 1937, Goldenson rose to prominence at Paramount by turning the Detroit branch into a profitable regional monopoly. Goldenson personally fired the previous Detroit manager George Trendle, and instated Earl Hudson as general manager. Also, as Goldenson candidly admitted in his memoirs, during the brief but bitter struggle with the Cooperative Theatres of Michigan, he threatened to fix prices unless the Cooperative relinquished control of the Michigan theater that would complete Paramount's monopoly. With his reputation enhanced at the studio, Goldenson then decided to make amends with the Cooperative for an even stronger position. As he said after the Cooperative battle, "we became good friends," creating the combine that SIMPP took to court.

In 1951, while the United Paramount-ABC merger was still pending FCC approval, Goldenson spearheaded a new corporate strategy. First of all, he involved the two companies in an executive shuffle that sent three of Goldenson's trusted United Paramount representatives immediately to ABC. One of these three was Earl Hudson, a defendant in *SIMPP v. United Detroit*, who became head of ABC west coast operations.

Another of Goldenson's main objectives was to bring movie showmanship to television. Contrary to the prevailing historical consensus, Hollywood was not always antagonistic toward the television industry. Early on, the major studios considered television as an important element in their diversification efforts into new entertainment media, and Paramount Pictures for instance found it in their best interest to help shape the television infrastructure. The hostility toward television developed as the FCC restricted the Hollywood studios from television due to the antitrust charges during the *Paramount* case that forced the film companies to sit on the sidelines as the radio broadcasters signal standards became adopted by the FCC. Only after Hollywood faced these setbacks that prevented them from dominating televison did the film establishment eschew the new medium as a rival.

For many years thereafter, Hollywood's anxiety toward television was evident in the reluctance of the majors to create original programming and the hesitation toward the sale of their old films to television. In 1951, the Screen Actors Guild, openly critical of the sale of Hollywood films to television, threatened to ban their performers from any producer who sold a recent (post-1948) movie to television. They carried out the boycott when independent producer Robert L. Lippert challenged the guild.

So by the time Leonard Goldenson looked for ways to integrate Hollywood production into the ABC network, he confronted a hostile film industry, and needed to look for an alternative outside of the major producer-distributors. He knew that the independent producers, on the whole, did not have the same reservations about television as many of the studio production heads. In fact, for most independents, the selling of their catalog of movies to television was seen as an extension of the profit-generating activities essential for their survival as independent filmmakers. Goldenson decided to pursue the independent producers of SIMPP to interest them in providing programming for the network.

FOR YEARS THE INDEPENDENT producers forecasted the oncoming of television. Mary Pickford and Sam Goldwyn's public predictions began no later than 1934. Their views spread amongst the independent population, and in a short time, figured into the United Artists studios policy, serving as the infamous deal-breaker that provoked Disney's exit from United Artists in 1937. "Remember that term," Gunther Lessing confided with Disney employees in the 1930s regarding television. "It's going to play a big part in this studio someday."

Moreover in the early days as the television medium was being defined, SIMPP considered it an important task of their members to be involved in the process that would ultimately determine whether the future of TV was seen as an appendage of broadcasting (radio-with-pictures) or as an extension of motion pictures (movies-in-the-home). Obviously the producers had their own set of aesthetic and economic opinions with a particular abhorrence of the reediting mutilation common in commercial television programming, not to mention their vehemence toward sponsor interruption that lowered their films' entertainment value.

To overcome this, SIMPP favored subscription telecasting—fundamentally similar to the modern pay television service—which the independent producers referred to as "Pay-As-You-See" TV. Several subscription services seemed practical, though primitive, including Phonevision, Telemeter (coincidentally 50 percent owned by Paramount Pictures), and Skiatron's Subscriber-Vision. SIMPP was pleased with the commercial possibilities of some of these systems, especially the ones that transmitted a scrambled signal to a decoder attached to a home television set. When the decoder was not in use, the channel would show trailers for the movies to be purchased. SIMPP believed that each territory should have at least one station devoted to Pay-As-You-See TV, opening up a market for quality, uninterrupted film viewing in the living room.

In June 1951, the Society of Independent Motion Picture Producers petitioned the FCC to immediately "license worthy systems of subscription television so as to afford the public a more abundant opportunity to enjoy quality feature length motion picture, educational and cultural programs." Arnall delivered the petition in person, hoping to revolutionize the limitations of the television medium and provide a way for producers to receive a percentage of in-home movie-watching revenue.

Unfortunately the FCC was not willing to provide the go-ahead. The FCC and Congress backed off of subscription television, afraid of inciting public indignation that television sets were purchased with the understanding that TV was free. Though SIMPP's efforts were unsuccessful at the time, as the television market matured over the years, subscription television eventually became a reality as envisioned by the independent organization.

LEONARD GOLDENSON OBSERVED that the independent producers' interest in television could provide him with a breakthrough television show that might evaporate Hollywood's resistance to television production. "I had to find a way to crack the market and get Hollywood into production," Goldenson said of his plans to bring film talent to TV. "Otherwise we'd be dead pigeons." He also pursued the independent producers because they were among the few behind-the-camera Hollywood personalities with household-name recognition, which would help elevate ABC's ragtag image.

Among the many Hollywood figures with whom Goldenson established close friendships over the years were his poker buddies Sam Goldwyn and David O. Selznick. But both of the prestige filmmakers were too wrapped up with their own feature film projects to consider a weekly television show. In the fall of 1950, ABC commissioned Walter Wanger to produce a fantasy television series *Aladdin and His Lamp*. The first episode was filmed, but the show failed to make it to broadcast when ABC had difficulty finding a sponsor for the ahead-of-its-time color program. And when Goldenson gave Orson Welles $200,000 and artistic freedom to create a pilot episode, the network deemed it un-airable.

In 1951, while the FCC still mulled over the ABC-Paramount merger, Goldenson visited the Disney studio to interest the Disney brothers in a television production deal. Walt Disney had already produced an hour-long program at NBC for Christmas 1950, and the success of this bold move would lead to another NBC special the following Christmas. The Disneys were unimpressed with ABC, which Walt called the "peanut network"—a distant third in television network rankings. Furthermore as an independent producer party to the pending Detroit lawsuit, Disney resisted a deal that would put him in a compromising situation.

Meanwhile the merger approval for ABC and the Paramount theaters finally came on February 9, 1953, in a five-to-two split decision by the Federal Communications Commission—the largest transaction ever in broadcasting. The FCC approved the merger on the basis that Paramount cash could enable a viable third network to provide additional competition that would in fact be in the public's best interests. American Broadcasting-Paramount Theatres was formed, and the head of the company Leonard Goldenson symbolized the new kind of media mogul that emerged as the Hollywood studio system was being swept away by industry change.

Back in Detroit, SIMPP was facing increasing frustration with the theater suit. Defense attorney Rockwell Gust claimed that the depositions and the subpoenaed SIMPP meeting notes indicated that James Mulvey was really the brains behind the lawsuit. Gust claimed that the discovery phase could not be concluded until Mulvey was interviewed. This time the interrogation would take place on SIMPP's terms. Mulvey would not be required to travel to Detroit; instead Gust would have to catch up with him in New York. In June 1951, Gust interrogated Mulvey for four days, and then asked for three more days in August, even though all of the other depositions had been given in less than one day each.

Still the defense was not satisfied. Gust said that the examination of Mulvey "proved to be highly disappointing from a discovery standpoint, in many respects, in view of the tremendous build-up he had received from preceding deponents, including Samuel Goldwyn." The defense attorney required more distribution details, and requested the booking records from RKO and the testimony of Ben Fish (Sam Goldwyn's brother) who served as principle traveling representative for Goldwyn.

SIMPP, finally fed up with the delays, claimed that after 38 months and 13 extensions, the Society had provided "adequate time for defendants to apprise themselves of any facts necessary to file Answers." The court agreed, and on November 20, 1951, the four main defendants were given 30 days to file their respective answers to the SIMPP complaint from 1948.

Twenty-nine days later the answers were filed by United Detroit, the Cooperative, Earl Hudson and James Sharkey. The most pointed words were submitted by Rockwell T. Gust on behalf of United Paramount. After denying all accusations of monopoly and refuting any conspiracy between United and the Cooperative, Gust attacked the hard-sell tactics of the independent producers for inflicting "excessive fees and unreasonable conditions." The document made mention of Samuel Goldwyn and James Mulvey as joint conspirators, acting in concert with other SIMPP members to fix prices. Thus, the attorney alleged, "under the guise of beneficial purposes therein alleged, the Society was actually formed and exists in furtherance of a conspiracy among its members directed against the exhibitors of motion pictures in the Detroit area and throughout the United States, to restrain trade and commerce therein . . . and to force such exhibitors to pay higher film rentals to said members of said Society. . . all in violation of Federal Anti-Trust Laws." Gust also added, "the plaintiffs do not come into this Honorable Court with clean hands and are entitled to no relief from this Court whatsoever." The defendants asked that the case be dismissed, and demanded that SIMPP pay recovery costs to the theater defendants.

The SIMPP attorneys reported to the president Ellis Arnall and the chairman Gunther Lessing early in January 1953 that they planned to accelerate their plans—still confident that the case would yield a SIMPP victory by 1954. SIMPP received permission to inspect the United Detroit records coincidentally at the same time that the United Paramount merger with ABC was finalized. But within a few months the independent producers' suit against United Detroit unexpectedly collided with Walt Disney's plans for Disneyland.

AS THE DISNEY STUDIO struggled to get back on its feet after World War II, Disneyland became Walt Disney's great postwar venture. Spending years trying to find backing for the park, Disney perceived that television could provide the financing and exposure necessary to get such a massive undertaking off the ground.

In 1952 Walt Disney formed a company originally called Walt Disney, Incorporated, which was renamed WED when Roy Disney convinced his brother to adopt a more low-profile name that would not cause confusion with the studio itself. WED set up shop on the Disney lot in Burbank in 1953, ostensibly to specialize in television production. At the time, the creation of WED was in harmony with other Hollywood production companies like Columbia and Republic which created subsidiaries, Screen Gems and Hollywood Television Service, respectively, to specialize in television while protecting the distinctiveness of their feature film trademarks. In actuality, WED was designed as Walt Disney's command-post for the Disneyland theme park since Walt Disney Productions' support for the unconventional project appeared questionable. Quite suitably for the maverick producer, he had to jump-start his dream by going independent from his own studio.

In September 1953, Roy Disney, took the WED concept sketches and six-page prospectus to New York to meet with television industry leaders. The two main networks CBS and NBC both expressed interest in a Disney-produced TV show but were unable to commit to the theme park as extra baggage in the deal.

Running out of options, Roy Disney returned to his Waldorf Astoria suite, and phoned Leonard Goldenson who, after two years of courting the Disney studio, was still enthusiastic about a deal between them and ABC. Desperately trying to become a major broadcaster, ABC was also willing to take a risk on the unusual Disney project. Goldenson immediately came to the hotel to discuss the proposal.

In exchange for Walt Disney's commitment to produce a weekly television series, ABC-Paramount would contribute $500,000 to the park, guarantee $4.5 million in loans, and become a 34 percent owner in Disneyland, Inc. (the company Walt Disney organized in 1951). Walt Disney Productions also invested in a one-third interest; and the remaining stock was split between Walt Disney himself and a publishing company that worked closely with Disney.

The ABC-Paramount board approved the Disney deal on March 29, 1954—one week after a memorable Academy Award ceremony where Disney came away from the night with an unmatched feat as the personal recipient of four Oscars. But in the Walt Disney Production board, last minute opposition within the company nearly killed the Disneyland deal. Eventually the contract with ABC was signed on April 2, and Walt Disney planned to begin his show for the fall season.

The ABC-Paramount deal put the independent producer Walt Disney in an interesting situation. His new commitments to ABC now made him the associate of the Paramount theaters whose ruthless tactics over the years had been the bane of the independents. Goldenson's active role in the Detroit monopoly made the dilemma even more awkward, as did Earl Hudson's position as head of ABC west coast operations. Not only was Hudson still a defendant in *SIMPP v. United Detroit*, but Walt Disney Productions sought millions of dollars in damages from the United Paramount theaters. The Disney company decided it was no longer prudent to be in a position of suing its television partner.

However, to avoid the unpleasantness of withdrawing from the case, Walt Disney encouraged a settlement between United Paramount and SIMPP. Disney, then in a race to build Disneyland and open the park before the summer of 1955, sent in Gunther Lessing to wrap up the case in Detroit. The penultimate record in the SIMPP case file in the National Archives and Records Administration of the Great Lakes Region in Chicago is the documented appearance of Gunther R. Lessing on September 13, 1954. Lessing, vice president of Walt Disney Productions and SIMPP chairman of the board, was entered as co-counsel for the plaintiffs on that date. According to court records, Lessing had no previous legal role in the Detroit lawsuit, and evidently had no other direct involvement in the SIMPP case since the affidavit he filed on Walt Disney's behalf in 1948 to dismiss the deposition requirement. Two weeks later, Gunther R. Lessing provided the leading signature on a stipulation agreement by both sides of the suit that dismissed the case *Society of Independent Motion Pictures, et al v. United Detroit Theatres, et al* on September 28.

None of the settlement terms were disclosed when the trade papers reported the end of the suit. *Daily Variety* claimed a victory for SIMPP, but the brief article was a far cry from the full-page banner headlines that SIMPP attracted when the suit was announced in

August 1948. Other accounts on September 28, 1954 favored neither side. In fact, the *Hollywood Reporter* story was overshadowed by other independent news—the expansion of the Walt Disney distribution company one week after terminating its ties with RKO. The juxtaposition of these two stories symbolized the circumstances at SIMPP itself, as the ambitions of prominent independents like Walt Disney Productions began to eclipse the industry status of the Society of Independent Motion Picture Producers.

No document of the settlement terms was included in the official court records either—only that the parties agreed that the case "be dismissed with prejudice and without costs to the parties or any of them." It is possible that SIMPP may have seen the case stalling months earlier and decided to back out gracefully. No action had been taken in the case since it was removed from pre-trial on November 14, 1953. Unquestionably the case had had its difficulties.

The independent producers may also have run into statute of limitations problems. The Paramount divorcement decree of 1949 contained provisions that protected the theater chains from further antitrust litigation. But since the SIMPP complaint was filed before the Paramount divorcement decree, the Society was entitled to pursue the case and to use the successful *Paramount* Supreme Court decision as evidence. Regardless, the statute of limitations—in some instances as short as four years—was still in effect, and the United Detroit defendants invoked the statute by saying that the SIMPP complaints were simply too old to make an effective case. This point was indeed arguable, and the case continued. However, the statute of limitations may have been viewed by SIMPP as a stumbling block in the suit.

On the other hand it is likely that, given the successful postwar antitrust cases, United Detroit was eager to settle for an amount that would satisfy the independent producers. This may have been a SIMPP victory after all, but one which was not accompanied with the customary dose of SIMPP ballyhoo because Disney would not have been in a position to gloat over his partners at ABC-Paramount. The specifics of the settlement were retired to the legal files of the Walt Disney studio. The legal collection of the Walt Disney Archives has been sealed off from the public, and the documents have been withheld from scholars and historians. Without these complete records, the significance of the Disney settlement in the Detroit lawsuit is largely speculative.

Contention between Society members increased after the *United Paramount* case folded, and the latent tendency of the independents to disagree amongst themselves reappeared. Only part of this was set off by the controversial conclusion to the Detroit case. The Society itself faced a reassessment of its purpose in the industry, as many of the preeminent independents embraced activities outside of traditional movie production.

This was most visible with Walt Disney. His was always a progressive enterprise, as evidenced by his long-time expansion into ancillary markets like merchandising, music, and publishing. In the 1950s when he constructed Disneyland, he moved into a field of amusement that was quite foreign to even the largest Hollywood studios. Television had provided him the vehicle in which to realize the massive outdoor project. But in so doing, several other Disney activities were reevaluated.

By way of example, during the early 1950s Walt Disney originated an extensive line of food products from bread to soft drinks. In addition to bringing further exposure to his name and company, Disney also considered this kind of diversification financially sound. Unfortunately when entering television, he was forced to curtail his food and beverage operation to avoid competition with potential advertisers. Only one significant remnant of the food line remained—Donald Duck orange juice.

Although choosing between the food industry and the theme park business was conceivably a lucid decision for Disney, it was still evidence of the unexpected alterations that Disney made as he continued to expand beyond that of a mere independent film producer. The situation with United Paramount was naturally an even stickier situation that seemed difficult to reconcile. Though Walt Disney and his studio expertly preserved relations with the ABC-Paramount combine without betraying the independent production movement, his predicament symbolized the kinds of ponderous circumstances that independents faced as they tried to diversify their independent operations. Some of the producers like David Selznick were turning their independent production companies into distribution outfits which further blurred the distinction between an independent and a major studio, and brought into question the ultimate destiny of the independents who battled the Hollywood establishment.

15

The Decline of SIMPP

IT WAS ONLY A SHORT TIME after the victorious *Paramount* case that an event took place at SIMPP which signified the inability of the independents to remain united. Internal dissension developed over the issue of film financing which would have had a conducive impact on the independent movement and arguably would have changed the future of SIMPP.

Independent producers from all film eras had been disadvantaged by financing. Banks provided some but not all of the money producers needed to finance their films. To minimize risks, the banks left the producers to find their own completion financing or "second money."

As the major studios warmed to independent production during the 1940s, they were able to lure independent production companies by offering cash advances that covered the entire movie costs. Essentially the major studios were reverting to a truer version of the Hodkinson distribution method, and in so doing were able to adapt to the industry changes as the studio system become outmoded.

United Artists had depended on independent films throughout its existence, and seemed perched to excel in the post-*Paramount* Hollywood. But UA only rarely participated in film financing, and when it had with Wanger and Stromberg for example, the distributor suffered heavy losses. Unwilling to encourage new producers with cash advances, UA's position in the industry diminished considerably during the 1940s.

SIMPP understood the importance of assisting the independents with cash-flow difficulties. The Society wanted to create a subsidiary to provide completion money to make independents less dependent on the major studios. The Bankers Trust Company, the prominent New York-based film lender, agreed to participate in a massive investment program that capitalized on the growing trend toward independent production. In the $20 million proposal, SIMPP would organize a company tentatively named Motion Picture Equity Corporation. Bankers Trust would provide $10 million in financing, and also float a stock subscription of one million shares at $10 each. Operated by independent producers, for independent producers, the subsidiary would provide much-needed second money for independent films. The plan was unanimously approved at a SIMPP meeting of over 70 participants on May 2, 1950.

However, before it could fund the corporation, the bank required a complete financial analysis of each independent production company during the previous 12 years. The survey was voluntarily, and to be done with extreme confidentiality; but many of the producers balked at the detailed questionnaire which asked for a number of intimate disclosures including budgets breakdowns, road show practices, and income. The producers who were the most forthcoming were obviously those who needed the financing most. The more established filmmakers—the Goldwyns, Selznicks and Disneys—had the least to gain, and were the most uneasy about bankers researching their books.

The Motion Picture Equity Corporation plans collapsed, to the detriment of many young independents. Consequently the independent trend toward studio-based financing continued. In many respects this made the new wave of independent producers less independent in the classic sense. The new producers were bankrolled by the studios, given space on the studio lots, and of course distributed by the majors—with the producer remaining independent in name only.

United Artists suffered as the major studios snatched away many would-be UA independents. Fewer and fewer of these kinds of producers felt a need to join with SIMPP, and this pattern cut into the authority of the independent organization. Frustratingly, many of the problems resulted from the inability of the established producers to reach out to the new generation of Hollywood production companies.

SAMUEL GOLDWYN'S COLLEAGUES realized early on that SIMPP's protests of the studio system gave Goldwyn a constructive target for his argumentative disposition. Without an outlet for his irascibility, Goldwyn would unavoidably combat his own partners as he had at Famous Players-Lasky, the original Goldwyn Pictures, and United Artists. Many who personally dealt with Goldwyn believed that his tendency to go against the grain was intrinsic, that he was fundamentally ill at ease with group consensus of any kind. Thus while the focus of SIMPP remained on monopoly fighting, Goldwyn's contradictory nature was subdued.

These qualities made Samuel Goldwyn ideally-suited for the Society of Independent Motion Picture Producers during its antitrust heyday. But when the unraveling of *SIMPP v. United Detroit* marked the end of the Society's antitrust activity, it directly resulted in one of the most prominent dissensions in the independent ranks when Sam Goldwyn decided to quit SIMPP.

As the Detroit lawsuit began in 1948, both Goldwyn and Disney planned to use the case as a springboard to other antitrust suits. In 1954, even though the case itself was not considered a complete loss for the independents, the results came as a disappointment, particularly to Goldwyn. The Detroit suit did not provide Goldwyn with the swift and definitive precedent that he was looking for. The outcome, along with other recent events, signified that Walt Disney, who was rapidly becoming the most prolific independent in the industry, was also taking a dominant position in the administration of SIMPP affairs.

For example, SIMPP supported Walt Disney in a personal dispute between Disney and actor Kirk Douglas which erupted in court in 1956. After Disneyland opened, Douglas was surprised to see 16-millimeter footage of himself and his family, photographed at the Disney home by Walt himself, broadcast on a Disney promotional television program. Then Douglas surprised Disney by filing an astronomical $415,000 lawsuit which became a courtroom showdown of freedom-of-expression versus right-of-privacy.

Following what he considered an unfavorable ruling in Los Angeles Superior Court, Gunther Lessing issued a statement on behalf of SIMPP which attacked the court opinion. The decision was later overturned, and the suit was settled following a reconciliation between the actor and the producer. The incident demonstrated, at least in appearance, how the Society was becoming the bailiwick of the Disney interests, particularly while Lessing held a key position as both SIMPP chairman and Walt Disney Productions vice president.

Though the Kirk Douglas incident took place after Goldwyn resigned from SIMPP (and in all likelihood Goldwyn agreed with Disney's position), he may have already seen these trends toward a more Disney-centric independent organization, and preferred not to remain a member. As reporter Alva Johnston wrote in the 1937 biography *The Great Goldwyn*, "He quickly gets out of anything he can't boss."

Moreover Goldwyn felt that independent production, like the Society itself, had changed considerably since 1942, when only a small number of high-profile producers were carving out a niche separate from the studios. Rather, as independent production grew, fewer took the road Goldwyn had blazed as his own financier and copyright holder. Of course, part of this was the inability of SIMPP to adapt to the new trends in independent production. Furthermore, because SIMPP dues were tabulated from box office profits, the majority of the Society revenue was supplied by the busiest producers like Goldwyn and Disney, leaving Goldwyn to wonder whether his membership was providing him with ample benefit.

On February 8, 1955 Samuel Goldwyn resigned from SIMPP, leaving Walt Disney by far the most active founding member. Goldwyn, who did not publicly announce his withdrawal until May, stated that changes in the structure of the industry had narrowed the Society's purpose. His statement was a courteous way of saying that though independent production had grown since the *Paramount* case, the Society no longer embodied the spirit for which the founders had designed it.

"The SIMPP has served a fine function over the years," Goldwyn said. "However, in recent years many of the independent producers who were among its original members have left the SIMPP and a large part of independent production is being financed by major companies. As a result, the SIMPP's area of activities has become quite limited. In view of these conditions, I felt there was no longer the purpose to be served by the SIMPP which formerly existed, and therefore on February 8 I submitted my resignation."

Sam Goldwyn had already begun to reassert his individuality on the antitrust front. He waged his own civil suit against his archenemy Fox West Coast—this time without SIMPP. He filed the Fox West Coast case in San Francisco in May 1950, when the Detroit suit was stalled by the deposition requirement. Goldwyn claimed that Twentieth Century-Fox, Fox West Coast Theatres, National Theatres, Charles P. Skouras, and several affiliated circuits including T. & D. Junior Enterprises had intentionally discriminated against independently-produced films.

Early on, the case transpired much like the Detroit suit. There were delays before the trial. Also the defendants were then in a state of flux as Twentieth Century-Fox completed its divestiture and Charles Skouras passed away. Likewise, as in Detroit, the suit was inhibited by statute of limitations problems that forced Goldwyn to scale back his suit from 28 films (treble damages of $6.75 million) to only seven films (seeking $1.75 million). Goldwyn was represented by Joseph L. Alioto, one of the triumvirate of SIMPP attorneys in the Detroit case, who would later become mayor of San Francisco. After the demise of the SIMPP Detroit lawsuit, Goldwyn revived his Fox West Coast case, and headed to pre-trial in September 1954.

The suit attracted attention off and on for several years. It was like the good-old antitrust days—the independent producer accusing the theater monopoly of eliminating competition by threatening to build on adjacent lots, price-fixing, and over-buying films which they never intended to show. Goldwyn gobbled up headlines when he brought in high-profile character witnesses on his behalf, including Mary Pickford and Cecil B. DeMille. James Mulvey became one of the heroes of the trial when he contributed his first-hand distribution information that turned the case in favor of Goldwyn. Eleven years into the suit, the decision finally came on May 5, 1961, and the judge awarded Goldwyn $300,000 in damages.

UNITED ARTISTS FACED deterioration due to management difficulties and internal dissension that mirrored the events at SIMPP. David Selznick had exited United Artists in 1947 to start his own distribution company, leaving Pickford and Chaplin the sole owners of United Artists. The two former silent stars entered into one of their most disagreeable times as partners. The company was already viewed as unstable. Now the banking community classified UA at-risk due to the $2 million repurchase of the Selznick stock. Adding further injury, the industry perceived that the distributor was losing its distinctiveness since the other major studios were building their own rosters of independent producers.

Several SIMPP members at UA including William Cagney, David Loew, Benedict Bogeaus, Howard Hawks, Harry Popkin, and Stanley Kramer withheld their films from United Artists in protest of the management crisis of the late 1940s. Many of these independents felt that United Artists' distribution presence had eroded, and they refused to release their movies until the studio could prove itself healthy.

During the ongoing Pickford-Chaplin feud, United Artists distribution company was continually rumored for sale. But the company leaders had been unable to come to terms to accept an offer. One of the failed purchases in 1949 would have vested United Artists in the hands of the independent-producing Nasser family lead by SIMPP member James Nasser. During that same time, the

Nassers were solidifying their control of the General Service studio property which likely would have become the new UA studio lot had Chaplin and Pickford actually sold the distribution company to the Nassers. The UA management remained at odds with their producers, and sustained heavy weekly losses until 1951 when Arthur B. Krim and Robert S. Benjamin, two entertainment attorneys formerly with Rank and Eagle-Lion, bought half of United Artists and took control of the company. Pickford and Chaplin each retained a 25 percent interest, and the Krim-Benjamin regime was given operating control of UA.

The new owners were the fortunate recipients of two blockbuster movies, *The African Queen* (1951) and *High Noon* (1952), produced by two of the most important SIMPP members during its later years—Sam Spiegel and Stanley Kramer, respectively.

AS INDEPENDENT PRODUCTION took off after the *Paramount* decision, the movement splintered, making it difficult for SIMPP to remain at the forefront. The major film companies could no longer justify keeping scores of talent contracts in an era without block booking. Now working off of the studio payroll, actors like Burt Lancaster, Kirk Douglas, and John Wayne, and directors like Otto Preminger and Alfred Hitchcock formed their own independent production companies to develop projects and negotiate with others. Suddenly there were more options than ever before even for those who did not wish to create their own corporate identity.

Some of the old Poverty Row distributors tried to use the independent movement to launch their studios into the majors. B-movie company Monogram formed a subsidiary in 1945 called Allied Artists Pictures Corporation, which sounded not-so-coincidentally like the United Artists tradename that was already synonymous with prestige filmmaking.

The president of Allied Artists was Steve Broidy who headed IMPPA, the Independent Motion Picture Producers Association—the organization that served as the independent-distributor equivalent of SIMPP. (IMPPA older than SIMPP, and with a confusingly-similar name, lacked the clout of SIMPP since it was mostly an organization of low-budget studios which concentrated on Westerns and "action dramas." But the 35-member independent distributor association still had a deal of influence in the industry in the 1930s and 1940s.)

Allied had an auspicious beginning as an A-movie producer-distributor, but like the other Poverty Row studios, was unable to make the conversion into the ranks of the majors. William Wyler produced and directed his classic *Friendly Persuasion* (1956) at Allied Artists. Walter Wanger, who signed with them 1951, praised the structure of Allied which had studio administration and filmmakers on the same coast. Without the split authority between east-coast executives and west-coast talent, filmmaking was less cumbersome and studio overhead decreased.

Allied Artists also spawned one of the most important independent production companies of the post-SIMPP era—the Mirisch Company, formed in August 1957 by the three brothers Harold, Marvin, and Walter Mirisch. The Mirisches controlled production at Allied for many years before going independent. They took some of the important Allied talent with them, promising their directors creative freedom in addition to liberal profit participation.

They envisioned the Mirisch Company as a haven for independent filmmakers who did not wish to deal with the business duties of an independent production company. Many actors, directors, and even other producers found stability and creative autonomy under the umbrella structure of the company. The brothers signed a 12-picture deal with United Artists in 1957, which was extended to 20 films two years later. The Mirisch Company moved to the Samuel Goldwyn Studios where they became the largest tenant, creating such films as *Some Like It Hot* (1959), *The Magnificent Seven* (1960), *West Side Story* (1961), and *The Pink Panther* (1964).

THOUGH THE SOCIETY of Independent Motion Picture Producers continued to add members well into the 1950s, such growth did not accurately relate to the health of the organization. Several of the busiest producers from the classic era, like David Selznick and

Walter Wanger, had curtailed their activities even though they were still SIMPP members. At the same time, many of the new independents were not joining SIMPP, finding the circumstances of the new independent-friendly Hollywood studios more to their liking. So even though SIMPP membership doubled in the first two years of Ellis Arnall's leadership, fewer films were produced by SIMPP members in 1950 than in 1948.

The difficulties at United Artists also had a domino effect on SIMPP's stability. Since the UA management had encouraged membership of all of its producers in SIMPP, this created strong ties between the Society and the Hollywood distributor. When United Artists faltered, this ate away at SIMPP revenue that was generated from the box office of its members.

Even the SIMPP membership dues seemed to work against the Society as new independents became dependant on studio financing. Before 1951 annual dues were based upon three-eighths of one percent of each producer's domestic theatrical gross. Unfortunately since the less-established independents usually had to surrender a large share of the box office to their distributor, the new wave of filmmakers were unwilling to base their SIMPP contributions on the total movie gross. To encourage more studio-based independents members, SIMPP modified its annual dues by charging three-eighths of one percent on the producer profits, known as "producers net gross," instead of the considerably-higher box office gross.

This concession hardly reversed the trend of independent producers operating away from SIMPP. The Society only represented a fraction of the industry's independent production in the 1950s. At the same time, it suffered financial difficulties. The Detroit lawsuit became a drain on the Society, and cut-backs were instated which hampered the Society's activities. Instead of the $40,000 annual salary for the president, Arnall agreed to work for the Society on a retainer basis, performing his SIMPP administrative duties from his private law practice in Atlanta.

SIMPP also had to scale back its ambitious international plans. In 1953 SIMPP had formed a subsidiary called the Independent Film Producers Export Corporation to compete with the MPAA's

Motion Picture Export Association. The independents planned to make themselves a cohesive international power to rival any major studio. "As the domestic market becomes less profitable," Arnall originally advised the producers, "it has become more essential that our people aggressively tap the potentialities of foreign income which might accrue from the proper distribution of their pictures in the world market." Their plans featured a sales headquarters in Paris, but the entire foreign enterprise had to be abandoned when SIMPP's financial problems set in.

With the producers no longer galvanized by the great antitrust battle against the major studios, the Society of Independent Motion Picture Producers desperately lacked direction in an era dominated by independent production.

During a week of conferences and meetings at Beverly Hills in the summer of 1958, SIMPP drastically scaled back its operations. For one last time, the Society drew front page headlines from the trade papers on August 1 after it announced the downsizing at a press conference the day before. The Society said that the retrenchment came "as a result of falling revenue from its members and changed conditions in Hollywood under which 'independent' producers have linked themselves to major companies."

Even though the independents tried to give the announcement a more upbeat spin, the press interpreted the news as the official end to the illustrious organization that once rivaled the MPAA. "We do not plan to completely dismantle the Society," Arnall explained. "It will be our purpose to maintain it in a more inactive status but, nevertheless, have the corporate structure available for use whenever we can render service to our members."

The executive secretary position, held by Marvin L. Faris for the previous 12 years, was disbanded immediately. Faris had leaned toward a career as an agent, and joined with William Morris soon thereafter. Later he worked at Creative Management Associates, and served as president of the Association of Talent Agents before he died in September 1981.

Arnall remained as president of SIMPP, with Gunther Lessing as chairman of the board. The SIMPP Beverly Hills office was closed in August, and, according to Arnall, "the corporate records, books and files of the Society will be in the custody and maintenance of Gunther R. Lessing" and kept "at the Disney Studios." The address of the Society of Independent Motion Picture Producers became 500 Buena Vista Street, the Burbank property where Walt Disney moved to in 1940, and where the Disney company has been headquartered ever since.

All membership dues since June 30, 1958 were remitted to the members, and no further dues were collected from that point on. Evidently the limited activities of the Society of Independent Motion Picture Producers were bankrolled by Walt Disney Productions, the company which stated that Walt Disney had no intention of abandoning the Society and continued to give it his full support until the end.

The industry publication *Film Daily* listed the Society among the industry's trade organizations through 1960, and according to a biography of Ellis Arnall written shortly before he died in 1992, the Society retained Arnall until 1963. Yet in the archives of the principal members, no SIMPP correspondence exists after 1959.

Some of the active SIMPP members also viewed the downsizing as the end of the Society and the end of an epoch. Walter Wanger wrote to Ellis Arnall, "I realize that it's due to idiots like myself that were too careless about our financial interests and got taken by the boys [the studio moguls] so that we couldn't support as worthy an organization as yours."

Arnall explained to the members, "It is my firm belief that independent motion picture production will continue as the backbone of the industry, and that ultimately new markets and new developments will open new opportunities for the production, sale and distribution of the quality films of our members." For this reason, he said that the Society would still be maintained so that it could, in fact, be reactivated at some future time when such an organization proved to be necessary to the industry.

16

Fade Out

PERHAPS IT WAS PARADOXICAL for the most independent-minded filmmakers in Hollywood to think that they could collectively sustain an organization that would unite the maverick producers over a lengthy period of time. As if the touch-and-go existence of the independents was not enough of a deterrent, the successful independents on the whole demonstrated a clear inability to take the unselfish steps necessary to reach out to other independents and construct a permanent niche for an independent film trade association.

The Society of Independent Motion Picture Producers, formed at the career high-points for many of the founders, also had to deal with the repose the classic Hollywood filmmakers. Most of the producers came away from SIMPP in a worse state than they had going in. Not surprisingly, the most prominent surviving member of SIMPP, Walt Disney, was also the creator of the most lasting corporate legacy. But Disney suffered through many bitter and challenging years that coincided with the antitrust struggle of the 1940s.

Walt Disney came into the Society in early 1942 in the wake of debilitating labor problems that interrupted his studio operation. The animators strike in the summer of 1941 was widely regarded as a major cause of the end of the Disney golden age that had been characterized by lavish production value and ground-breaking achievements in animation. The advent of World War II cut-off the studio's essential foreign revenue, and brought lean years for Disney. After sustaining heavy losses on *Pinocchio* and *Fantasia* (both 1940), Walt Disney announced in January 1942 that *Bambi* would be the last of his full-length animated features, as several projects were shelved to make way for the war effort.

In the 1940s, Walt Disney seemed to have lost his storytelling confidence. His films relied heavily on voice narration, a film style that contrasted starkly with the bold and innovative ideas that brought universal praise during the previous decade from the public, his peers, and the film intelligentsia. As his films lost their experimental edge, the Disney product moved to the mainstream. More and more his projects were supported by big-name talent like Bing Crosby, Edgar Bergen, and Dinah Shore, and his feature-length releases consisted of an unambitious string of animated shorts packaged together. Walt Disney had a difficult time finding saleable projects, while Roy Disney had similar problems keeping the studio finances afloat. In 1949 the company continued to show a fiscal loss. Walt Disney Productions stock, which had gone public in 1941 at the price of $25, bottomed-out at its all-time low $3 per share.

Though Disney reentered feature animation production with *Cinderella* (1950), studio insiders claimed that Walt Disney's fancy seemed to lie elsewhere. After having achieved what he considered to be the pinnacle of artistic and commercial success in animation in the late 1930s, he drifted toward live-action projects, nature documentaries, and of course theme parks—in a diversification effort that eventually saved his independent company.

With nearly $1 million in frozen funds accumulated in Great Britain, the Disney brothers briefly considered opening a cartoon studio in England, but instead formed Walt Disney British Films Ltd. to produce live-action films overseas. Their first British film, *Treasure Island* (1950), was also the first Disney feature without any animation, and established the Disney live-action division as a prestige outfit for literary-based A-pictures with broad appeal.

Disney's constant drive for quality, which had resulted in exorbitant losses on past animated films, proved to be a masterstroke that made his movies a rerelease gold mine. The timeless nature of his movies, and Walt Disney's insistence of keeping them out of the public view on a seven-year cycle, gave Disney a fresh and profitable rerelease franchise and resulted in a Disney stranglehold on animated features until the early 1990s when the home video releases of Disney films destroyed their theatrical value.

Like several other prominent independent production companies, Walt Disney Productions ventured into distribution. Dissatisfied with the RKO handling of their documentary features, the Disneys formed the Buena Vista Film Distributing Company in 1953 to handle domestic distribution of all of its films, beginning with *20,000 Leagues Under the Sea* and *Lady and the Tramp* (both 1954). Instead of operating a chain of expensive exchanges like the other distributors, Buena Vista pioneered a far more flexible distribution system by establishing sales offices in key territories, while a regional bureau called National Film Service was hired to physically transport the film prints to theaters. After decades of slow, constant growth, Buena Vista became one of the industry's most profitable distribution outfits.

Walt Disney's move into television also helped stabilize the company, not only by adding additional revenue, but by allowing the producer to plant stakes in the new and expanding medium. The 1954 deal between Walt Disney and ABC-Paramount went sour after a few years although both sides benefitted greatly from the partnership. ABC received several shows from the producer, while the deal enabled Disney to finance Disneyland.

Leonard Goldenson later said "the Disneys had turned out to be terrible business partners." Instead of splitting the Disneyland earnings amongst the investors, "Disney kept plowing his profits back into park expansion." The television network was unaccustomed to the Disney philosophy of long-term growth that had been practiced religiously by the brothers from the earliest days of their company.

"They're just a dollar-minded bunch," Roy Disney complained against ABC. "They run the business for money first."

Walt Disney also despised the arbitrary manner that ABC manipulated his television shows. When ABC canceled *The Mickey Mouse Club* but denied Disney the right to take it to another network, Roy Disney threatened an antitrust lawsuit against the American Broadcasting Company in an effort to force Disney's release from the contract.

The Disneys had demonstrated their business savvy in the original 1954 deal by giving Walt Disney Productions the option to repurchase the ABC-Paramount interest in Disneyland within seven years. In 1958, Walt Disney Productions reported a nine-month net profit of $2.9 million, due largely to the 65.52 percent interest in Disneyland, Inc. that the company had acquired through various stock purchases. One year before, Walt Disney Productions stock moved to the New York Stock Exchange where it traded for around $60 a share. The Disney brothers were determined to consolidate complete control of Disneyland in the hands of Walt Disney Productions.

In a 1959 deal brokered by SIMPP's Loyd Wright, Walt Disney sold part of his personal Disneyland holdings to Walt Disney Productions as "recompense for his independent work in developing the concept of Disneyland." Also around the same time, as Walt Disney moved to NBC, Walt Disney Productions began to exercise its option to buy the stock held by ABC-Paramount, and eventually paid $7.5 million to reacquire the one-third interest that had cost American Broadcasting only $500,000 originally. Though it came at a tremendous cash outlay, the maneuver put Walt Disney Productions in complete control of the theme park that became the bedrock of the company's financial future. By the time Walt Disney died on December 15, 1965, the Disneyland theme park represented a total investment of over $126 million.

SIMPP's Gunther R. Lessing remained a prominent Disney executive even after SIMPP folded. He retired in 1964, almost exactly 35 years after he joined the Disney brothers' family business. Walt Disney, who almost never attended any retirement parties for his employees, gave high praise to Lessing during his retirement roast in December 1964. Gunther Lessing died at age 80

on September 28, 1965, less than three months before Walt
Disney's death.

SAMUEL GOLDWYN, FOR HIS sheer longevity as a successful independent producer, remained a marvel in the industry, though his
success was achieved on quite a different level than that of Walt
Disney. With only brief interruptions in his production output over
a 30-year span, Goldwyn released his seventy-eighth film *Hans
Christian Andersen* (1952) which became his last RKO release, and
his final production as a SIMPP member.

He remained landlord of the 18-acre Hollywood studio at Santa
Monica Boulevard and Formosa Avenue, the former Pickford-
Fairbanks studio which had been called the Samuel Goldwyn
Studio since 1939. During the 1940s, Mary Pickford still retained
her share of the property, which meant that neither independent had
clear majority control. The joint owners continued to bicker over
the studio until their disagreement created a deadlock that landed
them in court, and put the lot up for sale at auction in 1955.

Goldwyn, assisted by James Mulvey, outbid Pickford, and
became sole owner of the property. But despite Pickford's many
frustrating encounters with Goldwyn over the years, she still helped
Goldwyn out as needed—as she did only a couple years later with
her appearance in the Fox West Coast case in 1957. The lot
provided a home for many independent production companies over
the years, and continued to be known as the Samuel Goldwyn
Studio until 1980 when Warner Bros. purchased the site as an
auxiliary to its Burbank headquarters, and renamed it the Warner
Hollywood Studio. After Warner sold the property to a private film
company in 1999, it remained in operation with a new identity
called The Lot.

The 82 year-old Sam Goldwyn retired from active filmmaking
after the $7 million musical *Porgy and Bess* (1959). He felt alien-
ated by the promiscuity of the cinema in general; though, interestingly, Goldwyn had spearheaded SIMPP's successful 1954 movement to modernize the 24 year old production code to avoid it
becoming outmoded. "I've tried to be honorable. I've tried to

behave decently," Goldwyn declared in 1959. "I've never done a picture that would offend anybody." Goldwyn was one of many Hollywood veterans who became distanced by the value shift in film as the censorship code eroded completely during the following decade.

After Goldwyn exited SIMPP, James L. Mulvey also relinquished his responsibilities from the Society. Then in 1960 Mulvey resigned from Samuel Goldwyn Productions to form a joint venture with a Canadian theater circuit to distribute foreign films with big-budget advertising campaigns. He had also taken an active interest in the Brooklyn Dodgers baseball franchise, serving as vice president since 1937. He became part owner of the team, and helped manage the Dodgers move to Los Angeles.

Goldwyn had a difficult time reclaiming the 5 percent interest Mulvey held in the Samuel Goldwyn film company. When litigation ensued between Goldwyn and Mulvey, the incident became a blunt reminder to Goldwyn why he had always resisted taking on partners over the years. Mulvey made the ironic accusation that Goldwyn had sold his films to television in a block sale that diluted the value of Mulvey's stock just when Goldwyn came to reclaim the shares. The court dismissed the block booking antitrust claim against Goldwyn, but awarded a $1 million settlement to Mulvey in 1972. He and Goldwyn instead settled in undisclosed terms out of court shortly before Mulvey died in December 1973.

Samuel Goldwyn, who had been wheelchair-bound after a stroke in 1969, died on January 31, 1974 at the age of 95.

DURING THIS SAME TIME, other independent producers were overtaken by the changes in Hollywood. David O. Selznick had orchestrated his corporate interests in the late 1940s to be able to flourish in the new era of independent filmmaking. However, despite his bold and auspicious entry into distribution, he was unable to make the same conversion from producer to distributor as Disney.

At United Artists in the 1940s, Selznick had spent most of his time developing film projects which he sold to other studios for a tidy profit. He realized that the sale of these film packages provided cash infusions that he could use to achieve his grand illusion to make a film that would top *Gone With the Wind* (1939). But in the meantime, the practice denied United Artists desperately-needed films from the producer.

After alienating his partners at UA, Selznick decided to form his own distribution company, the Selznick Releasing Organization (SRO) in 1946 with himself as sole stockholder. His plan was to release his western epic *Duel in the Sun* (1946) with a daring saturation-level release in simultaneous bookings across the country. Though the film and the distribution proved costly, *Duel in the Sun* became a blockbuster in spite of poor reviews and lackluster word of mouth.

For a brief time, Selznick expanded Vanguard and SRO by bringing in other producers, Dore Schary and Mark Hellinger. His executive vice president and SIMPP liaison Daniel T. O'Shea managed another of Selznick's privately-held companies called the Selznick Studio. O'Shea tried to get plans off the ground for a production facility to be called Selznick City. Years later O'Shea recounted to journalist Bob Thomas how the project became doomed by David Selznick's quixotic behavior. Some associates and later historians have wondered if Selznick's near-delusional impulsiveness was a sign that the producer had inherited the chronic mental instability that ran in the Selznick family. Though the Selznick organization in the late 1940s seemed like the harbinger of a new era of flourishing independent production, David O. Selznick's well-positioned empire was devastated by his habitual extravagance and his obsession in repeating past successes instead of moving into new areas as had Walt Disney.

In 1949 Selznick prepared to close down SRO. Dan O'Shea prepared a booklet containing the Selznick assets that would be shopped around to the highest bidder to provide money for Selznick's return to epic film production. The full-page headline on the front of the April 7 *Hollywood Reporter* shocked the industry and infuriated Selznick: "Selznick Studio Goes On Block."

O'Shea, who relinquished his duties with SIMPP, turned in his resignation as Vanguard president and executive director of the

Selznick Studio in April 1950. The trades announced that O'Shea intended on opening his own agency; instead he took an executive position at CBS, and them moved to RKO in 1955 to supervise RKO's fadeout as a production company. It was a fitting end to the executive who began his career at RKO three decades earlier as an attorney. Daniel T. O'Shea died in 1979.

As for David Selznick, he liquidated Vanguard in June 1951, and inadvertently triggered a stream of tax problems that precluded his later ambitions in the film industry. He made only three more films, all featuring the actress Jennifer Jones who became Selznick's second wife. His final production was *A Farewell to Arms* distributed by Twentieth Century-Fox in 1957. He died following a heart attack in 1965.

THE CAREER OF WALTER WANGER featured the extreme ups-and-downs typical of classic Hollywood independent film production—where prosperity came with each successful film, and insolvency loomed with every flop. In 1942, during SIMPP's first year, Wanger was the highest paid Hollywood figure behind Louis B. Mayer. His personal income tax for the year was an incredible $900,000 following the success of *Eagle Squadron* (1941) and *Arabian Nights* (1942).

Accordingly, Wanger took advantage of the postwar boom with a vast diversification and a brief sojourn into distribution. In 1946, during his reorganization of Walter Wanger Productions, he reactivated Walter Wanger Pictures to accelerate his plans to produce prestige pictures, and also formed Young American Films, Inc. to specialize in 16-millimeter educational movies. He joined forces with other independents like William and Edward Nassour who became SIMPP members in 1949 (not to be confused with the Nasser family which also joined SIMPP around the same time).

In 1949 Wanger organized his own distribution company in partnership with the Nassour brothers and Joseph Bernhard, the owner of Film Classics which had acquired most of the Selznick International film library. They formed the Wanger-Nassour Releasing Organization, but it was quickly stunted by Wanger's financial difficulties, including the unraveling of Diana Productions (with Joan Bennett, Fritz Lang, and Dudley Nichols) and Sierra Pictures (with Ingrid Bergman and Victor Fleming).

Wanger had approached *Joan of Arc* (1948) too ambitiously, and had overconfidently risked the subsidiary rights from his previous films in order to finance the new epic which he considered his equivalent of *Gone With the Wind*. The failure of *Joan of Arc* brought unforseen damage by costing Wanger the television rights to his film library at a time before the TV market had matured. In January 1951 Bank of America filed a petition of involuntary bankruptcy against Wanger for his outstanding debt from *The Reckless Moment* (1949), the film which incidentally had delayed Wanger's deposition-taking in *SIMPP v. United Detroit*. He protested the action, and started to put his production company back on its feet with a three-year, $5 million deal with Allied Artists.

Unfortunately the distinguished independent veteran became embroiled in one of the most sensational attempted murders in the history of Los Angeles. Wanger suspected extra-marital activity between his wife Joan Bennett and her agent Jennings Lang of MCA. On December 13, 1951, the gentle, silver-haired Wanger shot the agent with two bullets during a rendezvous between Lang and Bennett outside the Beverly Hills apartment of Marlon Brando. The SIMPP producers, including Goldwyn and Disney, came to Wanger's defense during the ensuing legal proceedings. The MCA agent recovered, and Wanger served four months in prison.

After his parole, Wanger produced other films including his best-remembered movie from this period, *Invasion of the Body Snatchers* (1956). A few years later he convinced Twentieth Century-Fox to film one of his pet projects, *Cleopatra* (1963). He served as a salaried producer for the feature which became one of the most problematic film productions in Hollywood history, held the record as the most expensive movie ever, and nearly brought ruin upon Twentieth Century-Fox. In 1965 Walter Wanger's marriage to Joan Bennett ended in divorce. The independent producer died from a heart attack on November 17, 1968, leaving behind an $18,000 estate.

ORSON WELLES SUFFERED from a recalcitrant image, which he claimed was thrust upon him shortly after he joined SIMPP, as his relations with RKO deteriorated. In hindsight, many of Welles' creative and financial difficulties came from his retreat from independence when he gave up final cut privileges in exchange for better studio terms after *Citizen Kane* (1941). As he became more dependant on studio financing, he found the carpet was repeatedly pulled out from under him.

Welles also blamed his difficulties on his good-will tour of South America that began in February 1942, one month after he cofounded the Society of Independent Motion Picture Producers. RKO took control of *The Magnificent Ambersons* (1942), reedited it in his absence, and forced the release of the $1 million film that went on to lose $600,000. Then in the midst of Welles' rumored extravagance in Brazil, RKO halted production on his unfinished South American-themed feature *It's All True*. When he returned to Hollywood, his Mercury production company was ordered off the RKO lot to make way for Sol Lesser's Tarzan unit.

Welles tried for many years to reclaim the unfinished *It's All True* footage from RKO, and worked as an actor and director for other producers in order to raise the money to purchase the film negative—which would have been his property all along had he taken the same course as the other independent producers.

"The basis of the whole enormous anti-Welles edifice dates exactly from South America. When I came back from there, I didn't get a job as a director for four years." The filmmaker claimed that his career never recovered from the reputation of recklessness with which the studios had branded him. Furthermore, his obsession with the unfinished *It's All True* kept his career from progressing. "I tried everything," he said in his efforts to wrestle control of the film footage from RKO. "I was near it, near it, near it. I wasted many years of my life. If I had turned my back the way they did on it, I would have been much better off. But I kept trying to be loyal to it. It began a pattern of trying to finish pictures which has plagued me ever since."

He struggled to keep Mercury Productions alive, and loaned himself out to independent producers including David O. Selznick (*Jane Eyre*, 1944), Sam Spiegel (*The Stranger*, 1946), Edward Small (*Black Magic*, 1949), and Alexander Korda (*The Third Man*, 1949).

In 1948 Orson Welles quit SIMPP as he prepared for an extended visit to Europe to find financing for his next films. He ended up an overseas resident for nine years before he returned to the United States to direct his final important Hollywood film, *Touch of Evil* (1958). Welles, the last surviving SIMPP founder, died from a heart attack October 10, 1985.

CHARLIE CHAPLIN, LIKE WELLES, also had his reputation tarnished by public misconception. Chaplin's problems were mostly political, and began when he and Welles were on a speaking tour together during World War II to cultivate support for the Allies on the Russian front. Chaplin's exuberance raised suspicions in the press which falsely branding the filmmaker as a communist sympathizer. The emotionally-charged political atmosphere agitated the controversy, and was one of the contributing factors to Chaplin's long hiatus from film production following *The Great Dictator* (1940). He was also sidetracked by a paternity suit that languished in court, even after his innocence was proved by a blood test administered by none other than SIMPP's Loyd Wright.

Chaplin selected *Monsieur Verdoux* (1947) as his next project, a black comedy based on an idea developed by Orson Welles. The film was poorly-received when it was released in April 1947, adding to the anti-Chaplin antagonism that marked his decline as an influential filmmaker. He resigned from SIMPP later that year.

In 1952 when he traveled to Great Britain to promote his next film *Limelight*, the Immigration and Naturalization Service barred Chaplin's return to the United States. Pickford and Goldwyn came to his defense by offering indignant public statements against the government. Instead, Charlie Chaplin and family took seclusion in Switzerland. He sold his Hollywood studio property on Sunset Boulevard and La Brea Avenue in 1953.

Anticipating further difficulties with the United States government, he hastily sold his shares in United Artists to the new owners Krim and Benjamin in February 1955 for only $1.2 million. He was knighted by Queen Elizabeth II in 1975, and died on Christmas Day two years later.

After her last starring role in the early 1930s, Mary Pickford remained a hands-on manager of United Artists and an active supporter of SIMPP from the beginning to the end of the Society. She fought for a progressive agenda at United Artists while the self-seeking attitude of her partners threatened to drive the distribution company into insolvency.

She also served as producer and executive producer in several production ventures to help with the UA product crises. In 1945, during the independent production boom at the end of World War II, she organized Comet Pictures to make medium-budget films with Ralph Cohn, the son of Columbia Pictures cofounder Jack Cohn. At Comet she produced probably her finest later film, the noir hit *Sleep, My Love* (1948). Later she became partners with SIMPP member Lester Cowan, the producer of *You Can't Cheat an Honest Man* (1939) and *My Little Chickadee* (1940) who was best known as an independent for the UA film *The Story of G.I. Joe* (1945). Pickford and Cowan produced *Love Happy* (1950), which received a drubbing from critics and audiences, but became famous as the final Marx brothers comedy and for the early cameo appearance of Marilyn Monroe.

By the time Goldwyn took over her share of the Formosa Avenue studio in 1955, Pickford had slipped away into film inactivity. One year later, she decided to sell her 25 percent interest in United Artists for $3 million, becoming the last independent producer of SIMPP to be completely divested of UA stock. In 1957 Krim and Benjamin, now the sole owners of the distributor, took United Artists into a new corporate era with a public stock offering.

Pickford became more reclusive after her retirement, and died May 29, 1979. Her legendary Beverly Hills estate known as Pickfair fell into disrepair and was later torn down.

THE GENERAL SERVICE STUDIOS continued to serve as a principle base of operation for the growing number of Hollywood independents. The studio owner Benedict Bogeaus undertook an aggressive expansion of the property during the postwar period, which turned out unexpectedly useful to the new wave of television producers that came to inhabit the lot.

In July 1946, Bogeaus invited William Cagney to become a one-fifth owner of the General Service Studio. Unfortunately James Cagney's career took a downturn toward the end of the 1940s. He continued to deplore the lack of distinguished material; the same criticism which drove him to independent production in the first place would also drive him into retirement. In 1949, Cagney moved out of the General Service Studios to rejoin with Warner Bros. In 1953 William Cagney produced his last film *A Lion Is in the Streets*. James Cagney's final fling as an independent came in the late 1950s when he formed Cagney-Montgomery Productions with actor-turned-director Robert Montgomery to make *The Gallant Hours* (1960).

In 1947 Bogeaus and Cagney began to sell their interests in the General Service Studios to their managers, the Nasser brothers. By 1950 James, George, and Ted Nasser gained control of General Service, and began to focus on television production. Tenants included Lucille Ball and Desi Arnaz, Ozzie and Harriet Nelson, and George Burns and Gracie Allen (Burns remained on the lot until his death at age 100 in 1996). The Arnazes used the General Service Studios as their Desilu headquarters between 1951 and 1953. The remodeled Stage 2, called the Desilu Playhouse, became the location for the filming of the earliest episodes of the seminal *I Love Lucy* television series.

The Nassers controlled the studio for the next three decades, with the exception of a few years in the late 1970s when the property was purchased by a Texas oil and gas firm which renamed the studio Hollywood General.

In 1979 independent producer-director Francis Ford Coppola bought the studio, and moved from his rented space on the Samuel

Goldwyn lot. Coppola purchased Hollywood General for $6.7 million to become the nucleus of the Zoetrope Studio. His ambitious plans suffered financial setbacks, and Coppola sold the lot in 1984 to a Canadian development company that renamed the property the Hollywood Center Studios.

HOWARD HUGHES, MUCH TO the relief of the Hollywood studio establishment, decided to get out of the film business in 1955 claiming "it represents 15 percent of my business and takes 85 percent of my time." The fortunes of RKO had diminished under the erratic leadership of Hughes, whose intolerable meddling drove many independent producers to other distributors while the studio incurred heavy liabilities. When the Disneys grew dissatisfied with their RKO distribution terms, Hughes offered to sell them the studio outright but the Disneys declined the offer.

In July 1955, Hughes sold his RKO holdings to the General Tire and Rubber Company, bringing to a close his sporadic but memorable run as recalcitrant independent producer and eccentric studio tycoon. General Tire, interested primarily in the RKO film library, decided to sell the studio lot in November 1957 to Desilu Productions. The sale reverberated throughout the industry as a symbol of the changing complexion of Hollywood brought by the independent filmmakers of the new television age.

Part of the Desilu purchase included the RKO-Pathé lot in Culver City on which still stood the old Selznick buildings and the dilapidated *Gone With the Wind* sets. Selznick International's colonial style studio became the new Desilu offices. Ironically, the $6.15 million deal was orchestrated by Daniel O'Shea, the former Selznick lieutenant who had been instated at RKO by General Tire. Desilu called the property a "haven for independents." And Lucille Ball reigned over a sprawling television empire that evoked comparisons to the career of Mary Pickford in old Hollywood.

FINALE

17

The Influence of SIMPP

DURING THE GOVERNMENT'S *Paramount* suit, the members of the Society of Independent Motion Picture Producers offered a dismal outlook for the studio system as the antitrust case triggered sweeping changes in the industry.

In the now-famous David O. Selznick declaration told by his long-time friend and collaborator Ben Hecht, the SIMPP founder denounced the hollow efforts of the Hollywood majors to preserve the studio system. "Hollywood's like Egypt," Selznick told the venerable screenwriter in 1951, "full of crumbled pyramids. It'll never come back. It'll just keep on crumbling until finally the wind blows the last studio props across the sand."

Charlie Chaplin also predicted the demise of the film industry giants. "I, Charlie Chaplin, declare that Hollywood is dying," he told the London press in 1947. "Hollywood is now fighting its last battle, and it will lose that battle unless it decides once and for all to give up standardizing its films—unless it realizes that masterpieces cannot be mass-produced in the cinema, like tractors in a factory. I think, objectively, that it is time to take a new road—so that money shall no longer be the all-powerful god of a decaying community."

SIMPP's Edward Small, who also said, "the studios are like dinosaurs. . . . still living and thinking in the past," described the independent revolution in 1948: "The day of the free ride is over. Hollywood will get down to business and independent organizations will lead this great industry back to the prosperity it so richly deserves when it serves the purpose of keeping the whole world entertained."

Sam Goldwyn, attacking the majors in November 1946, said, "Times have changed, but Hollywood hasn't. . . . Hollywood has run dry of ideas. It's living on borrowed time and borrowed ideas from the past."

Ellis Arnall predicted that the antitrust decrees would finally open the independent production floodgates. "Nothing has taken place within the industry as revolutionary or as far-reaching," the SIMPP president said. "Not only will independents move forward successfully in the days ahead, but they will soon have new converts and additional recruits. Before many years have elapsed, the so-called major producing companies will actually be independents themselves. The great difference between the independents and the majors has been that the majors have been in the real estate and theatre business of producing motion pictures. When divorcement is made absolute, then the majors will be independent producing companies."

The over-exuberant nature of the independent statements typified the actions of the Society of Independent Motion Picture Producers in the *Paramount* case. SIMPP members put the same showmanship in their antitrust grandstanding as they did in their moviemaking. But despite the exaggerated words, the influence of the independents during this transition period was undeniable. In assisting the government in its suit against the Hollywood studio oligopoly, SIMPP instigated a dramatic industry-wide metamorphosis, in a business already known for its constant state of flux. Furthermore, the vast economic changes that the antitrust verdicts brought to the structure of Hollywood coincided with the rise of television and its inevitable upheaval of the recreational habits of the American public. Both factors aided the filmmakers of SIMPP in their goal of bringing independent production to the fore. For example, just when the *Paramount* decision appeared to make full-scale B-movie production unfeasible, Hollywood executives began to view television production as a suitable means to keep a full-time studio lot operating profitably. In time, the theaters became the exclusive domain of the A-picture, and the cheapies were relegated to television. This brought about a shift where first-run exhibition concentrated solely on the big-budget movies that had been the mantra of SIMPP and the stock-in-trade of the classic independent producers.

Over the years the major distributors found it easier and more reliable to depend on independent producers for their prestige, big-budget films. Case in point—in 1939 MGM released two expensive Technicolor extravaganzas. One was the $4 million independently-produced *Gone With the Wind*, which made $14 million in only 12 months; the other prestige film was the $2.75 million in-house production of *The Wizard of Oz*. The latter film, after distribution and promotional costs, resulted in a million dollar loss that kept the film in the red until television broadcasts kicked-in years later. Film historian Thomas Schatz observed that the comparison of the two films signaled to the major studio heads "that the risks and headaches of gargantuan blockbusters were best left to independents like Selznick, Goldwyn, and Disney."

So when the block booking ban took away the pre-sold market for low-budget films, and television adsorbed studio overhead, the major distributors naturally increased their ties with the independents who would supply their studios with top grade pictures.

In the early 1950s, all major film distributors had released films by independents. In 1957, according to industry trade reporting, 71 percent—or over two-thirds—of all releases from the former Big Eight were independent productions.

By operating the studios in this manner, the distribution executives were spared the brain damage and chaos associated with film production. This brought about a change in the position of Vice President in Charge of Production, formerly inhabited by a creative executive like Irving Thalberg or Darryl Zanuck. The new studio production head became more of an administrator, usually with a background in law or business, who had a sharper deal-making acumen than story sense. As SIMPP filmmaker John Huston observed in his memoirs, "Studio heads now are accountants, tax experts, a sprinkling of financial wizards, and ex-agents. They are hardly a creative breed. . . . illiterate when it comes to making pictures."

As argued in previous chapters, the demise of block booking caused greater upheaval to the studio system than theater divorcement. Admittedly, no studio could release enough films to fill their theater chains with their own product alone. Furthermore there was some truth to the Big Five assertion that their theater subsidiaries were operated with a degree of autonomy from the parent company. Vertical disintegration may have widened the gap between studios and theaters, but it did not absolutely undermine the way movies were sold. Block booking, on the other hand, had been the bedrock of film distribution even before the Hollywood studios became large circuit owners. In the 1946 New York Equity Suit, it should be remembered, the Statutory Court actually protected vertical integration but refused to permit block booking. Outraged at the prospect of theater owning without block booking, the studios themselves were compelled to appeal to the Supreme Court.

Hollywood reduced its overall film output, as SIMPP had advocated for many years before the *Paramount* decision. In 1940 Sam Goldwyn said that there was not enough quality story material in Hollywood to justify the 500 movies released by the Big Eight, and he suggested that the industry voluntarily hold production to about 200 pictures or less. This began to take effect in post-antitrust Hollywood where even the largest studios like Paramount Pictures scaled back their annual releases from one feature every week, to about 15 or 20 features per year. The majors became more like United Artists which distributed an average of 19 films per year during the 1930s and 1940s—its movies for the most part supplied by independent producers.

"The studios now tried to make only those pictures they thought the theatre owners would fight to get," former SIMPP member Preston Sturges explained. "And the theatres owners, who were trying to predict what the public would pay to see, only wanted the pictures they thought would make them rich." As independent production flourished, the *event picture* became the norm.

The studio release schedule focused on—what would be termed in later years as—the "tentpole" movie: the A-picture film with grosses so high that it off-set the costs of other films. The tentpole movie usually provided a franchise that spilled over into ancillary revenue from television, consumer products, and perhaps sequels. What began as SIMPP's crusade for quality films turned into the blockbuster-oriented mindset of the industry at large.

BEFORE THE *Paramount* case, many of the independent exhibitors complained that they had been relegated to second-class status by the strict run-zone-clearance enforced by the studios. Following the antitrust case, former subsequent-run theaters decided to compete for the newest and most expensive films, creating a free-for-all first-run market. The elaborate system of subsequent runs faded away as more movie releases opened simultaneously across the country. The practice of mass booking the same film became known as "day-and-date" distribution.

Day-and-date became the favored practice of producers because it packed as many screens as the market could bear with a single movie in an effort to lure audiences into the theaters while the film was new and admission prices were therefore at their highest. The idea was not especially novel; the distributors had always viewed movies as "perishable" merchandise that diminished in value in proportion to its age. The independents, however, pioneered the day-and-date release as commonly practiced in modern Hollywood, by backing their films with hefty promotional campaigns that capitalized on the immediacy of the film release.

Howard Hughes realized that the event-value of his film *The Outlaw* (1943) would be enhanced by launching a mass-exhibition experiment with simultaneous showings in several cities. Selznick took the idea to the next level when he distributed *Duel in the Sun* (1946) with the first day-and-date nationwide campaign, and grossed $9 million in only six months. In 1951 the Disneys feared a disappointing reaction to their latest animated feature *Alice In Wonderland*. They cut their losses by orchestrating a saturation-level day-and-date release with an overactive advertising campaign that brought audiences to theaters before negative word-of-mouth set in.

Over the years, the situation became more drastic. Back in the studio era, an average feature film required approximately 350 copies to satisfy first run, and then the used prints would be passed down through the subsequent runs. Even the most popular films needed at most 500 film prints to be supplied by the distributor. Eventually, as day-and-date became standard practice, the typical Hollywood release opened in 2,000 or more screens simultaneously. By the 1990s, the largest day-and-date releases required over 6,000 film prints.

The rise of the drive-in theater also illustrated the shift away from run-zone-clearance as practiced by the studios. The drive-in theater, which began as an inexpensive way to cater to depression-era audiences that were enamored with the automobile, turned into a popular exhibition alternative to the four-wall movie house after World War II. From about 300 outdoor theaters in 1946, the drive-in craze grew to over 4,000 in 1954. According to *Film Daily* in June 1956, for the first time, more people attended drive-in theaters than walk-in theaters. The drive-ins forced the closure of the small subsequent-run theaters that used to inhabit the "neighborhood run."

By its nature, the drive-in attracted a more youth-based audience. The younger demographic on the whole changed the focus of the theatrical motion picture. Television, which brought visual entertainment into the living room, made the theater-going public more discriminating about which movies would draw them out of their homes. "Who wants to go out and see a bad movie," said Goldwyn in his famous quote, "when they can stay at home and see a bad one free on television?" So instead, Hollywood courted the rapidly-growing youth population that was more willing to spend discretionary dollars on movies.

Another youth-driven trend which indirectly resulted from the antitrust decrees was the advent of a new peak movie season—summertime. The movie industry had always been subject to seasonal fluctuation of receipts. However, during the studio era, summer showed a slackening of film revenue as outdoor recreation took patrons away from the movie theaters. (Traditionally-speaking, the slow summer months were also a distant hold-over from the early silent days when film companies spent their time making films during the favorable summer weather, and distributing them throughout the other months of the year.) As audiences got younger, movie grosses expanded during vacation periods. Summer became the most important blockbuster season, followed by the Christmas holiday. Naturally the new studio marketing schedules followed these patterns.

Industry analysts predicted that the *Paramount* decree, coupled with television, would eliminate all theaters except for the big downtown movie palaces. In actuality, quite the opposite took place. As walk-in movie-going began to retake the drive-ins in the 1960s, the first-run theaters moved away from the metropolitan centers and went into the suburbs, giving rise to the multiplex cinema that offered more movie variety and close proximity to shopping and recreational activities.

For example, the Mid-West Drive-In company expanded into shopping centers in 1951, and evolved into the General Cinema Corporation, one of the largest theater chains in the United States. In the early 1960s, the Durwood Theatres, a former Paramount-Publix affiliate in Kansas City opened the first multi-screen theater. The company renovated several large theaters including the Kansas City Paramount Theatre into multi-screens, and expanded its chain by building multiplex theaters in others states. In 1969 the company changed its name to American Multi-Cinema, Inc., also known as AMC.

DESPITE THE BRAVADO of the SIMPP producers, the *Paramount* decrees did not bring an end to industry domination by major distributors. More accurately, the studios became "stables for the independents," as Ellis Arnall referred to the former Big Eight. As a sign of the times, some of the old studio moguls even relinquished their executive responsibilities to become independent producers of A-class movies for their studios, like Darryl F. Zanuck and *The Longest Day* (1962) and Jack Warner with *My Fair Lady* (1962).

The radical transformations brought about an end of the studio system, but not the demise of the studios themselves. Only those companies which refused to change became casualties in the era of independent production. The most revealing contrast between success and failure came as the two giants Paramount and Metro-Goldwyn-Mayer entered the new age—one studio continued to prosper, the other dwindled.

In 1954 Loew's became the last of the Big Five film companies to agree to theater divorcement. (Twentieth Century-Fox and Warner Bros. each signed separate decrees in 1951.) Proving even more recalcitrant, Loew's would not even complete the divorcement until 1959, over a decade after the Supreme Court decision. But this made the transition even more painful for MGM, as the encroachment of television seriously devalued their movie theaters just at the time when they were forced to find buyers.

"The major companies," Arnall said in 1954, "are recognizing the advantages of independent production and decentralizing their operations so as to utilize more independent units." Instead, MGM clung to its past. It failed to develop a presence in television, and the company disregarded the shift to independent production. In the late 1940s, when Louis B. Mayer reorganized MGM, he re-instituted the central-producer system, which had been extinct at MGM since the days of Thalberg. Such an anachronistic reversal stunted the corporation. Producers, actors, and directors ended their contracts to become independent at other companies, and MGM had a difficult time absorbing the studio overhead.

Never able to rebound from divorcement, Metro-Goldwyn-Mayer stopped distributing in 1973, and announced that its domestic film operation would be handled by United Artists. Since then, MGM has made several attempts to try to regain its stature in the industry. The decline was a dramatic turn from the pre-*Paramount* days, when MGM stood as the only studio never to show a loss during any year before 1949.

In comparison, Paramount Pictures recognized the inevitability of divorcement early on. By starting its theater divorcement before the onslaught of television, they were able to get a more reasonable price for their divested theaters. As discussed in chapter 9, Paramount began to establish ties with some of the most important postwar independents like Liberty Films and Rainbow Productions. The company also aggressively pursued interests in television. As the studio era waned, Paramount cut-back on its annual releases and maintained a profitable long-term existence. The studio entered the conglomerate period in film history when it was purchased by Gulf+Western in 1966. Adolph Zukor, retained his honorary company title and his office on the studio lot until he died in 1976 at age 103.

Paramount Pictures and MGM, by virtue of their commanding vertical position, had formerly lead the industry in reported revenue during the studio era. No film corporation other than Paramount or Loew's took the top spot in annual profits for any year between 1919 and 1948. The *Paramount* case opened the way for the ascendance of other distributors. Warner Bros. announced the industry's highest profits in 1951, and then Fox in 1956. Even the former Little Three were able to compete, now that giants resembled the structure of United Artists. Steeped in the traditions of independent production, UA overcame its management difficulties and flourished with profits that outdistanced all other studios in the late 1960s. Such an event was unheard-of 20 years earlier. By the 1970s, the lowly Universal outperformed all of the other studios. And, even more remarkably, in the late 1980s Buena Vista reported the highest market share of any Hollywood distributor.

No studio in the independent era could maintain a continuity with their product, thus eliminating the *house style* that distinguished one studio from anther (i.e. the Warner urban drama, or the Lubitsch-esque high-society gloss of Paramount). Previously each studio style was defined by the creative staff that was marshaled under the production executives. Each studio had maintained a roster of screenwriters, an in-house art department, a corp of directors, and of course a legion of movie stars and contract actors. But as more of the creative personnel became involved with independent production, the studio hold on the industry talent rapidly eroded.

Hollywood talent became available on a freelance basis. And this became especially well-suited for the producers who set up movies as collapsible corporations—the practice that was popularized by Samuel Goldwyn who organized each of his film productions as a separate corporate entity. The collapsible corporation would hire its own staff, complete the picture, and then liquidate its profits. For example, Goldwyn made *Up in Arms* (1944) under the corporate identity of Avalon Productions, Inc., a company which produced only that one picture, then assigned the rights of the film to Samuel Goldwyn Productions, Inc. When Hunt Stromberg made *Guest in the House* (1944) he baldly named his collapsible corporation Guest in the House, Inc., and thus originated another industry trend that has continued to this day where single-film corporations share the name of the film production itself.

The collapsible corporation strategy began as a tax shelter for Goldwyn in the early 1940s, but eventually independents found that the collapsible corporation had its own organizational advantages. It became a tidy way to account for costs and negotiate with talent on a picture-by-picture basis. The practice helped make the independent-based Hollywood films fundamentally different from the mass-production method that typified the studio system.

As individual films became the order of the day, the power previously held by the studios was transferred to those who could package together script, director, and cast into a project that would attract a major distributor. The antitrust case set the stage for the rise of the agent as Hollywood power-broker. Lew Wasserman of MCA and Ray Stark, founder of Seven Arts, moved from talent agenting to commanding positions at the head of major studios, Universal and Warner Bros. respectively.

Moreover, the talent agent had historical ties to the classic Hollywood independent, as illustrated by the agent-producers like Edward Small, Charles K. Feldman, and even the archetypal

Myron Selznick who was directly or indirectly involved with several production companies at any given time in his career. His brother David O. Selznick, it should be noted, pioneered the role as film packager in the 1940s by profitably developing films to sell to the studios during the pre-production stage. Selznick received heavy compensation in these deals which foreshadowed the role of the modern agent-packagers that would take over the old-time studio function of assembling a creative film team.

Likewise Alexander Korda spent many years of his career on film-development profiteering. He made an art out of announcing numerous projects to the press, generating a great deal of buzz in the industry, in order to jack up the value of the project so that it could be sold to another producer at a considerable profit. "A film when it is not finished is an asset, but when it is completed it is a liability," Korda said after making more money on his story properties than on his full-fledged film productions.

The cost of filmmaking spiraled ever-upward because talent demanded more for each film in much the same manner that the SIMPP producers demanded higher booking fees for their highly-individualized pictures. In the groundbreaking deal arranged by Lew Wasserman on behalf of James Stewart for *Winchester '73* (1950), the star received $600,000 in salary and profit participation, making, in one film, double his entire annual salary as a contract performer for MGM.

Hollywood became a city of deal makers as each film production became a one-time alliance of various talent that was negotiated on a person-by-person, picture-by-picture basis. "We made pictures then, we didn't make deals," said director Billy Wilder, nostalgic for the old days of filmmaking. "Today we spend 80 percent of our time making deals and 20 percent making pictures."

WHILE THE INDEPENDENT PRODUCERS revolutionized industry practice, the role of the independent also changed considerably from the days of SIMPP. When the studios began to encourage independent filmmaking, what they really encouraged was closer ties between the independent production company and the studio-distributor.

Skeptics had always noted the self-contradictory nature of the classic Hollywood independent producer. But the new independents became even more subordinate under the standard distribution agreements that favored the studio.

Typically the distribution fee gave the studios 35 percent of all first money grosses. Only after the studio collected its own share and deducted its distribution expenses were profits then divided between the producer and the studio. The actual terms may have varied as some independents had enough clout to negotiate a lower distribution fee or higher percentage points, but regardless the distributors habitually took their cut of the money off the top. In addition, the distributor became accustomed to charging the producers exorbitant overhead expenses, especially if the deal involved the producer's use of the studio lot during production. This subjected the independent filmmakers to the notoriously creative bookkeeping of the studios that was done is such a way that some of the most successful movies would appear to fail to show a profit.

Finally, most of the new independent producers also surrendered their film copyrights to the distributors. This was quite contrary to the *modus operandi* of the empire-builders of SIMPP like Walt Disney and Samuel Goldwyn who viewed the long-term subsidiary rights of their films as an essential part of their livelihood. As the studios put up the money for independent producers, each major distributor became a depository of film copyrights. So that even though most films were no longer produced in-house, the majors still steadily accumulated a large and usually valuable film library.

Formerly, an independent was defined as an individual or an organization that was technically not on the studio payroll—and even with that old designation, the status of the independent was still a matter of interpretation. Therefore in an era when filmmakers were largely not under studio contract but still closely tied to the majors, the true distinction of the term independent was open to more circumspection than ever before. "Independent" became an industry by-word, since the Hollywood mainstream was comprised of independent production companies.

Over the years, a new definition of the term became prevalent, particularly as film schools brought widespread exposure to the art and craft of filmmaking. Many of the new filmmakers were pushed to the fringes of the industry, and the classification of *independent* was adopted by art-house film producers. During the studio era, independent producers were big-budget prestige filmmakers who had love-hate relations with the studios. In modern Hollywood, an independent was someone with no studio ties to speak of, usually with anti-Hollywood implications, making niche movies outside the mainstream on economical budgets. Thus two very-different segments of the industry claimed the title of independent: the companies and filmmakers which were part of the Hollywood mainstream, spiritually the descendants of SIMPP; and those who made "quality films with limited resources" and chose not to participate in Hollywood's wide-scale distribution mechanism.

Regardless of which distinction, the SIMPP victory over block booking became the charter of freedom for all strands of independent production. The independents struggled against block booking from the early days of Hollywood until finally the *Paramount* decision made it illegal for a distributor to sell a film contingent upon the sale of any other film. This allowed SIMPP to achieve its primary objective that all movie sales be done on a picture-by-picture and theater-by-theater basis, so that individual merit and not distribution size determine the success of the picture.

Interestingly, some of the immediate effects of the block booking ban aroused criticism from the independent theater owners. Back in May 1948, the leader of the Allied States theater organization, Abram F. Myers, who attacked SIMPP during the Unity Plans days in 1942, declared "tomorrow belongs to the independent exhibitors." However by 1953, the exhibitors complained that the Justice Department efforts to aid the small theater owners had backfired. Many small movie houses which could not afford to compete for first-run movies found that the Hollywood studios had eliminated the kinds of programmer pictures that sustained the neighborhood theaters in the past. The independent exhibitor associations claimed that the overall shortage in the number of films since the demise of block booking had brought irreparable damage upon the theaters. Even the large circuits found it difficult to fill their screens now that the studios concentrated on fewer, higher-budgeted films. And by 1954 some of the larger theater chains like National Theatres petitioned the government to allow the exhibitors to produce their own films.

With eerie recollection, the industry remembered how the major studios always claimed that block booking was done to benefit the theater owners. Years earlier, the Big Five defended block booking by claiming that the practice provided an umbrella of bulk films that the exhibitors would not be able to afford under normal, competitive circumstances. As demonstrated by the failed Unity Plan deal between the studio and the exhibitors, which SIMPP helped derail in 1942, the exhibitors wanted block booking reform not abolition. But SIMPP pressed so ardently, and worked so closely with the government, that eventually the independent producers got their way, and the theaters were left with conditions that seemed beneficial but ultimately proved less than ideal.

Another side effect of the end of block booking which has been lamented by industry reactionaries has been the decline of the short-subject and the demise of the theatrical animated cartoon. During the studio era, all of the Big Eight distributors maintained their own in-house animation units or developed intimate ties with independent animation producers like Leon Schlesinger (Warner Bros.), Max Fleischer (Paramount), Walter Lantz (Universal), and Walt Disney (United Artists and RKO). Live-action shorts also provided a useful function by providing a test venue for fresh faces on the verge of stardom or new directors looking for a break. Before full-line forcing was disbanded by the Consent Decree of 1940, the studios would block book an entire series of shorts along with the feature packages. But even with this built-in market, the shorts were always in jeopardy of being squeezed out of the program, especially with the rise of the double feature. When the distributors were forced to tighten their belts after the *Paramount* decision, the short subjects took the hit. The live-action shorts were quickly phased out, while the animated cartoons held on a little longer.

The problem with the animated shorts after the *Paramount* case was that the studios did not immediately disband their animation divisions but had imposed cut-backs that eliminated quality and allowed the cartoons to diminish. The studios stopped creating new animated characters, and without the influx of new cartoon super-stars, the market for animated shorts stagnated until the theaters removed the shorts altogether. In spite of surveys in recent decades that have indicated that theatergoers favor seeing extra shorts in addition to the regular feature, the return of cartoons to the theaters has been mostly speculative. The distributors have been unwilling to try to market new groups of shorts, and the major theater chains have been reluctant to try out a potentially lucrative cartoon series that would enhance the audience's theater-going experience.

Other critics of the over-commercialization of the film industry have identified another valid objection to the outlaw of block booking: after the *Paramount* verdict, Hollywood has concentrated not only on fewer films, but also on less variety of subject matter. It was actually quite an unexpected backlash because the independent movement had always promised to bring diversity to the formulaic studio-made films. However, block booking allowed the producer-distributors to spread out their profits and losses, making the studios more willing to sustain a diverse range of films. That is not to say that the classic Hollywood movies were all groundbreaking. On the contrary, without question, filmmaking formulas and censor-ship restrictions lead to an overall homogenization of film product during the studio era. Nevertheless, the old Hollywood studios had far more leeway to make an uncommercial film because even the smallest movies had a built-in market provided by block booking. This also allowed the industry of the past to sustain a number of genres which modern Hollywood no longer finds feasible to pro-duce as it chases after the largest audience demographic.

Without block booking, the modern Hollywood distributors have had to count on each film carrying its own box office weight. Figuratively speaking, the new studios tried to score more home runs than ever before, even though they were up at bat far fewer times. More careful than ever to avoid a big-budget failure, Hollywood did not abandon the formula approach to filmmaking, it merely adjusted the formula. With so much money riding on each film, the studios have continued to make production decisions based on focus-group research and perceived market value that has inevitably lead to a copy-cat approach to filmmaking.

A studio era Hollywood movie would typically spend months in the theaters, as some films took longer than others to find an audience. The new studios have gravitated toward ready-made blockbusters, spending their promotional dollars on films that already have built-in marquee value. Under the modern Hollywood system, dark-horse blockbusters have become infrequent occurrences because the success of each release is determined by an opening weekend box office report. The buzz surrounding the movie must be good, and the film must immediately hit, or it is buried by the studio in an effort to cut its losses and make way for another release.

In their efforts to maximize profits on every single film, the new Hollywood distributors have been compelled to drive hard deals at each theater engagement. The percentage-based deals that were previously championed by SIMPP have become standard for every major film released by the Hollywood distributors. Competitive bidding between theaters has also escalated film rental costs. And just as in the SIMPP days, a producer and distributor can expect to receive far less for their film in a region where theaters exist with little or no competition. This situation became another point of contention for exhibitors who claimed that exorbitant individual film costs have seemed more oppressive than block booking.

Only a few years after the Supreme Court case, the exhibitors petitioned the government to lift the ban on block booking and allow the practice to continue on a modified, regulated basis. But the Department of Justice continued to uphold the anti-block booking laws in full force. Occasional block booking outbreaks have made the news over the years when distributors overstepped their bounds.

In 1978 a federal grand jury in New York City indicted Twentieth Century-Fox for allegedly block booking some of its less-desirable films with the mega-hit *Star Wars* (1977). After a fine was imposed against Fox, the distributor promised to strengthen internal compliance procedures. Then in 1988, the aggressive selling methods of a Fox general manager brought additional fines to the studio for block booking several features in the mid-1980s. When Twentieth Century-Fox attempted to appeal the guilty verdict in 1990, the Supreme Court denied a hearing for the case.

THE GOVERNMENT WAS NOT as vigilant in defending against vertical integration, and has allowed the major distributors to return to exhibition in varying degrees. Most of the former major studios eventually found ways to reenter the exhibition business when theater-owning restrictions were relaxed in the 1980s.

The Paramount Theatres went through one such transformation that brought the remnants of the old chain back to the major studios. ABC Broadcasting decided to get out of the theater business in the 1970s, and sold off United Paramount to several separate buyers. In 1974 a high-ranking ABC-Paramount manager Henry Plitt purchased the northern tier of the circuit, which he renamed the Plitt Theatres. The Plitt chain later became part of the Cineplex Odeon Corporation. In 1986, Universal Studios Inc. purchased 49 percent of Cineplex Odeon.

Around 1985, years after Loew's Inc. was forced to sell Metro-Goldwyn-Mayer, the Loews Theatre chain was purchased by TriStar Pictures, the new studio formed by Columbia, CBS, and Home Box Office in 1983. TriStar subsequently merged with Columbia Pictures Entertainment to became the media arm of the soft-drink conglomerate, the Coca-Cola Company. In 1989 Coca-Cola sold Columbia Pictures Entertainment, along with its 1,000-screen Loews chain, to the Sony Corporation. When Loews and Cineplex Odeon merged in 1998, with over 2,700 combined screens, 51 percent of the chain was owned by Sony Pictures Entertainment and 26 percent by Universal.

Twentieth Century-Fox's former theater division, the National Theatres went through several owners, and even produced its own films for a time. The circuit became known as the Mann Theatres when Ted Mann, the husband of former Selznick contract performer Rhonda Fleming, took over the National General Corporation, and continued to produce and exhibit pictures. In 1973 he also acquired the legendary Grauman's Chinese Theatre, which he renamed Mann's Chinese. In 1986, Warner Bros. and Paramount became joint owners of Cinamerica Limited Partnership, the parent company of Mann Theatres and Festival Theaters in the west, and Trans-Lux Theatres in the east.

Even after Paramount Pictures was taken over by Gulf+Western and was transformed into Paramount Communications, the media giant still operated Famous Players Ltd., the formidable Canadian theater chain. Paramount also came in close contact with National Amusements, one of the largest privately-held movie circuits in the country, which controlled Viacom Inc. In 1994, Viacom purchased Paramount Communications, creating one of the premiere entertainment conglomerates in the world.

The Disney studio, after it went on to become a major distributor, also got involved in the theater business. SIMPP producer Sol Lesser sold his independent theater chain Principle Theatres in 1959 to the Pacific Drive-In Theatres Corp., which decided to use the Principle movie houses to expand into four-wall theaters. Pacific Theatres affiliated itself with several historic landmarks including the Cinerama Dome in Hollywood. In the late 1980s, the chain also became closely associated with the Walt Disney Company, which bought a controlling interest in part of the Pacific circuit. Pacific screens like the El Capitan, a former Paramount movie palace across the street from Grauman's Chinese Theatre, and the Crest, an art deco style prestige movie house in the Westwood Village district of Los Angles, were purchased by Disney to serve as flagship theaters for Disney's new road-show releases.

During the 1990s when telecommunications and entertainment legislation deregulated the major media companies, it seemed ludicrous to prohibit theater ownership since the main motion picture studios already had broad holdings in everything from broadcasting to publishing. As the massive scope of the major studios enlarged, the theaters continued to play an important role in the new media age. For those who predicted the demise of theaters at the hand of television (and then later with home video), theater exhibition has surprisingly remained at the forefront of the motion picture economic ladder.

In the same manner that the theaters once had numerous runs from first run to subsequent run, the diversification of media has allowed modern films to pass through several outlets from home video, to cable television, to network television, to syndication, etc. These runs that take a movie through other media have often been referred to as "distribution windows." So even though the subsequent-run theaters faded after the *Paramount* verdict, they were replaced by emerging ancillary markets.

As the exhibitors concentrated exclusively on first-run films, the movie theater maintained its position as the preeminent venue in which movies made their debut. Traditional theater-going has remained the trendsetting market in which the earning potential for each movie is established in a dynamic, large-screen setting. Even though a new movie stays in the theaters for a relatively short time, the film still takes months to play out through the various other media windows. Since the pattern of profitability established at the movie theater level follows every film as it travels through all of the subsequent distribution windows, it has not been a surprise that the modern Hollywood studios have been interested in getting back into the theater business.

Though the *Paramount* case rendered run-zone-clearance obsolete, the semblance of this old Hollywood studio practice remained in the new media market. In the decades following the *Paramount* verdict, when the distributors were barred from theater ownership, they readily entered the other media outlets from home video to cable television. Distributors even stipulate how long a movie will be in one window before moving on to the next—for example a six-month delay between theatrical debut and video release, then another six months or so before cable broadcast. With contracts such as these, the modern Hollywood distributors still use *clearance* in a similar manner as the old studios.

Furthermore, the modern distributors arrange output deals in which feature films are customarily sold in packages in various windows, especially television. Therefore the entertainment industry on a whole is not immune to the block booking plague that SIMPP fought to eliminate forever. Notwithstanding the fact that block booking is anathema in the theater market, the other media did not receive the same purging from the practice that had once served as the focal point of the old Hollywood studio system.

By curbing the studio control over the theaters, SIMPP inadvertently set Hollywood on a course where even larger leviathans hold dominion in the entertainment business. If upon the Society of Independent Motion Picture Producers rests a large share of the credit for instigating the independent revolution and for ending the stringent run-zone-clearance of the old studio system, then SIMPP also unintentionally propagated the next evolution of the industry's ideas about vertical integration.

18

Epilogue

DURING THE GREAT antitrust battle of the Hollywood studio era, there was a quote from a famous film industry figure which the press often reprinted. The person said, "If the business is to progress, it must advance upon the basis of free and unhampered selection of product for exhibitors, large and small, . . . by a resolute refusal to be drawn into any allied scheme, even if the results promised are of temporary benefit to themselves." The statement, however, was not from a SIMPP member or a government prosecutor. The quote came from Adolph Zukor, the titan of Paramount, who offered those words to the industry trades in October 1918 while he battled against the monopolistic threats of the First National theater combine. Yet the credibility behind Zukor's comment was erased within four months when Zukor took his own studio vertical and created his own trust-like combination.

The irony was not lost on those who opposed the Hollywood oligopoly. The Department of Justice proudly included the Zukor quote in its complaint against the *Paramount* case defendants in 1938, and the Society of Independent Motion Picture Producers borrowed it in their 1942 diatribe against block booking to reveal the arrogance and hypocrisy behind the major distributors. Furthermore it demonstrated that the monopolistic tendencies of the moguls were actually a product of their long struggle as one-time renegades.

From Sam Goldwyn, the pioneer who was a virtual cross-section of Hollywood history, to the second generation independent David O. Selznick, the SIMPP producers were a historically-minded bunch who viewed themselves as architects of a new epoch in filmmaking. This characteristic was further evident in SIMPP's public statements—like the 1947 article written by Society president Donald M. Nelson discussing the role of the independent producer in Hollywood in terms of grand historical sweep, beginning with *The Birth of a Nation* (1915) and continuing through to the Society of Independent Motion Picture Producers. The article was distributed to the main news outlets, and attracted attention in the industry even before it was published in the *Annals of the American Academy of Political and Social Sciences.*

Famed columnist Terry Ramsaye praised Nelson's essay, but sagaciously observed that the SIMPP leader neglected to address "the familiar evolutionary process, long demonstrated in the art, by which the successful independent of today becomes the major of tomorrow." Ramsaye, also a veteran producer and Hollywood historian, had chronicled the rise of the Hollywood tycoons in his voluminous *One Million and One Nights* published in 1925. In the book, he described how the founding fathers of Hollywood, Adolph Zukor, William Fox, Carl Laemmle and others, made their fortunes as independents by building on the ashes of the bloated Edison Patents Trust, which they outmaneuvered using a combination of artistic, economic, and legal means. When those early independents became moguls themselves, they simply replaced one monopoly with another, and continued the process of discriminating against the next generation of independents lead by SIMPP.

During the *Paramount* case, the Society of Independent Motion Picture Producers adhered to this pattern perfectly by rising up in opposition to the studio monopoly and prevailing against the anti-competitive menace in order to initiate a new mode of film production. But could it be said that SIMPP completed the circle by replacing the old studio system with a new form of monopoly?

The comparison of SIMPP with the former studio czars seems to break down on several key points.

To begin with, the relationship between SIMPP and the major studios was manifested in a far less adversarial manner than the outlaws who fought the Edison combine. The Patents Trust was famous for its violent enforcement of its monopoly, and the outlaws endeavored to keep as much distance as possible between themselves and the Trust. On the other hand, the SIMPP producers self-admittedly depended on the studio infrastructure for many of its fundamental services—especially distribution. Though they resented the terms the studios imposed, the independents worked within the Hollywood system to acquire talent, story properties, and financing.

In fact, many of the staunchest of independents found that their operations could not survive into the post-studio era, even though they vehemently complained that the studio system served as the greatest barrier to their independence. In particular, once David O. Selznick got his film duchy poised to enter the realm of the majors in the late 1940s, his enterprise rapidly deteriorated. The consensus among film historians was that as the movie business came out of the studio era, Selznick lost his foothold in the industry due primarily to the erosion of the inter-dependent relationship he had with old Hollywood. Similarly, by 1948 Walter Wanger was already lamenting the changes being made in post-studio era Hollywood: "There's not the old cooperation that used to exist between production, distribution and exhibition. . . . We shouldn't have to depend upon agents and lawyers and bankers and statisticians to run the business. What we need is showmen."

Even Orson Welles, one of the surrogate fathers of the modern anti-Hollywood movement, suggested that the old studio system had at least provided symbiosis for filmmakers like himself. "Hollywood died on me as soon as I got there," Welles said in 1970. "I wish to God I'd gone there sooner. It was the rise of the independents that was my ruin as a director. The old studio bosses—Jack Warner, Sam Goldwyn, Darryl Zanuck, Harry Cohn—were all friends, or friendly enemies I knew how to deal with. They offered me work. . . . I was in great shape with those boys. The minute the independents got in, I never directed another American picture except by accident. . . . I was a maverick, but the studios understood what that meant, and if there was a fight, we both enjoyed it. With an annual output of 40 pictures per studio, there would probably be room for one Orson Welles picture. But an independent is a fellow whose work is centered around his own particular gifts. In that setup, there is no place for me." Many of the SIMPP producers who clung to the past could not manage in the new Hollywood that they helped bring about.

With SIMPP there was another apparent breach in the historical pattern which indicated that the Hollywood renegades may not have fulfilled the model of independents becoming the new tyrants. Though unquestionably the studio system withered, the studios themselves—that is, the major distributors—did not die at the hand of the independents the same way that the Patents Trust companies had imploded during the 1910s. Put another way: the independents revolutionized the industry approach to Hollywood filmmaking, however they did not eliminate the need for effective distribution. To the credit of the old studio bosses, once the majors realized that the days of the studio system were numbered, they adapted to the new age of the independent. The moguls, recalling their own renegade roots, consciously remembered what had happened to the Edison monopoly once it became antiquated and unwilling to adapt. So the Big Eight transformed themselves. And those companies which did not, namely MGM, suffered the ruinous fate of any obsolete giant.

In an unintentional way, the industry innovations championed by SIMPP actually helped insure the continuance of the major distributors. The new blockbuster mentality of the industry, coupled with the acceptance of day-and-date theatrical releasing, required distributors to be increasingly adept or unfailingly deep-pocketed. Distribution, which had always stood as a deterrent for the producer since the early days of film, remained the critical branch of the film industry. Some independent producers formed their own distribution companies like Selznick, Wanger, and Disney, but few were able to sustain them with the consistency of product necessary in order to justify overhead expenses. Other independents like Goldwyn realized that, in order to expand their production outfits in such a manner, they would have to become more like the major studios, and thus decided to remain as producers only. So the surviving members of the former Big Eight continued to dominate distribution in the American film industry, while the independents produced about four out of every five major studio releases. Even at the end of the 1990s, the major studios, along with their various distribution labels and subsidiaries, commanded a combined market share of over 95 percent of the national box office—a figure comparable to the Hollywood oligopoly at its studio-era apogee.

Although the grand old studios were not wiped away by SIMPP, closer inspection of modern independent-based Hollywood reveals that the SIMPP members actually did begat a monopoly of sorts, as best exemplified by the one classic Hollywood independent that achieved the rank of major distributor during the 1970s and 1980s. Walt Disney Productions and its distribution arm Buena Vista struggled for many years until Walt Disney's long-term creative philosophy came to fruition in the form of a powerful multimedia corporation.

Granted, this corporate transformation of Walt Disney Productions was not realized until years after the death of Walt Disney. Nevertheless, he instituted the company ideals that enabled his successors to implement a new kind of vertical philosophy that later spread through all of the Hollywood studios. Walt Disney's innovations were not simply alterations to the studio system, but his ideas transcended the traditional Hollywood studio notions and pointed to an advanced method of building a diverse entertainment company.

Walt Disney encouraged a system of cross-promoting his projects. With television for example, he provided updates on his theme park construction, plugged his latest films, and peddled consumer products. Industry wags denounced Disney's shows as "the longest trailers ever made," and he continually drew upon recycled material. Yet each component of the Disney empire served to publicize the other, in a practice that became an overused buzzword in later Hollywood—*synergy*. For Walt Disney, the person, this came as an expression of his diverse interests: animation, live-action, theme parks, documentaries. For the rest of the industry, this became an explosive corporate philosophy where a vast number of unrelated activities became coordinated into a group that was far more valuable than its individual parts.

Of course some studios had explored the value of cross-promoting with other media years before Disney. In the early sound era, radio broadcasting was considered a viable source of new talkie talent. Likewise music publishing divisions also figured into studio strategy. However, the difference between old Hollywood's isolated attempts at synergy and that of the Disney model stemmed from the tendency of the major studios to continually return to their core business of film. Movie studio diversification generally followed the ebb and flow of the national economy, creating a cyclical pattern that restricted expansion into unrelated ventures. This resulted in mostly temporary alliances between old film studios and other media, as exemplified by the failed Paramount-CBS merger that was quashed by the Great Depression.

Rather, Disney demonstrated a new kind of enterprise where film revenue accounted for less than half of the overall company earnings; most of the income and long term stability came from television, merchandising, and of course outdoor recreation.

Notably, Walt Disney was also one of the rare producers from classic Hollywood whose films generated more revenue overseas than in the United States. (Chaplin, during the silent era, was another such filmmaker.) The reliance of the Disney company on international earnings, which contributed to the frustration of Disney's lean years during World War II, presaged the globalization of the rest of the Hollywood distributors. The *Paramount* decision forced distributors to search for new markets to recoup earnings from their increasingly expensive movies. The majors enlarged their presence overseas, and courted the foreign territories until all U.S. distributors reported more earnings from overseas box office than domestic. The new paradigm naturally favored those properties which, like Disney and Chaplin in the past, had tremendous international appeal.

This suggests a historical pattern in the broadening of the industry with the rise of each independent movement. In the previous upheaval lead by W. W. Hodkinson, he and the other outlaws like Adolph Zukor and William Fox took film from its regional states-rights origin favored by the Edison Trust, and moved the industry into a nationwide program with a coast-to-coast distribution network. Likewise, following the SIMPP success against the studios, Disney and the new independent Hollywood shifted the focus of the entertainment industry from its domestic national agenda into an international one, where worldwide integration became the name of the game.

In time, the Disney formula became a road-map for the makeup of the modern media company in which film was merely one element—albeit a very significant part—of a broad-based corporation that integrated movies with television, radio, cable broadcasting, publishing, music recording, home video, travel, sport franchises, retail stores, and the internet. In this regard, it seemed appropriate that when the Society of Independent Motion Picture Producers folded in the late 1950s, the organization's legacy was absorbed by the Disney enterprise.

In Walt Disney the grand historical pattern embodied by SIMPP has been fulfilled. He was a trendsetting filmmaker in the 1930s who became a Hollywood renegade in the 1940s. His company Walt Disney Productions redefined industry practice, and then its successor the Walt Disney Company, as it was renamed in 1986, assumed its position among the industry giants. Although the predatory corporate agenda of the modern Disney company has brought controversy from the public and provoked indignation from Walt Disney preservationists, the Disney studio has become a key player in recent show business history by creating one of the most complete vertical entertainment companies ever seen.

It is fitting that such an entity would emerge from the ranks of the independent producers of classic Hollywood—that, though the

Society itself and many of its members faded, their influence has lived on. Of course the Disney studio is not alone, but existing among the reorganized survivors of the former Big Eight. Like the old Hollywood studios, the new media conglomerates are both occasional partners and direct competitors in an industry of diverse corporate holdings. As with past independent movements, the Hollywood renegades' struggle against the Big Eight monopoly has resulted in a new multimedia cartel that continues to expanded as the modern movie titans leapfrog one another to maintain an entertainment operation that has dwarfed the old studio system.

APPENDIX

Acknowledgments
and Author's Note

Most of the founding members of the Society of Independent Motion Picture Producers were self-admitted packrats who kept volumes of documentary material. A famous Sam Goldwyn malapropism came from such an alleged incident where a Goldwyn bookkeeper asked the producer for permission to destroy some original studio documents to clear much-needed space. Goldwyn agreed, but added with further instructions: "Just be sure to keep a copy of everything." Likewise the biographies of the SIMPP members are replete with incidents that show the attentiveness that many of the independent producers paid in respect to their historical collections—from Charlie Chaplin's instructions to his studio to save his film out-takes, to Mary Pickford's eagerness in repurchasing the rights to her early films, to Walt Disney's extensive collection of personal and business-related documents.

In spite of this, however, modern historians of the Society of Independent Motion Picture Producers have had to overcome several research limitations. Some of the personal materials of the members, after they were collected religiously for years, no longer exist, as with the Alexander Korda papers that were destroyed shortly after his death. SIMPP president Ellis Arnall had his personal collection burned some time after his gubernatorial administration to avoid supposed political entanglements. A large portion of the Orson Welles collection was accidentally destroyed by fire.

Some materials are unavailable for other reasons. Despite the repeated and respectful requests from the author to gain access to the Disney studios collection of SIMPP material, the Walt Disney Archives has been unable to permit any public viewing of the SIMPP papers which have all fallen into the legal collection of the Walt Disney Company.

Fortunately, a large amount of SIMPP material exists in other collections. In

1972, the Walt Disney Archives donated part of the SIMPP collection, most of which were duplicates from the Disney papers, to the American Film Institute, which subsequently passed them on to the Academy of Motion Picture Arts and Sciences. Most of these papers dealt with the *United Detroit* lawsuit, and these duplicates formed the basis of the *SIMPP v. United Detroit* collection currently part of the Margaret Herrick Library at the Motion Picture Academy in Beverly Hills. The collection includes the valuable depositions of several key participants. Unfortunately, the material does not contain any of the papers dealing expressly with Walt Disney at the lawsuit, including his own deposition. The Walt Disney SIMPP documents, according to correspondence between the Disney archivist, AFI, and the Academy, were retained by the Disney Studio in Burbank. A more complete record of the *United Detroit* case, available at the National Archives in Chicago, was inspected by the author, and referenced liberally in chapters 14 and 15. However, the official court records do not contain a number of desirable documents such as the Disney deposition either.

Other independent producers kept SIMPP materials as part of their papers. An extensive collection pertaining to SIMPP is housed in the David O. Selznick Collection in Texas. And the Walter Wanger papers at the Wisconsin State Historical Society contain a comprehensive history of the Society that includes official SIMPP announcements, meeting notes, and press releases. Also, though not as significantly, there are a number of folders in the Mary Pickford Collection at the Margaret Herrick Library that contain correspondence between Pickford and the Society.

The author acknowledges special thanks to the following who provided a helping hand during the years of research for this book: Scott Curtis, Faye Thompson, and the Margaret Herrick Library staff at the Academy of Motion Picture Arts and Sciences; Dave Smith of the Walt Disney Archives; Becky Cape and Julia Simic from the Lilly Library, Indiana University; Steve Wilson at the University of Texas; and Dee Anna Grimsrud at the State Historical Society of Wisconsin.

THE REDISCOVERY OF the Society of Independent Motion Picture Producers has been sporadic. In the 1970s a few writers and journalists began to take note of the Society after its inactivity in the late 1950s had obscured SIMPP's influence on film history. In December 1976, Thomas M. Pryor, the veteran entertainment reporter who chronicled the earliest exploits of SIMPP for the *New York Times* back in the days of the UMPI in 1942, wrote a *Daily Variety* editorial on independent production that mentioned SIMPP and its illustrious roster of members who were unable to form a cohesive unit after the success in the *Paramount* case took away their unity of purpose. When the Pryor article was published, the industry was then in the first stage of a new wave of independent companies lead by the film-school generation that would profoundly effect modern Hollywood—among the most prominent were Francis Ford Coppola's American Zoetrope, George Lucas' Lucasfilm, and Steven Spielberg's Amblin. Pryor agreed that an independent organization seemed good ideally, but that since SIMPP had helped make independent production the industry norm, a set of reasons and concrete purposes for such an association would be necessary to avoid the same demise that SIMPP faced.

That same year, Arthur Marx wrote about the Society of Independent Motion Picture Producers in his book, *Goldwyn: A Biography of the Man Behind the Myth*. Marx's mention of the Society was brief but engaging, and set the stage for A. Scott Berg's elaboration on SIMPP in *Goldwyn: A Biography*. Later, Marc Eliot brought up the Society of Independent Motion Picture Producers in *Walt Disney: Hollywood's Dark Prince*, but unfortunately several inaccuracies in the Eliot work (which put SIMPP's founding in 1938 instead of 1942 and mixed up the *Paramount* case with the *United Detroit* lawsuit) diminished the scholarly value of the book. In 1998, Bob Thomas' biography of Roy Disney, *Building a Company: Roy O. Disney and the Creation of an Entertainment Empire*, briefly discussed the role that SIMPP played in the end of the studio system, and mentioned Roy Disney's activity in the group.

Hollywood Renegades—the most complete chronicle of the Society of Independent Motion Picture Producers yet written—has been prepared by the author with the hope that this book will provide a springboard for future research dealing with the independent producers' struggle to bring the classic Hollywood studio system to an end. The citations that follow have been provided in a comprehensive manner, though the source material has been consolidated in an effort to avoid endnote over-citation. A more expansive version of the author's research notes have been published to the Cobblestone Entertainment website located at *http://www.cobbles.com*. All readers are encouraged to reference the on-line database for additional information. The author welcomes all correspondence and questions via the same web address.

JAA

ABBREVIATIONS

AMPAS	Academy of Motion Picture Arts and Sciences: Margaret Herrick Library, Beverly Hills, California.
DOSC	David O. Selznick Collection: University of Texas, Austin, Texas.
DV	*Daily Variety*
HR	*Hollywood Reporter*
LAT	*Los Angeles Times*
MPC	Mary Pickford Collection: AMPAS.
MPH	*Motion Picture Herald*
NARA	National Archives and Records Administration: Great Lakes Region, Chicago.
NYT	*New York Times*
WDA	Walt Disney Archives, Burbank, California.
WWP	Walter F. Wanger Papers: Wisconsin State Historical Society, Madison.

Notes and Sources

Chapter 1: Introduction

Hollywood studio control of 95 percent of film industry: Big Five, 73 percent; Little Three, 22 percent. Conant, *Antitrust in the Motion Picture Industry*, p. 44.

"There are two kinds": Berg, *Goldwyn*, p. 108.

"It is my opinion": David O. Selznick to John Wharton and John Hay Whitney; Behlmer, *Memo From David O. Selznick*, p. 100.

"I can't afford": Kulik, *Alexander Korda*, p. 224.

In 1939, it is worthy to note, the four mentioned studio-made films *The Wizard of Oz*, *Mr. Smith Goes to Washington*, *Union Pacific*, and *Dark Victory* were all produced by former or future independents who, at the time, were under studio contract—respectively Mervyn Le Roy, Frank Capra, Cecil B. DeMille, and Hal B. Wallis.

Wanger quote—"an independent producer is someone dependent upon the banks, the trade press, the lay press, the radio critics, the theatre men, distributors and, lastly, upon the public": Walter Wanger, "Mr. Wanger on the Stand: The Prominent Producer Has His Say About American and Foreign Films," *NYT*, May 15, 1938, sec. X, p. 4.

The Big Five controlled 2,600 theaters (about 16 percent of the domestic theaters) with 126 of the 163 first-run theaters (about 77 percent on the first-run market) in the largest 25 metropolitan areas: Huettig, *Economic Control of the Motion Picture Industry*, pp. 6, 77.

Independent financing contingent upon a Big Eight distribution agreement: Donald M. Nelson, "The Independent Producer," *The Annals of the American Academy of Political and Social Sciences*, 254 (November 1947), p. 49.

U.S. Justice Department initiates the Paramount suit; "divest themselves of all interest": "Big Film Concerns

273

Accused In U.S. Suit of Acting As Trust," *NYT*, July 21, 1938, p. 1.

Chapter 2: "Bust the Trust—Go Independent"

"Bust the Trust": slogan popularized in 1909 by the defectors from the Motion Picture Patents Company; see Bowser, *The Transformation of Cinema*, p. 73, and Dick, *City of Dreams*, p. 22.

Information on the Motion Picture Patents Company, General Film Company, and Motion Picture Distributing and Sales Company from Bowser, pp. 27-36, 79-85, 221; Lahue, *Dreams for Sale*, pp. 19- 22; Stanley, *The Celluloid Empire*, pp. 12-18; Hampton, *History of the American Film Industry*, pp. 64- 82; Jacobs, *The Rise of the American Film*, pp. 81-94, and Ramsaye, *A Million and One Nights*, pp. 526- 527.

"Is the independent market controlled by a trust too?" Revier Film trade advertisement protesting the Sales Company: *Moving Picture World*, January 7, 1911, p. 55.

Collapse of Triangle—Zukor outlines his plans for the former Triangle contract talent: Adolph Zukor to Jesse L. Lasky, telegram, June 26, 1917, Cecil B. DeMille Archives, Harold B. Lee Library, Brigham Young University, Provo, Utah.

Hodkinson business material taken from W. W. Hodkinson, *Memorandum To Mr. George Seaton, President Academy of Motion Picture Arts and Sciences*, March 5, 1958, AMPAS: including some personal history, *Plan For Adjusting Rental of Licensed Film in San Francisco, California*, dated

April 1911 (p. 1), and "predicting, in one chart . . ." and "knowing that it would . . ." (p. 2).

Paramount history: Hodkinson, *Memorandum*, pp. 2-6; *Federal Trade Commission Decisions, November 5, 1926 to January 29, 1928, Volume XI*, United States Government Printing Office, Washington, D.C., 1930, pp. 193-208; Irwin, *The House That Shadows Built*, pp. 209-221; Zukor, *The Public Is Never Wrong*, pp. 124-126, 176-181.

Zukor opposes Hodkinson—"I did not believe that distributors ought to control production.": Zukor, p. 125; "The man has ice in his veins": Lasky, *I Blow My Own Horn*, p. 124.

Lasky described the events of the takeover of Paramount in a series of letters to DeMille in 1916. Between April and July, the merger discussions were tenuous, and the plans were canceled as late as June before they were resumed again: Jesse L. Lasky to Cecil B. DeMille, June 9, 1916, pp. 2-3; Jesse L. Lasky to Cecil B. DeMille, June 20, 1916, p. 1. Cecil B. DeMille Archives, Harold B. Lee Library, Brigham Young University, Provo, Utah.

Hodkinson after Paramount: "William W. Hodkinson - Born: Independence, Kansas - August 16, 1881," oral history (unpublished), AMPAS; "Hodkinson Re-Enters Picture Field with Distributing Co.," *Dramatic Mirror*, November 3, 1917, p. 14; "Hodkinson Has Plan 'To Save' the Movies," *NYT*, July 14, 1932, p. 24; "W. W. Hodkinson, 90" (obituary), *Variety*, June 9, 1971; Lahue, *Dreams For Sale*, pp. 150-168.

Conant, *Antitrust in the Motion*

Picture Industry, p. 22, attributes Zukor with the origination of the A-pictures, B-picture, etc. classification of films. Early block booking involving Chaplin films at Essanay: Conant, p. 8. Laemmle had a similar film scale, instead of A-pictures, B-pictures, and so on—Jewels (later called Super Jewels), Bluebirds, and lastly Red Feathers (later Butterflies): see Dick, pp. 46-47.

Formation of First National and battle with Zukor: Hampton, *History of the American Film Industry*, pp. 170-196. Koszarski, *An Evening's Entertainment*, pp. 72-77; Pickford, *Sunshine and Shadow*, pp. 185-189.

Paramount-First National alleged merger and the formation of United Artists: Balio, *United Artists: The Company Built by the Stars*, pp. 11-24; Chaplin, *My Autobiography*, pp. 219-226; Pickford, p. 110-116. "We also think that", *Moving Picture World*, February 1, 1919, p. 619, also quoted in Balio, p. 13.

Zukor claims that he was "laughed at" by exhibitors when he threatened to move Paramount into the theater business: Adolph Zukor, "Origin and Growth of the Industry," from Kennedy, *The Story of the Films*, p. 71.

Zukor theater-buying and Paramount corporate policy: *Federal Trade Commission Decisions* (1930), pp. 205-208; Zukor, p. 238. The five states without Paramount theaters included Delaware, Montana, Wyoming, Washington, and Oregon: Gomery, *The Hollywood Studio System*, pp. 28-29, 34.

"Adolph Zukor had now": Irwin, *The House That Shadows Built*, pp. 279-282.

United Artists Studio lot: Carey, *Doug and Mary*, p. 90.

United Artists Theatre Circuit and the battle with Fox West Coast: "Movie Stars Fight Fox Chain in West," *NYT*, November 7, 1930, p. 32; "Fox Replies to Artists," *NYT*, November 8, 1930, pp. 8; also see Balio, pp. 64-65, 113.

Chaplin quote "for the purpose of": Balio, p. 196.

"I shall devote my life": William Fox, "Reminiscences and Observations," from Kennedy, *The Story of the Films*, p. 317. *Time* magazine called William Fox the new Zukor: "Greatest Film Man," *Time*, April 8, 1929.

Paramount and Warners merger: "Unite $200,000,000 in Movie Merger," *NYT*, October 10, 1928, p. 31; "$400,000,000 Union In Movies Reported," *NYT*, August 20, 1929, p. 16; "Paramount Plans Race With Radio," *NYT*, August 21, 1929, p. 36; "Paramount Deal With Warner Pends," *NYT*, September 26, 1929, p. 35.

Movie attendance 1929—"Long lines waiting to gain admission are usual sights at the entrances of the more important talkie and movie theatres." See "Vast Movie Crowds Key To Prosperity," *NYT*, August 18, 1929.

Paramount troubles 1930-1933: "Paramount," *Fortune*, 15 (March 1937), pp. 86-212. Profit/loss figures: Finler, *The Hollywood Story*, p. 151.

The erstwhile "Big Three" as predicted by the *New York Times*: "Contest To Divide Amusement Field," *NYT*, September 22, 1929, sec. II, p. 14.

Fox and Twentieth Century merger: Allvine, *The Greatest Fox of Them All*, pp. 149-154; Gomery, pp. 86-88, 178-179; Balio, pp. 118-130.

For more information on unit and

independent production during the Depression see Bordwell, Bordwell, Staiger, and Thompson, *The Classical Hollywood Cinema*, pp. 316-330. For additional background and insight on this subject the author recommends: Schatz, *The Genius of the System*.

"Pictures lose their individuality": Bernstein, *Walter Wanger, Hollywood Independent*, p. 94.

Capra's anti-block booking deal: "Frank Capra" *Boxoffice*, November 15, 1935.

Capra's views on unit-production—see Frank Capra, "By Post From Mr. Capra," *NYT*, April 2, 1939, sec. X, p. 4. Article excerpt available online at *The SIMPP Research Database:* <http://www.simpp.com>.

Goldwyn deal with RKO for 17.5 percent distribution fee worldwide: "Hollywood Inside," *DV*, January 26, 1942, p. 2.

For more information on the major studios accepting independent deals see Douglas W. Churchill, "Unit Production on the Rise," *NYT*, April 21, 1940, sec. IX, p. 9.

Chapter 3: Box Office Poison

Block booking information is discussed in several important published sources that prove variously concise and comprehensive, including Conant, *Antitrust in the Motion Picture Industry*; Huettig, *Economic Control of the Motion Picture Industry*; of particular interest is the detailed study: Benjamin Werne, "The Neely Anti-Block Booking and Blind Selling Bill—An Analysis," *Contemporary Law Pamphlets*, Series 6, Number 1, New York University of Law, New York, 1940.

Hodkinson's views on block booking: W. W. Hodkinson, *Memorandum To Mr. George Seaton, President Academy of Motion Picture Arts and Sciences*, March 5, 1958, p. 3, AMPAS.

Federal Trade Commission investigation of Paramount and block booking: *Federal Trade Commission Decisions, November 5, 1926 to January 29, 1928, Volume XI*, United States Government Printing Office, Washington, D.C., 1930, pp. 193-208; "Government Sues Film Distributors," *NYT*, April 28, 1928, p. 4; "Paramount Enters Denial," *NYT*, May 9, 1928, p. 3; Middleton, New York: "$5,130,000 Damages Asked In Film Suit," *NYT*, November 25, 1930, p. 22; Paramount compliance rejected: "Rejects Film Plea on Block Booking," *NYT*, May 8, 1928, p. 30.

Film Boards of Trade and the film arbitration system: "Film Arbitration Praised," *NYT*, April 30, 1928; "Film Arbitration Is Praised By Hays," *NYT*, June 6, 1928, p. 11; "Producers Defend Film Arbitration," *NYT*, June 21, 1928, p. 29; "Government Sues Film Distributors," *NYT*, April 28, 1928, p. 4.

Famous Players-Lasky antitrust case: Associated Press, "Will Ask Court Order To Stop Block Booking," *NYT*, May 15, 1928, p. 2; "Government Rests Second Film Suit," *NYT*, March 15, 1929, p. 25; "Anti-trust Decree Filed in Film Suit," *NYT* January 23, 1930, p. 20; "Government Appeals Movie Film Case," *NYT*, April 30, 1930, p. 28; "Movies in a Trust High Court Finds," *NYT*, November 25, 1930, pp. 1, 22; *Paramount Famous*

Lasky Corporation et al v. United States, 282 U.S. 30 (1930); *United States v. First National Pictures, Inc., et al,* 282 U.S. 44 (1930). The ten defendants were Paramount-Famous-Lasky Corporation, First National Pictures Inc., Metro-Goldwyn-Mayer Distributing Corporation, Universal Film Exchanges Inc., United Artists Corporation, Fox Film Corporation, Pathé Exchange, Inc., FBO Pictures Corporation, Vitagraph, Inc., and Educational Film Exchanges, Inc.

Hollywood and the NIRA: Balio, *United Artists: The Company Built by the Stars,* pp. 96-104; Schatz, *Genius of the System,* pp. 159-161.

Cancellation privilege discussed in Benjamin Werne, "The Neely Anti-Block Booking and Blind Selling Bill—An Analysis," pp. 10-12.

Legion of Decency and civic opposition to block booking: Balio, *Grand Design,* pp. 59-69; also mentioned in French, *The Movie Moguls,* p. 79. Pickford's comments: Mary Pickford, "The Big Bad Wolf Has Been Muzzled," from *HR,* circa 1934, reprinted in Wilkerson and Borie, *The Hollywood Reporter, the Golden Years,* pp. 234-236.

Coalition of 35 groups at a conference called by former First Lady Grace Goodhue Coolidge—complete list of conference participants available at *The SIMPP Research Database:* <http://www.simpp.com>. See also "35 Groups To Fight Blind Film Booking," *NYT,* October 5, 1934, p. 29.

Anti-Block Booking and Blind Selling Bill: H. R. 6472 [1935] by Cong. Pettengill (Ind.); S. 3012 [1935] by Sen. Neely (W. Va.); S. 153 [1937] by Sen. Neely (W. Va.); H. R. 1669 [1937] by Cong. Pettengill (Ind.); S. 280 [1939] by Sen. Neely (W. Va.); Benjamin Werne, "The Neely Anti-Block Booking and Blind Selling Bill—An Analysis," *Contemporary Law Pamphlets*; Senate Report on S. 280, 76th Congress, 1st Session, U.S. Government Printing Office, 1939.

Selznick quote from statement of C. C. Pettijohn, in opposition to H. R. 6472, Before the Sub-Committee on Interstate Commerce, 7th Congress, 2nd Session, 1936, p. 7.

P. S. Harrington, "Give the Movie Exhibitor A Chance," *The Christian Century,* June 1935, p. 819; C. C. Pettijohn, "What Price Neely Bill?", talk given before Associated Motion Picture Advertisers at New York City, December 14, 1939.

Matthew M. Neely, State Papers and Public Addresses, Charleston, West Virginia, 1948; Samuel Barret Pettengill, *My Story,* privately published by Helen M. Pettengill, Grafton, Vermont, 1979.

Congress and block booking: "Sample Letter For Actors and Actresses" (1939), AMPAS block booking file; Associated Press (Untitled), *NYT,* April 4, 1939, p. 29; "Gives Movie Booking Plan," *NYT,* April 5, 1939, p. 31; "Kent Backs 'Right' of Block Booking," *NYT,* April 7, 1939, p. 25; "Report Approves Neely Movie Bill," *NYT,* June 4, 1939, p. 17; "Senate Votes Ban on 'Block-Booking'," *NYT,* July 18, 1939, p. 14; Thomas M. Prior, "Some Arguments Pro and Con the Neely Bill," *NYT,* January 14, 1940, sec. IX, p. 5; "Senator Neely Rides Again," *NYT,* April 21, 1940, sec. IX, p. 4; "Denounces Movie Bill," *NYT,* May

28, 1940, p. 29; "unworkable": "Neely Bill Definitely Dead," *HR*, June 6, 1940, p. 1.

Chapter 4: Hollywood Trust

"A railroad receivership" and the reorganization of Paramount: "Paramount," *Fortune*, 15 (March 1937), p. 87. More information on Paramount holdings given in Gomery, *The Hollywood Studio System*, p. 33.

Studio-owned theater chains divide the country into regional monopolies: see Conant, *Antitrust in the Motion Picture Industry*, pp. 51-52; Huettig, *Economic Control of the Motion Picture Industry*, pp. 74-84, Gomery, pp. 13, 29, 58, 85; and United Press, "Clark Asks Court End 'Monopoly' in Films," *NYT*, February 10, 1948, p. 26.

During the late 1930s, the average Paramount ownership in the theaters the studio controlled was 70 percent: "Paramount," *Fortune*, p. 208.

Theater pooling and Paramount-RKO pool in Minnesota: Conant, pp. 52, 62-64.

Definitions of "open" and "closed" situations: "Paramount," *Fortune*, p. 211.

Hollywood in slump 1938: *Variety*, December 14, 1938.

"Everywhere I go": Thomas M. Prior, "Uncle Carl Speaks As He Pleases," *NYT*, September 4, 1938, sec. X, p. 3.

"Also, there was a period": Bosley Crowther, "In the Opinion of Mr. Schenck," *NYT*, September 11, 1938, sec. X, p. 3.

Profits decline for Big Eight: "47% Decline Shown In Picture Profits," *NYT*, June 12, 1938, sec. III, p. 1.

Justice Department initiates the *Paramount* suit: *United States v. Paramount Pictures, Inc. et al*, 334 U.S. 131 (1948); "The independent producer": *United States v. Paramount*, petition filed July 20, 1938, p. 71; "Big Film Concerns Accused In U.S. Suit of Acting As Trust," *NYT*, July 21, 1938, p. 1; "Govt. Files Anti-Trust Action: Eight Majors, Subsidiaries, Officers, Directors, Named In Justice Dept. N. Y. Bill," *HR*, July 20, 1938, p. 1; "U.S. Wallup for Film Majors," *DV*, July 20, 1938, p. 1; "Pic Stocks Down In Suit Reaction; Para. Pfd. Off $10," *HR*, July 21, 1938, p. 1: Paramount stock down $10 to $90, Loews down 3 ¾ to 52 ¼.

A complete list of the corporate and individual defendants in the case *United States v. Paramount* available at *The SIMPP Research Database*: <http://www.simpp.com>.

Sidney Kent's conciliation committee: "Film Heads Seek To Aid Exhibitors," *NYT*, June 29, 1938, p. 14; "The Statement Issued by Will Hays," *NYT*, July 21, 1938, p. 6; "Picture Industry Pushes Its Inquiry," *NYT*, July 26, 1938, p. 25; "Film Committee To Go On," *NYT*, July 25, 1938, p. 18; "Business As Usual During Altercations," *MPH*, July 30, 1938, pp. 14-15.

The three independent theater antitrust suits: *United States v. Griffith Amusement Co.*, 223 U.S. 100 (1948); *United States v. Schine Chain Theatres*, 334 U.S. 110 (1948); *United States v. Crescent Amusement Co.*, 323 U.S. 173 (1944); "Movie Chain Here Faces 'Trust' Suit," *NYT*, August 7, 1939, p. 10; Associated Press, "Schine Movie Chain Sued As Monopoly," *NYT*, August 8, 1939, p. 19; "Third Movie

Suit Is Aimed at South," *NYT*, August 11, 1939, p. 2; "Independents' Day," *Time*, May 17, 1948, p. 91; Conant, *Antitrust in the Motion Picture Industry*, pp. 88-94.

Paramount trial commencement and adjournment: "Movie Suit Comes Up For Trial Tomorrow," *NYT*, June 2, 1940, sec. III, p. 5; "Govt. Stops Anti-Trust Suit," *HR*, June 8, 1940, pp. 1, 4; "Movie Negotiations Continue," *NYT*, June 13, 1940, p. 29; Douglas W. Churchill, "Hollywood Looks For the Rainbow," *NYT*, June 16, 1940, sec. IX, p. 3.

Costs of the *Paramount* trial: "Anti-Trust Trial Starts Today: Millions Will Be Spent by Majors in Legal Battle to Dispose Charges of Govt.," *HR*, June 3, 1940, pp. 1, 3. Mentions that the heads of legal counsel alone cost an estimated $20,000 per day.

Goldwyn and the double feature: Bosley Crowther, "Double Feature Trouble," *New York Times Magazine*, July 14, 1940, pp. 8, 20: the article also mentions that about 60 percent of U.S. theaters customarily showed multiple features. Comments on *The Saturday Evening Post* article: "Goldwyn Slams Double Features in SEP Article," *HR*, July 10, 1940, p. 7. Gallup poll: "Gallup Find 57 P.C. Off Duals," *HR*, August 8, 1940, p. 1. On CBS radio: "Goldwyn In Air Debate on Duals," *HR*, August 13, 1940, p. 3.

Selznick against blind bidding: "Plan Worked Out To End Film Suit," *NYT*, August 24, 1940, p. 15. Also see "DOS Incorporates New Producing Co.," *HR*, August 8, 1940, p. 1.

Consent Decree of 1940: "Govt. Approves Basis for Decree," *HR*, June

12, 1940, pp. 1, 6; "Film Monopoly Trial Put Off," *NYT*, July 23, 1940, p. 22; "Divorcement Threat If Para. and 20th Don't Sign," *HR*, August 20, 1940, p. 1; "Plan Worked Out To End Film Suit," *NYT*, August 24, 1940, p. 15; "Exhibs' Squaks Won't Sway Decree Decision," *HR*, September 10, 1940, pp. 1, 4; "Accord Is Reached On Film Legislation," *NYT*, October 23, 1940, p. 26; Theodore Srauss, "Peace! Isn't It Wonderful," *NYT*, January 19, 1941, p. 4; *The Consent Decree: With the Interpretive Statement of the Department of Justice and Arbitration Rules With Map of Jurisdiction* (New York: Quigley Publications, 1941).

The Little Three dissent: "Decree by August 1 or Trial Goes on, Says U.S.," *HR*, July 15, 1940, pp. 1, 9.

Minnesota block booking: Thomas M. Prior, "By Way of Report," *NYT*, May 4, 1941, sec. X, p. 4; new Neely bill: "Congress Receives Big Grist of Bills," *NYT*, January 7, 1941.

"Not since the talkies came": Adela Rogers St. John, "Who Runs Hollywood Now? Consent Decree Jitters!," *Liberty*, November 29, 1941, p. 24.

Chapter 5: Unity

Paramount film surplus: Sherwin A. Kane, "Paramount Feature Total 36 To 40 For New Year," *Motion Picture Daily*, May 11, 1942, p. 1; also see "Para. to Continue Policy of Building Pic Backlog," *HR*, July 2, 1940.

Decrease in B-film production: Samuel Goldwyn, "Mr. Goldwyn Takes Up the Cudgels," *NYT*, May 3, 1942, sec. VIII, p. 4.

"The inevitable purging" (quote

from Loyd Wright): "Chaplin and Other Independents Oppose New Plan for Block Booking of Films," *NYT*, April 14, 1942, p. 16.

Higher film rentals: Huettig, *Economic Control of the Motion Picture Industry*, p. 140.

Big Five released from Schine case: "Requests Dismiss Writ," *NYT*, March 11, 1941, p. 41.

Motion Picture Industry Conference Committee, the Unity Plan, and the United Motion Picture Industry: "Industry Unity Program Looms As Film Branches Meet Today," *HR*, January 21, 1942, pp. 1, 2; "Industry Branches in Accord," *HR*, January 22, 1942, pp. 1, 8; "Anti-Trusters Report Swings Attention of Pix Unity Meet," *HR*, January 23, 1942, p. 1, 9; Thomas M. Prior, "By Way of Report," *NYT*, March 1, 1942, sec. X, p. 3; "New Sales Plan For Films Urged," *NYT*, March 4, 1942, p. 22.

Biographical information on Loyd Wright: "Loyd Wright" (obituary), *Variety*, October 30, 1974; *Los Angeles Examiner*, December 21, 1961; *LAT*, March 10, 1954.

James Allen: "Mellett Sets Allen Here," *HR*, February 4, 1942, p. 1.

SIMPP early history: *Statement of Receipts and Disbursements of Society of Independent Motion Pictures, Handled By Loyd Wright From Inception of Society To Date*, March 1, 1943, pp. 1-7, WWP.

Pre-SIMPP rumors mentioned: "Independent Producers Form an Association," *Boxoffice*, January 31, 1942.

Formation of SIMPP: Loyd Wright to Walter Wanger, telegram, December 16, 1941, WWP; "Film Producers

Form Independent Society," *NYT*, January 29, 1942, p. 24; "Indie Producers Filing Org Papers, Wright Prez," *DV*, January 29, 1942, p. 1.

Hollywood Reporter scoop: "Top Indie Producers In Setup: Organizes Away From Hayes Influence; Loyd Wright Prez, Jim Allen in Washington," *HR*, January 23, 1942, pp. 1, 4.

SIMPP opposes Unity Plan—"to consider desirability": Loyd Wright to SIMPP, telegram, March 26, 1942, WW; Loyd Wright, SIMPP, untitled, (press release), April 13, 1942, WWP; "Chaplin and Other Independents Oppose New Plan for Block Booking of Films," p. 16.

SIMPP v. UMPI: Thomas M. Prior, "In This Corner: Presenting a Three-Sided Fight Over Proposed Changes in Selling Films," *NYT*, April 19, 1942, sec. VIII, p. 4; Samuel Goldwyn, "Mr. Goldwyn Takes Up the Cudgels," p. 4.

In no known instances had a SIMPP founding member block booked a package consisting of their own features. However, early SIMPP member Hunt Stromberg reissued *Lady of Burlesque* (1943) and *The Guest in the House* (1944), sometimes as a unit, sometimes separately according to the Hunt Stromberg *United Detroit* case deposition: *The Society of Independent Motion Picture Producers, et al v. United Detroit Theatres Corp., et al*, case number 7589, District Court of the United States for the Eastern District of Michigan Southern Division, *Deposition of Hunt Stromberg*, April 8, 1949, p. 86, AMPAS.

SIMPP meeting notes April 29: John C. Flinn, May 1, 1942, WWP.

SIMPP anti-block booking: Society

of Independent Motion Picture Producers to Thurman Arnold, "Shall Block Booking of Motion Pictures Be Permitted to Return?" An Open Letter, published by SIMPP, New York, June 1, 1942.

Unity Plan makes progress: "UMPI Has New Sales System," *DV*, March 2, 1942, p. 1; "UMPI Plan Gets Tentative O.K.: Speedy Approval Is Seen," *HR*, July 9, 1942, pp. 1, 10; "Para, Warners, RKO Will See New Season Pix in 3 Blocks," *HR*, July 13, 1942, pp. 1, 4.

Goldwyn press conference July 20, 1942: "Goldwyn Blasts Trade Evils," *HR*, July 21, 1942, pp. 1, 6; "40% Cut In Films Asked by Goldwyn," *NYT*, July 21, 1942, p. 22; "Goldwyn Calls Twin Bills Unpatriotic," *NYT*, July 26, 1942, sec. VII, p. 6.

Unity Plan regress: "UMPI Sales Plan Faces Hurdles," *HR*, July 17, 1942, p. 1 (Consent Decree amendments given in full: Sections III-A, IV-A and VII); "UMPI Plan Seems Doomed," *HR* July 22, 1942, p. 1; "UMPI Handed K.O. by Arnold," *HR*, August 18, 1942, p. 1. "Am more encouraged": John Flinn to Loyd Wright, telegram, July 22, 1942, WWP.

Double-feature Gallup poll: "Public Okays Single Bill," *HR*, September 14, 1942, p. 1.

Big Five maintain block booking: "Five Majors Will Continue Blocks of 5 If UMPI Fails," *HR*, July 31, 1942, p. 1; "Metro Selling Blocks of 8," HR, August 14, 1942, p. 1; "4 Majors Continue Blocks of 5," *HR*, August 19, 1942, p. 1.

Chapter 6: Moving In

Hunt Stromberg—biographical information: "Hunt Stromberg," (press release), c. 1944, AMPAS; "Hunt Stromberg Dies at 74; Prolific Producer One of Metro's 'Big Four'," *Variety*, August 25, 1968, p. 22; Joyce Haber, "Hunt Stromberg, Ex-Movie Producer, Dies," *LAT*, August 25, 1968; "Hunt Stromberg Announces His Future Plans for Productions," *New York Morning Telegraph*, February 12, 1922, p. 2; "Bull Montana in 'A Ladies' Man," *New York Morning Telegraph*, February 26, 1922; "Booking Record for Stromberg," *New York Morning Telegraph*, April 30, 1922; "Stromberg Gets Metro Release," *DV*, February 9, 1942, p. 1; "Stromberg Resignation Made Official," *MPH*, February 14, 1942; "Stromberg With U. A." - "Stromberg Picks Veterans for His Production Staff" - "'Fame' Cites Champion Producers; Stromberg 'Firsts' Recalled," *Hollywood Film Forecast* (booklet), September 1942, pp. 1-4 AMPAS; *The Society of Independent Motion Picture Producers, et al v. United Detroit Theatres Corp., et al*, case number 7589, District Court of the United States for the Eastern District of Michigan Southern Division, *Deposition of Hunt Stromberg*, April 8, 1949, AMPAS; Schatz, *The Genius of the System*, p. 253; Eames, *The MGM Story*, p. 46, 121; French, *The Movie Moguls*, p. 52.

Organization of Hunt Stromberg Productions, Inc. given in: *The Society of Independent Motion Picture Producers, et al v. United Detroit Theatres Corp., et al*, case number 7589, District Court of the United States for the Eastern District of

Michigan Southern Division, *Deposition of Hunt Stromberg*, April 8, 1949, p.5, AMPAS. In addition to Stromberg, organizers included "Lester Roth, Lowell Calvert, and Myron Selznick who owned 70% of the stock."

James and William Cagney—biographical information from McCabe, *Cagney* and Schickel, *James Cagney*; Cagney, *Cagney by Cagney*; Goldwyn and Selznick's reluctance to hire Cagney mentioned in Schickel, p. 105; Grand National Films: Balio, *Grand Design*, p. 323; joining UA, providing financing: Balio, *United Artists: The Company Built by the Stars*, pp. 191-193.

Sol Lesser: *Biography of Sol Lesser*, AMPAS; "Sol Lesser, 90, Predated Nearly All Industry Pioneers; 117 Features," *Variety*, September 24, 1980, p. 4; "Producer Sol Lesser, 90, Movie Industry Pioneer, Dies," *LAT*, September 20, 1980, sec. II, p. 1; "Sol Lesser Busy in Chicago," *New York Morning Telegraph*, January 16, 1921; "Sol Lesser, Benedict Quit RKO," *DV*, February 2, 1942, pp. 1, 6; Hildy Crawford, "Sol Lesser: History of Films," *Palm Springs Life*, January 1965, p. 20; Essoe, *Tarzan of the Movies*, pp. 72-82; Lasky, *RKO*, pp. 166-167.

Edward Small: "Pioneer Indie Producer Edward Small, 85, Dies," *DV*, January 26, 1977, p. 1; "Small Sez Big Studios Going," *DV*, December 8, 1948; "Eddie Small Puts Up Bid His Bid for E-L," *Variety*, May 12, 1949; "Edw. Small Leaving Col for UA," *DV*, April 30, 1952, p. 1.

Edward A. Golden: "Edward Golden, Pioneer, Dies," *DV*,

September 28, 1972; "Silence Is Not a Golden Trait," *NYT*, October 31, 1943, sec. II, p. 3.

Income tax reform: Jim Marshall, "Nothing To It," *Collier's*, May 18, 1946, p. 96; Ernest Borneman, "Rebellion in Hollywood," *Harper's*, October 1946, pp. 337-339. The liquidation of Selznick International Pictures and the loss of *Gone With the Wind*: Thomson, *Showman*, pp. 379-380.

McCarey and Roach film profile: Bogdanovich, *Who the Devil Made It*, pp. 379-383; Dardis, *Harold Lloyd*, pp. 54-55; also see Maltin and Bann, *Our Gang*, pp. 10-12.

Benedict Bogeaus biographical information: Bill Peirce, Jr., "Biography: Benedict Bogeaus," (press release), c. 1946, AMPAS; "Producer Bogeaus Dies After Stroke," *Los Angeles Herald-Examiner*, August 24, 1968; UPI, "Benedict Bogeaus, 64, Is Dead; An Independent Film Producer," *NYT*, August 25, 1968; "Ben Bogeaus, 64, Dies of Heart Attack," *DV*, August 26, 1968; Thomas M. Prior, "Rags to Riches: Or the Hectic Saga of Benedict Bogeaus, Producer and Many of Many Affairs," *NYT*, November 25, 1945, sec. X, p. 3. "Bogeaus Joins U. A.," *HR*, July 24, 1942, p. 1.

"All independent producers": quoted in UPI, "Producer Bogeaus Is Dead," *Hollywood Citizen-News*, August 24, 1968.

History of the General Service Studio, now known as the Hollywood Center Studios: "The Beginning," *Hollywood Center Studios*: <http://www.hollywoodcenter.com/history>; Schumacher, *Francis Ford Coppola*, pp. 268-269; Harold Lloyd information from Dardis, *Harold Lloyd*, pp. 140-141

David L. Loew: "David L. Loew," *Variety*, March 28, 1973; *Daily Variety Tenth Anniversary Issue*, October 29, 1943; Bergan, *Jean Renoir*, pp. 249-251.

Constance Bennett: see Bennett and Kibbee, *The Bennett Playbill*.

Harry Sherman: Eyles, *The Western*, pp. 132-133.

Arnold Pressburger: Balio, *United Artists: The Company Built by the Stars*, pp. 189, 272; McGilligan, *Fritz Lang*, pp. 291-301.

Seymour Nebenzal: "Seymour Nebenzal," *DV*, September 27, 1961; "Nebenzal, 62, of Films, Dies in Berlin," *Los Angeles Examiner*, September 27, 1961; McGilligan, pp. 145-146, 173.

Andrew L. Stone: "Andrew and Virginia Stone, Biography," (press release), c. 1955, AMPAS.

Charles R. Rogers (not to be mistaken with actor-producer Buddy Rogers, the third husband of Mary Pickford): "Charles R. Rogers, Biography," (press release), September 4, 1940, AMPAS; "Injuries Fatal To Film Producer Chas. R. Rogers," *Hollywood Citizen-News*, March 30, 1957; "Charles Rogers, Producer, 64, Dies," *NYT*, March 31, 1957; "Charles R. Rogers," *DV*, April 1, 1957.

SIMPP annual dues before 1945: Loyd Wright to Walter F. Wanger, "To Membership dues," November 1, 1944, WWP.

Chapter 7: Halls and Armories

Mellett visit to Hollywood, denunciation of the double feature: Frank S. Nugent, "Double, Double, Toil and Trouble," *New York Times Magazine*, January 17, 1943, pp. 11, 21.

War time figures: Finler, *The Hollywood Story*, p. 34.

"You could run film backward" mentioned in: Jim Marshall, "Nothing To It," *Collier's*, May 18, 1946, p. 96.

"Present conditions": John C. Flinn to Loyd Wright, January 20, 1943, WWP. Also mentions the violations of the Consent Decree that have frozen first-run play dates.

Goldwyn outspoken—"The art of showmanship": Fred Stanley, "Blast At Hollywood," *NYT*, July 30, 1944, sec. II, p. 1; Theodore Strauss, "Why Keep The B's?," *NYT*, July 26, 1942, sec. X, p. 3. Goldwyn fights Florida theaters: "Goldwyn Tell Fans Via Ads Why They Can't See 'Foxes'," *HR*, January 22, 1942, p. 4. History of Sparks circuit: Dick, *City of Dreams*, p. 57. Goldwyn refuses other independent theaters: *HR*, July 24, 1944.

SIMPP discussions with Department of Justice, actions in interim: John C. Flinn to Loyd Wright, January 26, 1943, WWP; Loyd Wright to John C. Flinn, January 28, 1943, WWP.

Tom C. Clark: "Government Is Free To Move In Film Case," *NYT*, November 21, 1943, p. 27.

Walt Disney animation for *Up In Arms*: Solomon, *The Disney That Never Was*, pp. 76-77. The *Up in Arms* animation, which was believed to have been destroyed, resurfaced in a film print uncovered by the Disney company in the late 1990s.

Goldwyn at the Woods versus Balaban & Katz: Fred Stanley,

"Discord In the West," *NYT*, August 27, 1944, sec. II, p. 1.

West Coast and Balaban & Katz antitrust violations: Conant, *Antitrust in the Motion Picture Industry*, pp. 85, 105. *United States v. West Coast Theatres*, C.C.H. Trade Regulation Reports, Supp. IV, 4206, Southern District of California, 1930; *United States v. Fox West Coast Theatres*, (1932); *United States v. Balaban and Katz Corp.*, C.C.H. Trade Cases, Northern District of Illinois, 1932.

T. & D. Theatres and *Up in Arms* in Reno, Tuesday, August 22, 1944: "Goldwyn Denounces Theatre Monopoly," *HR*, August 22, 1944, pp. 1, 6; "Pickford, Disney Support Goldwyn in Monopoly Fight," *HR*, August 23, 1944, pp. 1, 3; "Goldwyn Fights Film Exhibitors," *NYT*, August 23, 1944, p. 16; "The Battle of Reno," *Time*, September 4, 1944, pp. 78, 80; also see Berg, *Goldwyn*, pp. 384-387; Marx, *Goldwyn*, pp. 301-302; Marill, *Samuel Goldwyn Presents*, p. 235.

Pickford speech: Transcription from radio station KEO, FBI report, October 19, 1944, Salt Lake City, FBI 60-86—see Trethewey, *Walt Disney: The FBI Files*, pp. 117-120.

Goldwyn speaking at *Up In Arms* opening: "Pickford, Disney, Cagneys, Welles Back Goldwyn Fight," *DV*, August 23, 1944, pp. 1, 8.

Producers threaten to show their own movies—"Movie Stars Fight Fox Chain in West," *NYT*, November 7, 1930, p. 32; "even if I had": Chaplin, *My Autobiography*, p. 393; "I'll show it in": Lasky, *RKO*, p. 165.

Welles' *Citizen Kane* fight with Fox-West Coast: Welles and Bogdanovich, *This Is Orson Welles*,

pp. 87-88, quoted from *NYT*, September 7, 1941.

Goldwyn and Selznick with the Astor Theatre: *The Society of Independent Motion Picture Producers, et al v. United Detroit Theatres Corp., et al*, case number 7589, District Court of the United States for the Eastern District of Michigan Southern Division, *Deposition of David O. Selznick*, April 28, 1949, pp. 45-48, AMPAS.

FBI investigation of T. & D.: Office memorandum from A. Rosen, FBI 60-3020, November 4, 1944; see Trethewey, *Walt Disney: The FBI Files*, pp. 123-124.

"The reason the picture": "Goldwyn Fights Film Exhibitors," p. 16.

SIMPP objects to new consent decree 1944: Tom C. Clark to Loyd Wright, January 28, 1944, WWP; John C. Flinn to Loyd Wright, February 3, 1944, WWP.

"As long as the independents": Assistant Attorney General Wendell Berge from press release quoted in A. Rosen, FBI 60-3020; see Trethewey, p. 123.

Department of Justice reactivates the *Paramount* case: Department of Justice (press release), August 7, 1944, pp. 1-5, WWP; "Govt. Readying Anti-Trust Case," *HR*, August 7, 1944, pp. 1-2; "U.S. Renews Battle On Film Monopolies," *NYT*, August 8, 1944, p. 15.

Chapter 8: Of Merit Instead of Power

MPPDA Title Registration Bureau: John C. Flinn to Walter Wanger, March 19, 1943, WWP; Will H. Hays to John

C. Flinn, May 21, 1943, WWP; John C. Flinn to Walter F. Wanger, May 27, 1943, WWP; John C. Flinn to Walter F. Wanger, February 29, 1944, WWP; Chaplin, *My Autobiography*, pp. 391-392.

"That the matter of a free screen": Fred Stanley, "Hollywood (Dis)Unity," *NYT*, June 24, 1945, sec. III, p. 3.

Near resignation of UA from MPPDA: John C. Flinn to Mary Pickford—see John C. Flinn to Grad Sears, September 25, 1944, WWP; UA and Bagnall join SIMPP: Loyd Wright and John C. Flinn to SIMPP producers, January 8, 1945, pp. 1-4, WWP.

Death of John Flinn: Mary Pickford to Courtney A. Flinn, 1946, MPC.

James A. Mulvey biographical information: "Mulvey Luncheon Marks 30 Years With Goldwyn," *MPH*, April 25, 1953; "James A. Mulvey, Retired Goldwyn Co. Prez, Dies in Fla.," *DV*, December 4, 1973, pp. 1, 9; Thomas M. Prior, "James Mulvey, 74, Dies In Fla., Goldwyn Partner & Litigant," *Variety*, December 5, 1973, pp. 4, 28.

Gunther R. Lessing biographical information: "Gunther Lessing" (obituary), *LAT*, September 29, 1965; *DV*, September 29, 1965, p. 11; *HR*, December 30, 1964.

"The only Mister we": Thomas, *Walt Disney*, p. 191.

Lessing and Pancho Villa: Brownlow, *The Parade's Gone By*, p. 18.

Lessing credited with the "Walt Disney" trademark idea: Tytle, *One of "Walt's Boys,"* p. 74.

The Disney Studio Strike of 1941—Lessing on the Short Subjects Committee: Shale, *Donald Duck Joins Up*, p. 41. Animator Ward Kimball's statement "Lessing died an outcast, of old age, a broken-hearted old man": see R. Fiore and Klaus Strzyz, "The Disney Strike From Inside and Out," *The Comics Journal*, 120 (March 1988), pp. 74-96. Also see Thomas, *Building a Company*, pp. 219-220 for Disney loyalty to Lessing in his later years.

SIMPP finances 1946: *Financial Status of Society of Independent Motion Picture Producers As of Dec. 31, 1946*, WWP.

SIMPP dues and membership requirements: *By-laws of The Society of Independent Motion Picture Producers As Unanimously Approved By the Executive Committee, August 28, 1945*, pp. 11, 14, WWP.

New SIMPP members 1945: John C. Flinn to Walter Wanger, telegram, April 29, 1945, WWP; "Donald Nelson in Film Post," *Los Angeles Examiner*, June 13, 1945.

Annual production $40 million, SIMPP first organization to rival MPPDA: Stanley, "Hollywood (Dis)Unity," p. 1; "Film Market Hampered By U.S. Edict, Nelson Says," *Hollywood Citizen-News*, January 10, 1947.

The *Crescent* case—"while the Supreme Court": Loyd Wright and John C. Flinn to SIMPP, January 8, 1945, WWP; "somewhere in the background": *United States v. Crescent Amusement Co., et al*, 323 U.S. 173 (1944); also John C. Flinn to Loyd Wright, November 4, 1943, p. 3, John C. Flinn to Eric Cleugh, December 28, 1944, and John C. Flinn to Walter Wanger, June 7, 1945, WWP.

New York Equity Suit: "Film Quality Tied To Theatre Chains," *NYT*, October 10, 1945; "Zukor Denies Film Pact," *NYT*, October 24, 1945, p. 23; *HR*, October 24, 1945, pp. 1, 10; "5 Movie Producers To Retain Theatres," *NYT*, June 12, 1946, p. 29; results of the trail recounted in *Film Daily Yearbook 1947*, p. 41 and briefly in Mast, *The Movies in Our Midst*, pp. 596-598.

SIMPP reaction: Joe Alvin, *Public Relations*, letter to SIMPP, January 9, 1947, pp. 1-5, "Film Market Hampered By U.S. Edict, Nelson Says," *Hollywood-Citizen News*, January 10, 1947.

Chapter 9: New Blood

Goldwyn and Wanger denounce the Hollywood studio system before the press on November 18, 1946: "Goldwyn and Wanger Agree Hollywood Films Are Lagging," *HR*, November 19, 1946, pp. 1, 16; "Goldwyn Decries Heavy Production," *NYT*, November 19, 1946, p. 41.

"Clutching the banner of": Ernest Borneman, "Rebellion in Hollywood," *Harper's*, October 1946, p. 337.

SIMPP membership rise and decline: "Top Indies to Spend $88,950,000," *HR*, June 9, 1947, pp. 1, 7; William R. Weaver, "Produce More For Less: Nelson," *MPH*, May 17, 1947, p. 29; additional membership figures in *Film Daily Yearbook 1949*.

Frank Capra information: Capra, *The Name Above the Title*, pp. 214-219, 290-308; McBride, *Frank Capra: The Catastrophe of Success*, pp. 269-273, 427-443; Balio, *United Artists: The Company Built by the Stars*, pp.

176-177, 181-183.

Capra-McCarey plans—"couldn't see eye to eye": Bogdanovich, *Who the Devil Made It*, p.389. McCarey's statement seems to suggest that he and Capra planned to form a company together shortly before McCarey organized Rainbow in 1944. However, it is also likely that McCarey referred to a prewar Capra-McCarey plan that never materialized.

Capra on producer-directors: Frank Capra, "By Post From Mr. Capra: Directors Without Power," *NYT*, April 2, 1939, sec. X, p. 4.

Liberty Films: Capra, pp. 371-374; McBride, pp. 506-508; Anderegg, *William Wyler*, pp. 293- 299. "Undoubtedly there will": Frank Capra, "Breaking Hollywood's 'Pattern of Sameness'," *New York Times Magazine*, May 5, 1946, pp. 18, 57, also see Koszarski, *Hollywood Directors, 1941-1976*, pp. 88- 89.

"I guess there is": McBride, p. 533.

Dissolution of Liberty Films: Capra Termination Agreement, March 20, 1951, pp. 1-2, (Butterfields internet auction, November 1999, lot 019).

International Pictures: Dick, *City of Dreams*, pp. 135-139; Gomery, *The Hollywood Studio System*, pp. 152-154; Schatz, *The Genius of the System*, pp. 463-465; Thomson, *Showman*, pp. 348-349.

Howard Hughes, Preston Sturges, and California Pictures: Thomas, *Howard Hughes In Hollywood*; Barlett and Steele, *Empire*; Sturges, *Preston Sturges*; Curtis, *Between Flops*; Lasky, *RKO*, pp. 204-219.

"I became an independent": Curtis, p. 219.

Hughes complains to William

Cagney: Sturges, pp. 304-305. Story retold at *The SIMPP Research Database*: <http://www.simpp.com>.

Chapter 10: The Independent Directory

Argosy (John Ford and Merian C. Copper): Sinclair, *John Ford*, pp. 135-146 ; Ford, *Pappy*, pp. 209-218, 227-232, 250-251; Bernstein, *Walter Wanger, Hollywood Independent*, pp. 146-150, 163- 169; Renowned Artists mentioned in Gallagher, *John Ford*, p. 119-220. John Ford Productions: see Davis, *John Ford*, pp. 194-199, 278.

Monterey (Howard Hawks, Charles Feldman, and H-F): McCarthy, *Howard Hawks*, pp. 401- 434, 468-469; Schatz, pp.424-425.

Transatlantic Pictures (Alfred Hitchcock and Sidney Bernstein): see Taylor, *Hitch*; Leff, *Hitchcock and Selznick*; Spoto, *The Dark Side of Genius*; Auiler, *Vertigo*, pp. 14-15; Rebello, *Alfred Hitchcock and the Making of Psycho*, p. 27; Schatz, p. 489.

Sam Spiegel biographical information: Sinclair, *Spiegel*, and James Fixx, "The Spiegel Touch," *Saturday Review*, 29 December 1962.

"Perhaps, the last authentic": Brownlow, *David Lean*, p. 247

Horizon Pictures: Sinclair, *Spiegel*; Huston, *An Open Book*, pp. 163-187, 210; Kaminsky, *John Huston*, pp. 39, 62, 87, 118.

Stanley Kramer biographical information: Kramer, *A Mad, Mad, Mad, Mad World*; and Spoto, *Stanley Kramer, Film Maker*.

"To use film": Kramer, p. 232.

Kramer defies blacklist: "Stan

Kramer Admits Employing 'Many' of Those 'Subpoenaed,'" *HR*, August 4, 1958, pp. 1, 9.

Cyrano de Bergerac road show release: Thomas F. Brady, "Dark Days For Independents: Legal Threat," *NYT*, January 21, 1951, sec. II, p. 5.

High Noon gross: Balio, *United Artists: The Company Built by the Stars*, p. 235.

Enterprise Productions and David Loew: Bowers, *The Selznick Players*, p. 79; Bergman and Burgess, *My Story*, pp. 163-164; "probably the greatest commercial failure": Balio, *United Artists: The Company Built by the Stars*, p. 217; "Movie Producer Quits, Make Good as Painter," *LAT*, November 28, 1953.

Sierra Pictures and En Corporation: Bernstein, pp. 237-247; Bergman and Burgess, p. 283; Bowers, p. 80. The name for Bergman's company was taken from the Swedish word *en*, meaning "one."

Joan of Arc, largest single film loan ever: SIMPP, "Leading Coast Banks Give Full Vote of Confidence To Independent Producers," (press release), May 5, 1948, p. 2. Other figures from Bernstein, pp. 238, 444.

"It should never have": Bernstein, p. 257.

Nelson article on independents: Donald M. Nelson, "The Independent Producer," *The Annals of the American Academy of Political and Social Sciences*, 254 (November 1947), pp. 49-57. Also see "Nelson Tells How Indies Have Lifted Film Standards," *DV*, October 20, 1947; "Nelson Cites Progress Due To Independents," *Box office*, October 25, 1947; Joe Alvin to SIMPP members, November 19, 1947,

WWP.

"If there are risks": "The Independent Producer," p. 55.

"On the decision": Ibid, p. 56.

Nelson hospitalized: SIMPP to SIMPP members, telegram, July 23, 1947, WWP.

Nelson resigns from SIMPP presidency—Letter of resignation: Donald M. Nelson to SIMPP members, December 1, 1947, pp. 1-3, WWP; "Nelson Resigns Industry Post," *NYT*, December 10, 1947, p. 44; "Nelson To Quit Independents," *NYT*, December 14, 1947, sec. II, p. 5.

Meeting on January 9, 1947: Donald M. Nelson to Walter Wanger, January 13, 1947, WWP; "Film Market Hampered By U.S. Edict, Nelson Says," *Hollywood Citizen-News*, January 10, 1947.

Chapter 11: Independent's Day

"Great care should be taken": Morris L. Ernst to Donald M. Nelson, January 3, 1947, WWP.

Robert L. Wright visits with SIMPP: Donald M. Nelson to Walter Wanger, April 9, 1947, WWP.

Robert J. Rubin information—joins SIMPP in latter 1947: see Marvin L. Faris to Walter Wanger, January 29, 1948, WWP; biographical information: *HR*, April 28, 1948.

SIMPP *amicus curiae*: Donald M. Nelson to SIMPP members, December 1, 1947, pp. 2, WWP; "Indie Prods Demand Big 5 Be Divorced From Theatres," *DV*, December 3, 1947, pp. 1, 11; *Film Daily Yearbook 1948*, p. 47.

"Declaration of independence as": "Ruling Opens U.S. Market for Indies, Says SIMPP Chief," *HR*, May 5, 1948,

pp. 1, 4.

Goldwyn and Schenck reactions to the Supreme Court ruling: "Ruling 'Boon' To Movie Fans, Goldwyn Says," *Hollywood Citizen-News*, May 5, 1948; "Film Leaders Split On Merits of Ruling," *NYT*, May 5, 1948, p. 29.

SIMPP telegram of protest: "Indies Fight Trust Suit 'Deal'," *HR*, September 14, 1948, pp. 1, 9; "Independents Wary of Major Film 'Deal'," *NYT*, September 14, 1948, p. 34; "SIMPP Fights Majors' Consent Decree Bid," *Hollywood Citizen-News*, September 14, 1948; "SIMPP Protests Any New Decree; Urges U.S. Force Theatres Sale,: *DV*, September 14, 1948, pp. 1, 11.

Justice Department concurs: "Movie Firms Asked To Drop Theatres," *NYT*, October 2, 1948, p. 10.

"Opinion in trade circles": A. H. Weiler, "Supreme Court Decision Summary," *NYT*, May 9, 1948, sec. II, p. 5.

RKO divorcement decree: "RKO Will Divorce Theatres," *HR*, October 27, 1948, p. 1; "RKO Board Agrees To Split Its Stock," *NYT*, October 31, 1948, p. 79; "Ruling Against RKO Ready For Court," *NYT*, November 2, 1948, p. 39; "Thomas F. Brady, "RKO Divorcement Plan May Set Pattern For Entire Industry," *NYT*, November 7, 1948, sec. II, p. 5.

Paramount consent decree 1949: Lewis Wood, "Paramount Consent Decree Splits Film Firm, Theatres," *NYT*, February 26, 1949, pp. 1, 10; Thomas M. Prior, "Paramount Split Will Be Tax Free," *NYT*, February 26, 1949, p. 10.

Paramount and television: "'Trust'

Background Makes 'Big 5' Unfit for TV, Senate Told," *HR*, April 21, 1949; Gomery, *The Hollywood Studio System*, pp. 35-38, 85, 129.

Paramount Pictures corporate split: "Paramount Stockholders Vote Approval of Split Into 2 Units," *NYT*, April 13, 1949, pp. 45, 47; "Paramount Ending Joint Ownership," *NYT*, December 8, 1949, p. 55; "Paramount Splits Into Two Companies," *NYT*, December 30, 1949, p. 13; "Paramount Reorganization Plan Completed 2 Months Ahead of Time," *NYT*, December 31, 1949, pp. 19, 21.

Reactions from the major studio holdouts—"Warner Says He Won't Sign," *NYT*, February 26, 1949, p. 10; "Loew's Fights Divorcement," *HR*, March 28, 1949, p. 1; Twentieth Century-Fox proposed consent decree and Loew's 154-page brief: "Ten Years Later: Movie Antitrust Action Draws to Close," *NYT*, March 6, 1949, sec. II, p. 5.

Government pursues case: "U.S. Hits At Trust 'Holdouts'," *HR*, April 4, 1949, pp. 1, 13; "Loew's, 20th Battle Renewed On U.S. Divorcement Demand," *HR*, April 22, 1949, pp. 1, 8; "Big 3 Get U.S. Divorce Terms," *HR*, April 25, 1949, pp. 1, 9; "U.S. Seeks Loew Houses Sale," *HR*, April 29, 1949, pp. 1, 11.

"It will be necessary": "Independents' Day," *Time*, May 17, 1948, p. 91.

"This consent decree marks": Prior, "Ten Years Later," p. 5.

Chapter 12: Diplomacy

Casting agreement with AMPP: William R. Weaver, "Produce More For Less: Nelson," *MPH*, May 17, 1947, p. 29.

The Great Anglo-American Film War: Thomas M. Prior, "British Film Boycott," *NYT*, August 29, 1948, sec. II, p. 3; Balio, *United Artists: The Company Built by the Stars*, pp. 221-223; Korda, *Charmed Lives*, pp. 218-221.

British negotiations with MPAA and SIMPP: MORE Thomas M. Prior, "Independent Producers Sound Battle Cry," *NYT*, August 29, 1948, sec. II, p. 3; M. A. Slater to Walter M. Wanger, September 3, 1947, WWP; Marvin L. Faris to SIMPP producers, July 16, 1948, WWP.

Disney telegram to George C. Marshall: "Disney Protests New Quota 'Pact'," *NYT*, August 23, 1948, p. 14.

SIMPP opposes French deal: George Mercader to Walter Wanger, interoffice communication, August 18, 1948, WWP; WWP also contains Mercader's handwritten notes from the August 17, 1948 SIMPP meeting.

Johnston alleges SIMPP division: "Film Makers Split Over London Talks," *NYT*, August 21, 1948, p. 8.

SIMPP counters: Prior , "Independent Producers Sound Battle Cry," p. 3.

"On the contrary": "Johnston Mistaken, Says Goldwyn: SIMPP In Accord," *HR*, August 24, 1948.

The SIMPP Executive Committee in 1948: "'Freedom of Enterprise' To Be SIMPP Goal In New Setup," *HR*, January 22, 1948.

Mulvey addresses SIMPP regarding leadership: "Mulvey To Spur SIMPP To Action," *DV*, November 15, 1948, pp. 1, 9.

SIMPP meeting with Arnall,

November 18, 1948: "Producers Confer With Ellis Arnall," *LAT*, November 19, 1948, p. 24.

Arnall biographical information— see Henderson, *The Politics of Change in Georgia*; *Georgia v. Pennsylvania Railroad Co.*, 324 U.S. 439 (1945); Scott E. Buchanan, "Georgia's Three Governors Controversy," *Gordon College, Barnesville, Georgia*: <http://www.gdn.peachnet.edu/faculty/s_buchanan/arnall.htm>.

"A lot of fun": "Arnall Declares 'Open War' On Big Theatre Monopolies," *HR*, December 14, 1948.

"The survival of democracy": "Arnall To Fight As SIMPP Head," *MPH*, December 18, 1948, p. 16.

Arnall chosen as SIMPP president: "Arnall Is Elected To High Film Post," *NYT*, December 13, 1948, p. 18; "Arnall Gets Film Post," *Los Angeles Examiner*, December 13, 1948, p. 3.

Arnall press conference, December 13, 1948—"the greatest fight raging", "Hollywood has a certain": "Arnall Pledges War Against 'Monopoly'," *Los Angeles Examiner*, December 14, 1948. Also see "Arnall To Fight Film Monopolies," *NYT*, December 14, 1948.

Hollywood blacklist: Donald M. Nelson to All SIMPP Members, December 1, 1947, WWP; the letters gives a brief account of the conference, SIMPP attendance, a transcription of the declaration, and mentions Wanger on the Committee of Five; also see French, *The Movie Moguls*, pp. 119-124.

"The most un-American activity", Goldwyn at the conference, and letter to Wanger: Berg, *Goldwyn*, pp. 433-439, 549.

Free World Association, Wanger at the conference, and views on HUAC: Bernstein, *Walter Wanger, Hollywood Independent*, pp. 193, 227, 268; Schary, *Heyday*, pp. 164-167.

Motion Picture Alliance and Free World Association: Confidential Report, September 21, 1944, FBI 100-22299—see Trethewey, *Walt Disney: The FBI Files*, pp. 53-57. "Linked throughout the nation": see "Erred, Wanger Letter Admits," *LAT*, September 8, 1950, p. 18. "To bury old disagreements": "Wanger Assured of MPA Cooperation," *Hollywood Citizen-News*, September 11, 1950.

Wanger on Disney: see Walter Wanger, "Mickey Icarus, 1943: Fusing Ideas with the Art of the Animated Cartoon," *Saturday Review of Literature*, September 4, 1943, pp. 18-19; reprinted in Smoodin, *Disney Discourse*, pp. 44-46. Wanger on the polo field with Disney: see Finch, *The Art of Walt Disney*, p. 118.

Eyewitness accounts of the Waldorf-Astoria blacklist meeting from November 1948 available at *The SIMPP Research Database*: <http://www.simpp.com>.

SIMPP accused of blacklist, denies blacklist: "Movie Companies Sued By Writers," *NYT*, June 2, 1948, p. 22; "SIMPP Denies 'Ten' Blacklist," *HR*, December 16, 1948, p. 1, 10, includes statement by Lessing, and plaintiff's reaction.

Arnall speaking at dinner for Alben Barkley: see "Arnall Named SIMPP Prez.", *DV*, December 13, 1948.

"It is the State Department's": "Arnall Blasts Monopoly Again," *DV*, December 17, 1948.

Johnston-Balaban-Schenck:

"SIMPP Sizzles At Snubbing From Anglo-U.S. Council," *DV*, March 28, 1949, pp. 1, 10.

Meeting with Secretary of State Acheson: "Arnall Pleased With State Dept. Talks On Quota Action," *HR*, April 13, 1949.

SIMPP meeting with President Truman: "Arnall Promised Indies Change By Britain To Aid U.S. Films," *DV*, April 15, 1949; detail of visit retold in Ellis Arnall, transcript of speech delivered at a meeting of the Motion Picture Industry Council, June 15, 1949, pp. 3-4, courtesy of Wisconsin State Historical Society, Madison.

Response from Secretary of State Acheson: Ellis Arnall to Walter Wanger, April 14, 1949, pp. 1-2, WWP.

SIMPP files complaint with Clark: "SIMPP Members Back Arnall Assault On U.S.-Anglo Pact," *DV*, May 13, 1949; "SIMPP Takes Beef To Gov't: U.S.-Anglo Pact Termed Monopoly," *DV*, May 17, 1949, pp. 1, 7.

"In spite of the fact": J. Mulvey to Gunther Lessing, June 6, 1949, WWP.

Response from Secretary of State Acheson: Ellis Arnall to Walter Wanger, April 14, 1949, pp. 1-2, WWP. MPAA and SIMPP settle: "Arnall 'Delighted' To Puff Peace Pipe With Johnston," *HR*, June 3, 1949, p. 9; "SIMPP, MPAA Bury Hatchet on Asking U.S. To Fight Quota," *HR*, June 6, 1949, pp. 1, 4; "Arnall Will Spurn Anglo-U.S. Meet," *DV*, June 8, 1949, p. 3.

"Have stopped one of": Gunther R. Lessing to SIMPP members, June 9, 1949, WWP.

Frozen Funds: "Indie, MPA British Split Indicated," *DV*, January 11, 1950,

pp. 1, 5; "SIMPP Gloomy Over British Movie Terms," *Hollywood Citizen-News*, May 27, 1950; "Independent Movie Producers Give Arnall Right to Make Final Decision on British Agreement," *NYT*, June 16, 1950, p. 29; "British Pact Is Approved By SIMPP," *MPH*, August 19, 1950.

Chaplin using British funds: "Chaplin Preps Starer To Be Made in Britain," *HR*, April 22, 1949, p. 1.

"Any system that requires": Ellis Arnall, transcript of speech delivered at a meeting of the Motion Picture Industry Council, June 15, 1949, p. 6, courtesy of Wisconsin State Historical Society, Madison.

Israel Motion Picture Studios of Tel Aviv: Marvin L. Faris to Walter Wanger, March 27, 1950, WWP; Italian shipbuilding: Marvin L. Faris to All SIMPP Members, June 16, 1955, WWP

"It would be suicide": Roy O. Disney to James A. Mulvey, June 9, 1949, WWP.

"He has grasped our problems": J. Mulvey to Gunther Lessing, June 6, 1949, WWP.

Reelection of Arnall, Lessing as new chairman: "Ellis Arnall Re-elected To Presidency of SIMPP," *Hollywood Citizen-News*, June 23, 1949; see also *Film Daily Yearbook 1950*, p. 61.

New membership regulations: see *By-laws of The Society of Independent Motion Picture Producers* (As Unanimously Approved By the Executive Committee at a Special Meeting On August 28, 1945 and Thereafter Assented To By All the Members, as Revised and Amended By the Members By Written Assent in November, 1950), pp. 1-2, MPC; and

later SIMPP By-laws Amendment:
Article III Membership (As Amended
March 12, 1951, May 7, 1951 and
January 28, 1952), WWP.

Goldwyn resigns from the
MPAA—"I find myself unable": Marx,
Goldwyn, pp. 330-331.

**Chapter 13: The Little Paramount
Case**

Goldwyn "it will be necessary":
"Independents' Day," *Time*, May 17,
1948, p. 91.

Arnall "one-half set up": "Arnall
Declares 'Open War' On Big Theatre
Monopolies," *HR*, December 14, 1948.

Arnall "relatives and friends":
"Arnall Says MPEA Hits Independent," *MPH*, July 23, 1949.

Arnall "Divorcement is a step":
"New Decree Boosts Chances Prods,
Sez Arnall," *DV*, February 28, 1949.

*The Society of Independent Motion
Picture Producers, et al v. United
Detroit Theatres Corp., et al*, case
number 7589, District Court of the
United States for the Eastern District of
Michigan Southern Division [hereafter: SIMPP v. United Detroit].

Meeting at Samuel Goldwyn's
house: SIMPP v. United Detroit,
Deposition of David O. Selznick, April
28, 1949, pp. 96-100, AMPAS.

Rubin report on monopolies: *Proof
of Combination-Proof of Damage*,
Richard V. Gilbert, consulting economist at Washington, D.C., to Robert
Rubin, April 13, 1948, AMPAS;
"Indies Plan Screen Time Fight," *HR*,
April 28, 1948, pp. 1, 3.

Producers authorize SIMPP to initiate Michigan case: Walter Wanger
Pictures, Inc. to The Society of

Independent   Motion   Picture
Corporation, July 21, 1948, pp. 1-2,
WWP.

SIMPP announces Detroit case:
"Producers Allege Movie House
Trust," *NYT*, August 25, 1948, p. 29;
"SIMPP Sues Exhibs For Millions,"
HR, August 25, 1948, pp. 1, 4;
"Independent Film Producers File
Anti-trust Theater Suit," *Daily News*,
August 25, 1948; "pound or two" and
"without precedent": "Exhibitors
Monopoly, Too, Says SIMPP, Filing
Suit," *MPH*, August 28, 1948, p. 13.

Goldwyn-Disney press conference—"The antitrust suit is":
"Goldwyn Hits Theater Chains," *Los
Angeles Examiner*, August 26, 1948;
"We do not intend": "60 Films Figure
In Indie Suit," *DV*, August 26, 1948;
"routine entertainment turned out" and
"we now feel": "Free Screen Object of
SIMPP Suit, Assert Goldwyn, Disney,"
HR, August 26, 1948, pp. 1, 11. Also
see "Exhibitors Monopoly, Too, Says
SIMPP, Filing Suit," p. 13.

Jackson Park case: see Conant,
*Antitrust in the Motion Picture
Industry*, pp. 161-177. *Bigelow v. RKO
Radio Pictures*, 327 U.S. 251 (1946).

History of the United Detroit
Theatres and Cooperative Theatres of
Michigan: SIMPP v. United Detroit,
Complaint, August 24, 1948, pp. 19-
24, NARA.

Rise of cooperative buying and
booking agencies for independent
exhibitors: see Conant, *Antitrust in the
Motion Picture Industry*, p. 57, which
also mentions the predatory tactics of
the Co-operative Theatres of
Michigan.

John H. Kunsky (a.k.a. John King)
and George W. Trendle: Kunsky in

1905 and 1911, see George B. Catlin, *The Story of Detroit*, and Koszarski, *An Evening's Entertain-ment*, p. 10. Apparently Trendle was kept on as manager of the Paramount theater holdings in Detroit until 1937 when he was fired for negligence, see Goldenson, *Beating the Odds*, pp. 36-37, 299. Information on the Kunsky-Trendle Broadcasting Company: see "History of Michigan AM Broadcasting," *Michigan Broadcast Guide*: <http://www.michiguide.com/history>; George Trendle and the Lone Ranger: Fran Striker, Jr., "The Real Lone Ranger: Fran Striker," excerpted speech given at the South Jersey Series Collectors meeting, Cherry Hill, New Jersey, February 25, 1995; Jack French, "The Miser of Motown: George W. Trendle," *Old-Time-Radio, The Vintage Radio Place*: <http://www.otrsite.com>.

United Detroit and Cooperative Theatres antitrust allegations: SIMPP v. United Detroit, *Complaint*, pp. 25-30; independent theater opposition: *Colonial Theatrical Enterprise, Inc., et al v. Cooperative Theatres of Michigan, et al*, no date (c. 1934), case number 6476, four-page decision by Edward J. Moinet - United States District Judge, courtesy of AMPAS; run, zone, clearance in Detroit: SIMPP v. United Detroit, *Complaint*, pp. 17-18; the "highly artificial and restrictive": "Independent Film Producers File Anti-trust Theater Suit."

"Indies War on Majors," *DV*, August 27, 1948, pp. 1, 6.

House of Representatives Small Business Committee: "House Detroit Inquiry," *DV*, August 27, 1948, p. 6; "House Committee Will Probe Alleged

Detroit Monopoly," *HR*, August 27, 1948, pp. 1, 9.

"The Society is certain": Ellis Arnall to Walter Wanger, May 12, 1949, WWP.

SIMPP complaint against Fox West Coast: "FWC Monopoly, Asserts SIMPP," *HR*, November 9, 1949, pp. 1, 8. SIMPP continues to investigate monopolistic exhibitors: "IMPP [sic] Plans Study of Film Monopoly," *NYT*, October 15, 1949, p. 11.

"Long experience has proved": Bosley Crowther, "In the Opinion of Mr. Schenck," *NYT*, September 11, 1938, sec. X, p. 3.

"I thought that the exhibitors" and "I see no reason": SIMPP v. United Detroit, *Deposition of David O. Selznick*, pp. 33, 35.

Chapter 14: Conflicting Interests

The Society of Independent Motion Picture Producers, et al v. United Detroit Theatres Corp., et al, case number 7589, District Court of the United States for the Eastern District of Michigan Southern Division [hereafter: SIMPP v. United Detroit].

Rockwell T. Gust information: SIMPP v. United Detroit, *Affidavit in Opposition* (Rockwell T. Gust), October 15, 1948, pp. 1-3, NARA.

Defendants given 20 days to respond: SIMPP v. United Detroit, *Summons*, September 15, 1948, NARA. Extension granted: SIMPP v. United Detroit, *Order Extending Time To Plead*, September 28, 1948, NARA.

Plaintiffs protest depositions with "serious hardship": SIMPP v. United Detroit, *Affidavit* (Robert J. Rubin), October 6, 1948, p. 2, NARA; "simply does not warrant": SIMPP v. United Detroit, *Memorandum In Support of Motions To Vacate or Modify Notice of Taking Depositions*, October 11, 1948, p. 11, NARA.

"Should Mr. Walt Disney" and "radical reorganization": SIMPP v. United Detroit, *Affidavit* (Gunther R. Lessing), October 1948, p. 2, WWP.

"It is embarrassing me": A. Stewart Kerr to Robert J. Rubin, March 24, 1949, WWP.

Stromberg in Detroit: SIMPP v. United Detroit, *Deposition of Hunt Stromberg*, April 8, 1949, AMPAS.

Selznick in Detroit: SIMPP v. United Detroit, *Deposition of David O. Selznick*, April 28, 1949, AMPAS. "I have never been in Detroit before today." p. 94; SIMPP meeting attendance: "Not for a long time." p. 100; favorite films: *Gone With the Wind* above all, then "a toss-up between *A Star Is Born* and *Rebecca*," then after that *The Prisoner of Zenda, Little Lord Fauntleroy*, and *The Adventures of Tom Sawyer*, p. 25.

Wanger delays—"the only picture that": George Mercader to Robert Rubin, April 13, 1949, WWP; Walter Wanger to Ellis Arnall, May 17, 1949, WWP; Walter Wanger to Robert J. Rubin, May 23, 1949, WWP; "The defense was lucky" and "I think that now": Roy O. Disney to Walter Wanger, August 2, 1949, WWP.

Extensions granted on February 21, 1949; May 20, 1949; September 22, 1949; January 5, 1950; April 10, 1950; June 23, 1950; October 12, 1950; November 10, 1950; November 27, 1950; December 8, 1950; defense given until 30 days after the end of the discovery period: SIMPP v. United

Detroit, *Order Extending Defendant's, United Detroit Theatres Corporation, Time to Plead in the Above Cause*, January 8, 1951, NARA.

Robert J. Rubin exits SIMPP: "Arnall Plans Action to Aid Independent," *MPH*, September 30, 1950; *Film Daily Yearbook 1951*, p. 1066.

Paramount divides television holdings: "Paramount Reorganization Plan Completed 2 Months Ahead of Time," *NYT*, December 31, 1949, pp. 19, 21.

Theater television: "A.B.C., United Paramount Merge in $25,000,000 Deal," *NYT*, May 24, 1951, pp. 1, 54; Bosley Crowther, "Anybody's Guess," *NYT*, June 3, 1951, sec. II, p. 1.

United Paramount-ABC proposed merger: "A.B.C., United Paramount Merge in $25,000,000 Deal," p. 1, 54; "Sharper Rivalry in TV Field Seen," *NYT*, May 25, 1951, p. 40; "Officers Named in Proxy Statement for Vote on ABC-United Paramount Theatres Merger," *NYT*, June 30, 1951, p. 20; "Merger Plan Filed," *NYT*, July 15, 1951, sec. III, p. 4.

Leonard Goldenson history and United Detroit in 1937: Goldenson, *Beating the Odds*, pp. 34- 40.

"We became good friends": Ibid, p. 37.

Earl Hudson becomes ABC administrative head: Ibid, p. 103.

For additional information on the early history of the Hollywood studios' interest in television: see Christopher Anderson, "Television and Hollywood in the 1940s," chapter 13 from Schatz, *Boom and Bust*, pp. 422-444.

Screen Actors Guild and Robert L. Lippert: "Actors Move To Bar From TV Films Made Since 1948," *MPH,*

July 7, 1951, p. 17. Lippert, who owned a chain of theaters in California and Oregon, branched into production and began feeding his theaters with his own B-features in the late-1940s.

Pickford on television: Mary Pickford, "The Big Bad Wolf Has Been Muzzled," from *HR*, circa 1934, reprinted in Wilkerson and Borie, *The Hollywood Reporter, the Golden Years*, pp. 234-236.

"Remember that term": Tytle, *One of "Walt's Boys,"* p. 113.

SIMPP subscriber television: "SIMPP Okays Pay-at-Home TB: Asks FCC To License System," *HR*, June 28, 1951, pp. 1, 10; "Indies Yen TV's Potential B. O.," *DV*, June 28, 1951, pp. 1, 10; "SIMPP and Television," *MPH*, July 7, 1951, p. 1; "Pay Vision Gets Spur From SIMPP Stand," *MPH*, July 7, 1951, p. 17. Also, in the mid-1950s, Walter Wanger was among the filmmakers who sat on the board of directors for a closed-circuit, large-screen operation called Box Office Television: see Bernstein, *Walter Wanger, Hollywood Independent*, p. 315.

"I had to find" and Goldenson visit to Disney in 1951: Thomas, *Building a Company*, pp. 184-185. Also see Schickel, *The Disney Version*, p. 313-314, and Mosely, *Disney's World*, p. 233. Goldenson with independent producers Goldwyn, Selznick, and Welles: Goldenson, *Beating the Odds*, pp. 63-64, 143. Wanger television pilot episode: Bernstein, pp. 266-267, 270.

ABC-Paramount merger approved: "Paramount, A.B.C. Cleared To Merge," *NYT*, February 10, 1953, pp. 1, 36, 43.

Gust delays Detroit trial in 1951:

SIMPP v. United Detroit, *Affidavit in Opposition to Plaintiffs' Motion To Vacate This Court's Order of November 8, 1951* (Rockwell T. Gust), November 15, 1951, pp. 1-6; deposition of James Mulvey and "proved to be highly", p. 4.

SIMPP fed up: SIMPP v. United Detroit, *Motion of Plaintiffs to Vacate Order of January 8, 1951 and for Entry of New Order*, October 22, 1951, pp. 1-3.

Answers filed—"excessive fees" p. 11: SIMPP v. United Detroit, *Answer of Cooperative Theatres of Michigan, Inc.*, December 19, 1951, NARA; "under the guise" p. 2, and "the plaintiffs do not" p. 13: SIMPP v. United Detroit, *Answer of Defendant, United Detroit Theatres Corporation*, December 20, 1951, NARA.

SIMPP predicts victory in Detroit: Ellis Arnall to SIMPP members, January 22, 1953, p. 2, WWP.

Disneyland and WED: Thomas, *Building a Company*, pp. 178-185; Schickel, *The Disney Version*, p. 313-314, Thomas, *Walt Disney*, pp. 248-249 and Mosely, *Disney's World*, p. 233.

Disney deal with ABC-Paramount: Thomas M. Prior, "Disney to Enter TV Field in Fall," *NYT*, March 30, 1954, p. 24; Thomas M. Prior, "Disney Pact Delayed," *NYT*, March 31, 1954, p. 38; Thomas M. Prior, "Disney and A.B.C. Sign TV Contract," *NYT*, April 3, 1954, p. 19.

Lessing ends Detroit case: SIMPP v. United Detroit, *Appearance* (Gunther R. Lessing), September 13, 1954, NARA; "be dismissed with prejudice": SIMPP v. United Detroit, *Stipulation* (Gunther R. Lessing, A.

Stewart Kerr, William Henry Gallagher, James E. Haggerty, David Newman, Rockwell T. Gust), September 28, 1954, NARA; SIMPP v. United Detroit, *Order* (case dismissal: Arthur A. Koscinski), September 28, 1954, NARA.

Trade papers announce the SIMPP-United Detroit settlement: "SIMPP Wins Settlement in UPT Suit," *DV*, September 28, 1954, pp. 1,4; "Detroit Suit Ended," *HR*, September 28, 1954, p. 1; "Disney Is Opening Three New Offices in Expansion Step," *HR*, September 28, 1954, pp. 1, 4.

Statue of limitations: SIMPP v. United Detroit, *Answer of Defendant, United Detroit Theatres Corporation,* December 20, 1951, paragraph 46, p. 13, NARA; see Conant, *Antitrust in the Motion Picture Industry*, pp. 191-195. Even though the divorcement decrees gave same protection to the Hollywood studios, the government suspended the statute of limitations making it possible for many civil suits against the studio-defendants. However, the government did not suspend the statute of limitations against the divested theater chains that were previously owned by the major studios. This made the statue of limitations issue moot in *SIMPP v. United Detroit.*

Chapter 15: The Decline of SIMPP

Financing for independents: see Balio, *United Artists: The Company Built by the Stars*, pp. 191- 193, 203, 216-217.

SIMPP's proposed Motion Picture Equity Corporation: "SIMPP Okays Finance Plan," *HR*, May 3, 1950, pp. 1, 4; Thomas F. Brady, "Film Men Are Told of Financing Plan," *NYT*, May 3, 1950, p. 37; Thomas F. Brady, "Loans for Independent Production," *NYT*, May 7, 1950, sec. II, p. 5; sample of questionnaire: "Suggested Information Requested for Study of Independently Produces Pictures Released During 12 Year Period Ending December 31, 1949," George L. Bagnall to Walter Wanger, September 19, 1950, WWP. Arnall designated Bagnall to gather the surveys, see "SIMPP Gets $10,000,000 Finance Plan," *MPH*, May 6, 1950; questionnaire details also given in: "Indie Financial Probe Details," *HR*, September 27, 1950, pp. 1, 6. Failure of the proposal: "Bank Quiz Draws Nix by SIMPP," *DV*, November 7, 1950, pp. 1, 7.

Douglas versus Disney: "SIMPP Statement Attacks Ruling in Douglas-Disney Suit," *HR*, December 11, 1956; also see Tytle, *One of "Walt's Boys,"* pp. 119-121, and Farber and Green, *Hollywood Dynasties*, p. 210.

"He quickly gets out": Johnston, *The Great Goldwyn*, pp. 35.

Goldwyn resigns from SIMPP: "Goldwyn Leaves Producers Group," *NYT*, May 11, 1955, p. 35. "The SIMPP has served": "Goldwyn Explains SIMPP Resignation," *HR*, May 11, 1955, p. 1. Also see "Goldwyn Resigns From SIMPP," *DV*, May 11, 1955, pp. 1, 4.

Goldwyn versus Fox West Coast—suit filed: "$6,750,000 Is Asked by Goldwyn in Suit," *NYT*, May 17, 1950, p. 35; delayed by depositions: "Goldwyn Gains in Theatre Suit," *NYT*, February 26, 1955, p. 13; statute of limitations: "Antitrust Trial on Fox Films Is On," *NYT*, July 11, 1957, p. 21; "Goldwyn Loss on Films Told at

Antitrust Trial," *LAT*, July 11, 1957; Skouras stock deal: Thomas M. Prior, "Hollywood in Court," *NYT*, July 14, 1957, sec. II, p. 5; appearances from Pickford and DeMille: Lawrence E. Davies, "Mary Pickford Stars for Goldwyn in Suit Against Fox Film Interests," *NYT*, August 8, 1957, p. 25, and "DeMille Lauds Goldwyn," *NYT*, September 18, 1957, p. 37; "Sam Goldwyn Appears Briefly In Trust Suit," *Hollywood Citizen-News*, November 19, 1957; "Film Trust Trial Ends First Phase," *NYT*, November 21, 1957, p. 38; Marx, *Goldwyn*, pp. 331-333; Berg, *Goldwyn*, p. 387.

United Artists difficulties: Thomas F. Brady, "Dark Days for Independents," *NYT*, January 21, 1951, sec. II, p. 5; Balio, *United Artists: The Company Built by the Stars*, pp. 215-219; Nasser brothers: "No UA Purchase at Deadline," *HR*, April 22, 1949, pp. 1, 10; *Variety*, April 21, 1949, p. 1; and Balio, p. 230.

Wanger at Allied Artists: "William R. Weaver, "Wanger's Allied Artists Deal Excites Interest," *MPH*, August 4, 1951.

IMPPA: Fred Stanley, "More About the Hollywood Scene," *NYT*, August 27, 1944, sec. II, p. 3.

Growth of SIMPP membership, reduction in film production: Ellis Arnall, "The Indies' Position in War Economy," *Variety*, January 3, 1951.

SIMPP modifies dues and expenditures: "Revise Arnall SIMPP Pay on Retainer Basis," *Variety*, July 25, 1951, pp. 3, 16.

The Independent Film Producers Export Corporation: "SIMPP Sets Up Its Own Export Assn.," *DV*, June 25, 1953, pp. 1, 3; "As the domestic mar-

ket": Ellis Arnall to SIMPP Members, July 17, 1953, WWP; "Seeking 'Reputable' European Reps For SIMPP Members," *DV*, March 26, 1954, p. 9; "SIMPPProducers Brief Foreign Sales Rep On Prod'n Plans Prior To O'seas Expansion," *DV*, December 27, 1956; "SIMPP Showcasing at Cannes," *HR*, May 13, 1957, p. 1.

SIMPP downsizing: "SIMPP Tightening Belt; Marv Faris Out After 12 Years," *HR*, August 1, 1958, pp. 1, 4; "SIMPP Shutter Its Coast Offices," *HR*, August 4, 1958, p. 4; "SIMPP Will Shutter Coast Office Aug. 30," *HR*, August 21, 1958.

"As a result of falling": "Trend to Majors Trims SIMPP," *DV*, August 1, 1958, pp. 1, 4.

Marvin Faris information: "Marvin Faris Resigns," *NYT*, August 2, 1958, p. 11; and Marvin Faris obituary, *DV*, September 11, 1981.

Last known whereabouts of SIMPP: *Film Daily Yearbook 1960*, and Henderson, *The Politics of Change in Georgia*, p. 206. Ellis Arnall died on December 13, 1992—44 years to the days after he became president of SIMPP.

"I realize that it's": Walter Wanger to Ellis Arnall, August 6, 1958, WWP, p. 1; "It is my firm belief": Ellis Arnall to Walter Wanger, Aug 6, 1958, WWP, p. 3.

Chapter 16: Fade Out

Information on the transformation of Walt Disney Productions: Miller, *The Story of Walt Disney*; Thomas, *Building a Company*; Thomas, *Walt Disney*; Schickel, *The Disney Version*;

Mosely, *Disney's World*; Holliss and Sibley, *The Disney Studio Story*; Watts, *The Magic Kingdom*.

End of the Disney animation Golden Age: "Disney Shelves Four Pictures," *HR*, January 5, 1942, pp. 1, 6.

Disney losses in 1949 at $93,899: Holliss and Sibley, p. 59.

Disney stock declines from $25 to $3: Diane Disney Miller, as told to Pete Martin "Mickey Mouse Becomes a Secret Weapon," *The Saturday Evening Post*, December 29, 1956, p. 73.

For information on Buena Vista Film Distributing Co., Walt Disney British Films, Ltd., and National Film Service: "Disney Moves Away From RKO," *DV*, September 21, 1954, pp. 1, 4.

"The Disneys had turned": Goldenson, *Beating the Odds*, p. 124.

"They're just a dollar-minded bunch": Thomas, *Building a Company*, p. 208.

The deal to repurchase ABC's Disneyland stock: Thomas M. Prior, "Land of Fantasia Is Rising on Coast," *NYT*, May 2, 1954, p. 86.

Disney financial status in 1958: "9-Month Disney Net $2,900,094," *HR*, July 29, 1958, pp. 1, 14. The article also mentions that Walt Disney Productions owned 65.52 percent of Disneyland since June 29, 1957.

"Recompense for his independent": Schickel, pp. 313-314.

Walt Disney turns 1,555 shares of Disneyland over to Walt Disney Productions: Walter E. Disney to Loyd Wright, "Re: Disneyland, Inc. stock escrow," October 1, 1959, Scott J. Winslow Associates, New Hampshire,

Historical Stocks, Bonds and Financial History, December 1999, p. 32. Loyd Wright, who served as Disney's personal lawyer, acted as escrow holder in the deal.

Value of Disneyland in 1966: Holliss and Sibley, p. 90.

Gunther R. Lessing retirement party and obituary: *LAT*, September 29, 1965; *DV*, September 29, 1965, p. 11; *HR*, December 30, 1964.

Samuel Goldwyn Studio— "History," *Warner Hollywood Studios*: <http://www.warnerhollywood.com>. In 1999, Warner Bros. agreed to sell the property to a real estate investment firm for $65 million: Chris Gennusa and David Robb, "Warner Hollywood Sold," *HR*, December 9, 1999, pp. 1, 34.

SIMPP involvement in 1954 censorship crisis: Thomas M. Prior, "Goldwyn Backed on Code Revision," *NYT*, February 12, 1954, p. 22; "8 Studio Chiefs Uphold Film Code," *NYT*, February 15, 1954, p. 19. The production code had created another rift between the major studios and the independents. The controversy was aggravated when Howard Hughes' *French Line* (1954) and Otto Preminger's *The Moon Is Blue* (1953) were released by member companies (RKO and UA respectively) without a production code seal of approval. SIMPP recommended a complete overhaul of the MPAA-controlled Breen code, essentially unchanged since 1930. Eight industry stalwarts upheld the code, and protested revision of any kind: Nicholas M. Schenck (Loew's), Barney Balaban (Paramount), Spyros P. Skouras (Twentieth Century-Fox), Harry Cohn (Columbia), Albert

Warner (Warner Bros.), Herbert Yates (Republic), and Steve Broidy (Allied Artists). Later the MPAA caved to pressure and approved code alterations in September 1954, permitting filmmakers to use the words "damn" and "hell." ("Majors 'Loosen Up' Prod'n Code," *DV*, September 14, 1954, p. 1). Joseph Breen retired the following month. As a historical side-note, the idea for the rating system (G, PG, R, etc.) that replaced the production code in 1968 is credited to SIMPP's Sol Lesser in an obituary from *Time* magazine, October 6, 1980.

"I've tried to be honorable": Loudon Wainwright, "The One-Man Gang Is In Action Again," *Life*, February 16, 1959, pp. 115-116.

Mulvey versus Goldwyn: "Mulvey Heads New Company With Canadian Group; Hutner in Setup," *HR*, October 17, 1960; "Court Dismisses Antitrust Angle, Orders Mulvey Suit vs. Goldwyn To Trial," *DV*, January 8, 1969, pp. 1, 8; "Similar Elements In Mulvey-Goldwyn Suit," *DV*, October 24, 1979; also Berg, *Goldwyn*, pp. 501-502.

At David O. Selznick's Vanguard, the board of directors in 1947 included himself, Daniel O'Shea and Loyd Wright. Selznick as the sole stockholder of SRO: see SIMPP v. United Detroit, *Deposition of David O. Selznick*, April 28, 1949, p. 49, AMPAS.

For O'Shea's humorous account of the short-lived plans for Selznick City, see Thomas, *Selznick*, pp. 251-252. On Selznick's mental instability and the O'Shea resignation, see Thomson, *Showman*, p. 554-556.

Dan O'Shea parts with Selznick:

"O'Shea Leaving Selznick; Will Open Agency," *Variety*, April 19, 1950; "Film Executive Given New Post by Radio System," *LAT*, November 25, 1950.

"Selznick Studio Goes On Block," *HR*, April 7, 1949, pp. 1, 3.

Walter Wanger's reorganization— Walter Wanger Pictures, Young American Films, Diana Productions, Sierra Pictures: "Wanger Pictures Reorganized," *LAT*, April 15, 1946. Also "Wanger Sets Up Film Budget of $14,00,00," *LAT*, February 11, 1946; "Wanger Schedules 10 Big Films," *Los Angeles Examiner*, February 11, 1946.

The Wanger-Nassour Releasing Organization: see "First Film Pacted by Wanger-Nassour," *HR*, June 7, 1949.

Allied Artists deal with Wanger: "Wanger Will Produce For Allied Artists Release," *MPH*, June 16, 1951.

Shooting of Jennings Lang: "Joan Bennett Sees Mate Shoot Agent," *LAT*, December 14, 1951, p. 1; "Shooting Story Told by Wanger," *LAT*, December 15, 1951; "Joan and Lang Held Trysts at Brando Home," *Los Angeles Examiner*, December 21, 1951. Also see McDougal, *The Last Mogul*, pp. 170-173.

Wanger obituary: "Film Producer Walter Wanger Dies at 72," *LAT*, November 19, 1968, pp. 3, 16.

"The basis of the whole": Welles and Bogdanovich, *This Is Orson Welles*, p. 134.

"I tried everything": Les Films Balenciaga and Paramount Pictures, *It's All True*, (video documentary), 1993. Also see Welles and Bogdanovich, pp. 164-165.

Orson Welles and Mercury:

"Welles Brazilian Film 1st Under Whitney Plan," *DV*, January 28, 1942, p. 6; "'All True' May Be Free Film Orson Welles Owes RKO Studio," *DV*, February 2, 1942, p. 7; Thomas F. Brady, "More on Welles vs. RKO," *NYT*, July 26, 1942, sec. II, p. 3.

"Hollywood died on me": Welles and Bogdanovich, p. 204.

The Chaplin-Welles lecture tour: "Artists Front to Win the War," advertisement for the Carnegie Hall "Win the War Meeting" on October 16, 1942.

Chaplin defended by Pickford and Goldwyn: McCabe, *Charlie Chaplin*, p. 223.

The Chaplin studio was built in 1918 after Chaplin signed an independent production deal with First National. After Chaplin sold it in 1953 to a New York real estate firm for $650,000, several TV shows were produced there including the George Reeves *The Adventures of Superman* series, *The Red Skelton Show*, and the original *Perry Mason*. The lot was briefly owned by Red Skelton from 1958 to 1962, then by CBS until 1966 when it became the home of A&M Records and Tijuana Brass Enterprises, Inc. In February 2000, the Henson family announced that they bought the property for $12.5 million to become the headquarters of their independent production operation the Jim Henson Company. Historical information from Charles Champlin, "The House That Charlie Built," *A&M Recording Studios*: <http://www.amstudios.com/pages/welcome_history.html>; "Modern Times: Hensons Buy Storied Chaplin Lot," *HR*, February 11, 2000, pp. 1, 43.

Chaplin sale of UA stock: see Balio, *United Artists: The Company That Changed the Film Industry*, p. 82-83.

Lester Cowan: "Lester Cowan" (obituary), *DV*, October 24, 1990; "Lester Cowan, 83; Movie Producer" (obituary), *LAT*, October 25, 1990.

Mary Pickford sold her United Artists stock for $2 million in cash, plus an additional $1 million debenture: see Balio, pp. 82-85.

Historical information on the General Service (now the Hollywood Center) Studios in Los Angeles: "Hollywood Center Studios History," *Hollywood Center Studios*: <http://www.hollywoodcenter.com/history>; "Premium," *NYT*, April 13, 1947; Sanders and Gilbert, *Desilu*, pp. 43, 76; Cowie, *Coppola*, pp. 148, 161.

Cagney-Montgomery Productions: McCabe, *Cagney*, p. 318.

"It represents 15 percent": French, *The Movie Moguls*, p. 102.

Hughes offers RKO to Disney: Thomas, *Walt Disney*, pp.238-239.

Emergence of Desilu, O'Shea sells RKO backlots, and "haven for indies": Sanders and Gilbert, pp. 136-139; Ball, *Love, Lucy*, pp. 253-254.

Chapter 17: The Lasting Influence of SIMPP

"Hollywood's like Egypt.": Hecht, *A Child of the Century*, p. 467.

"I, Charlie Chaplin, declare": A. H. Weiler, "Chaplin's Swan Song?," *NYT*, December 14, 1947, sec. II, p. 5.

"The studios are like dinosaurs": "Producer Assails 'Slide Rule' Movies," *Hollywood Citizen-News*, April 17, 1970.

"The day of the free ride": "Small Sez Big Studios Going," *DV*,

December 8, 1948.

"Times have changed": "Goldwyn and Wanger Agree Hollywood Films Are Lagging," *HR*, Nov. 19, 1946, p. 1, 16.

"Nothing has taken place" and "Not only will independents": see "Divorcement Means Easier Indie Financing, Says Arnall," *HR*, January 10, 1950, p. 4, and " Arnall Sees Big Future For Indies," *DV*, January 10, 1950.

"That the risks": Schatz, *The Genius of the System*, p. 269.

Independent production percentages in 1957: see *MPH*, October 5, 1957, p. 11; and Conant, *Antitrust in the Motion Picture Industry*, p. 117.

"Studio heads now": Huston, *An Open Book*, p. 353.

Goldwyn suggests limiting Hollywood to 200 features annually: "Goldwyn Slams Double Features in SEP Article," *HR*, July 10, 1940, p. 7.

"The studios now tried": Sturges, Preston Sturges, p. 310.

Film as perishable merchandise: see Sidney R. Kent, "Distributing the Product," from Kennedy, *The Story of the Films*, p.222.

Day-and-date releases for Hughes and Selznick discussed in Donald M. Nelson, "The Independent Producer," *The Annals of the American Academy of Political and Social Sciences*, 254 (November 1947), p. 55. For Disney and *Alice in Wonderland* (1951): see Thomas, *Building a Company*, pp. 221-222.

Average number of film prints between 200 and 500: Conant, *Antitrust in the Motion Picture Industry*, p. 59; e.g. Schatz, *Genius of the System*, p. 198. In 1997, Steven

Spielberg's *The Lost World: Jurassic Park* opened simultaneously on more than 6,000 screens (or approximately one-quarter of all U.S. screens): *1999 International Motion Picture Almanac* (New York: Quigley Publishing), p. 652.

Drive-in theater statistics—1946-1954: see *Film Daily Yearbook 1955*, p. 106. In June 1956: see *Film Daily*, June 29, 1956, p. 6, quoted in Conant, *Antitrust in the Motion Picture Industry*, p. 15.

"Who wants to go": French, *The Movie Moguls*, p. 13.

Low summer box office in studio era: Joseph P. Kennedy, "General Information to the Course," from Kennedy, p. 22.

Mid-West Drive-In becomes General Cinema Corporation: Christopher Grove, "Showbiz Runs in the Family," *Variety*, December 22, 1997, pp. 38, 54.

Stan Durwood theaters, Durwood, Inc., becomes American Multi-Cinema, Inc.: see "Small Beginnings, Big Dreams," *AMC Theatres*: <http://www.amctheatres.com/amc/amc_history.html>.

"Stables for independents": "Indies Ask Part in Code Policy," *HR*, May 9, 1955, p. 4.

"The major companies are recognizing": Thomas M. Prior, "Goldwyn Backed on Code Revision," *NYT*, February 12, 1954, p. 22.

Collapsible corporations for Goldwyn and Stromberg named in the SIMPP's complaint from *SIMPP v. United Detroit*. After 1946, Goldwyn restricted the practice due to the increasing tax scrutiny.

"A film when it": Kulik, *Alexander*

Korda, p. 127.

"We made pictures then": French, *The Movie Moguls*, p. 129.

"Quality films with limited resources"—a definition supplied by Dawn Hudson, the executive director of Independent Feature Project/West, see *Variety*, January 27, 1998.

"Tomorrow belongs": "Myers Says Theatre Empires Doomed by Court's Decision," *HR*, May 5, 1948, p. 4.

Independent theaters complain since the end of block booking: "Movie Antitrust Actions Hit by Exhibitor at Inquiry," *LAT*, April 1, 1953; W. R. Wilkerson, "Tradeviews," *HR*, July 14, 1954, p. 1.

National Theatres petitions for permission to produce: "NT Asks Gov't Okay To Produce," *HR*, September 24, 1954, p. 1; "Skouras Plans Pix Prod'n by NT," *DV*, September 24, 1954, pp. 1, 4.

Big Five studio leaders claiming that block booking had previously aided exhibitors—Sidney Kent: "Kent Backs 'Right' of Block Booking," *NYT*, April 7, 1939, p. 25; C. C. Pettijohn: "Neely Bill Called Threat To Public," *NYT*, December 15, 1939, p. 32.

Block booking and the animated short: Over the years, while block booking has remained strictly enforced, the industry has made an exception on several occasions to permit a distributor to sell one feature with one animated cartoon as a package deal, as Buena Vista has done with the "Roger Rabbit" series of shorts from 1989 through 1993. Though technically in violation of antitrust law, the practice has been permitted to provide a boost to the near-extinct theatrical

short market. Unfortunately, this new form of block booking has shown to hurt rather than help the chances for a general theatrical short revival because of the manner in which each short has been tied to the feature. With a new cartoon that is inseparably linked to a feature, the short stands or falls solely in accordance with the main attraction. This glass ceiling has kept each animated short from proving its own value, and has continued to undermine the future of the theatrical cartoon for the same reasons that SIMPP opposed block booking many years ago.

Twentieth Century-Fox guilty of block booking in later years: Will Tusher, "Fox Charged With Block Booking," *DV*, October 7, 1988, pp. 1, 28; Will Tusher, "Fox Found Guilty of Block Booking," *DV*, December 5, 1988, pp. 1, 19; Will Tusher, "Fox Appeal of Block-Booking Verdict Denied," *DV*, January 9, 1990. The Justice Department initiated its latest investigation of block booking in April 1999, according to *Boxoffice* magazine, when the government requested information regarding the block booking and clearance practices of Disney, Fox, MGM, Paramount, Sony, Universal, and Warner Bros. back to 1996. No major allegations have resulted.

ABC sells Paramount theaters: Goldenson, *Beating the Odds*, p. 231.

Cineplex Odeon and Loew's Theatres information: "Company History," *Loews Cineplex Entertainment*: <http://www.loewscineplex.com/corporate/lcp_corp_history.htm>.

Warner and Paramount interest in Mann Theatres: Matthew Doman, "WB, Par to Aid Drowning Mann,"

HR, October 4, 1999, pp. 1, 6. The two studios started to drift away from exhibition in 1997, but by 1999 stepped back in during Mann Theatre's receivership.

Progressive and Pacific Theatres: "Sol Lesser, 90, Predated Nearly All Industry Pioneers; 117 Features," *Variety*, September 24, 1980, p. 4.

Chapter 18: Epilogue

"If the business is to progress": see "Justice Department Statement on Suit Against Leading Movie Interests," *NYT*, July 21, 1938, p. 6; and Society of Independent Motion Picture Producers to Thurman Arnold, "Shall Block Booking of Motion Pictures Be Permitted to Return?" An Open Letter, published by SIMPP, New York, June 1, 1942, p. 4. See the complete Adolf Zukor quote on monopolies at *The SIMPP Research Database*: <http://www.simpp.com>.

SIMPP and film history: Donald M. Nelson, "The Independent Producer," *The Annals of the American Academy of Political and Social Sciences*, 254 (November 1947), p. 49-57.

"The familiar evolutionary process": Terry Ramsaye, *Nelson on Independents*, October 25, 1947, WWP.

"There's not the old": "Hollywood Sold Short," *MPH*, September 11, 1948, p. 18.

"Hollywood died on me": Welles and Bogdanovich, *This Is Orson Welles*, p. 204.

As of 1999, the eight largest distributors were listed in the *Hollywood Reporter* as Buena Vista, Warner Bros., Universal, Paramount, Twentieth Century-Fox, Sony, DreamWorks, and MGM, accounting for 83.5 percent of the annual $7 billion box office. A number of the most prominent independent distributors including Miramax (Buena Vista), New Line (Warner), Gramercy (Universal), Fox Searchlight (Twentieth Century-Fox), Sony Pictures Classics (Sony), and Samuel Goldwyn Films (MGM), and other "independent distributors" that are owned by major studios, raise the majors' share to more than 95 percent. See *HR*, January 5, 2000.

"The longest trailers ever made": Diane Disney Miller, as told to Pete Martin, "Small Boy's Dream Come True," *The Saturday Evening Post*, January 5, 1957, p. 82.

For additional information on the corporate transformation of Walt Disney Productions into the Walt Disney Company, see Grover, *The Disney Touch*; Taylor, *Storming the Magic Kingdom*; and Flower, *Prince of the Magic Kingdom*.

Acknowledgments and Author's Note

"Just be sure": Marx, *Goldwyn*, pp. 4-5.

Thomas M. Prior, "Indie Producers Org Seems Good Idea, But a Set of Aims Must Be Established," *DV*, December 13, 1976.

Bibliography

Acker, Ally. *Reel Women: Pioneers of the Cinema 1896 to the Present.* New York: Continuum, 1991.

Allvine, Glendon. *The Greatest Fox of Them All.* New York: Lyle Stuart, 1969.

Anderegg, Michael A. *William Wyler.* Boston: Twayne, 1979.

Anderson, Christopher. *Hollywood TV: The Studio System in the Fifties.* Austin: University of Texas, 1994.

Armes, Roy. *A Critical History of the British Cinema.* New York: Oxford University Press, 1978.

Allen, Robert C.*Vaudeville and Film, 1895-1915.* New York: Arno Press, 1980.

Armour, Robert A. *Fritz Lang.* Boston: Twayne, 1977.

Auiler, Dan. *Vertigo: The Making of a Hitchcock Classic.* New York: St. Martins Press, 1998.

Balio, Tino, ed. *The American Film Industry.* Madison: University of Wisconsin Press, 1976.

_____. *United Artists: The Company Built by the Stars.* Madison: University of Wisconsin Press, 1976.

_____. *United Artists: The Company That Changed the Film Industry.* Madison: University of Wisconsin Press, 1987.

Ball, Lucile, with Betty Hannah Hoffman. *Love, Lucy.* New York: G. P. Putnam's Sons, 1996.

Barlett, Donald L. and James B. Steele. *Empire: The Life, Legend, and Madness of Howard Hughes.* New York: Norton, 1979.

Barnouw, Erik. *A Tower In Babel: A History of Broadcasting in the United States to 1933.* New York: Oxford University Press, 1966.

_____. *The Golden Web: A History of Broadcasting in the United States 1933-1953.* New York: Oxford University Press, 1968.

_____. *The Image Empire: A History of Broadcasting in the United States from 1953*. New York: Oxford University Press, 1970.

Barrier, Michael. *Hollywood Cartoons*. New York: Oxford University Press, 1999.

Behlmer, Rudy, ed. *Inside Warner Bros.: 1935-1951*. New York: Viking Press, 1985.

_____. *Memo From David O. Selznick*. New York: Viking Press, 1972.

Bennett, Joan, and Lois Kibbee. *The Bennett Playbill: Five Generations of the Famous Theater Family*. Octavio, NY: Holt, Rinehart & Winston, 1970.

Berg, A. Scott. *Goldwyn: A Biography*. New York: Ballantine, 1989.

Bergan, Ronald. *Jean Renoir: Projections of Paradise*. Woodstock, NY: Overlook Press, 1992.

_____. *The United Artists Story*. New York: Crown, 1988.

Bergman, Andrew. *We're in the Money: Depression America and Its Films*. New York: New York University Press, 1971.

Bergman, Ingrid, and Alan Burgess. *My Story*. New York: Delacorte Press, 1980.

Bernardoni, James. *The New Hollywood: What the Movies Did With the New Freedom of the Seventies*. Jefferson, NC: McFarland, 1991.

Bernstein, Matthew. *Walter Wanger, Hollywood Independent*. Berkeley, CA: University of California Press, 1994.

Bernstein, Walter. *Inside Out: A Memoir of the Blacklist*. New York: Alfred A Knopf, 1996.

Best, Marc. *Those Endearing Young Charms; Child Performers of the Screen*. New York: A. S. Barnes, 1971.

Billingsley, Kenneth, Lloyd. *The Hollywod Party: How Communism Seduced the American Film Industry in the 1930s and 1940s*. Rocklin, CA: Prima Publishing, 1998.

Biskind, Peter. *Seeing is Believing: How Hollywood Movies Taught Us to Stop Worrying and Love the Fifties*. New York: Pantheon, 1983.

Bogdanovich, Peter. *Who the Devil Made It: Conversations With Robert Aldrich, George Cukor, Allan Dwan, Howard Hawks, Alfred Hitchcock, Chuck Jones, Fritz Lang, Joseph H. Lewis, Sidney Lumet, Leo McCarey, Otto Preminger, Don Siegel, Josef von Sternberg, Frank Tashlin, Edgar G. Ulmer, Raoul Walsh*. New York: Alfred A. Knopf, 1997.

Bordwell, David, Janet Staiger, and Kristin Thompson. *The Classical Hollywood Cinema: Film Style and Mode of Production to 1960*. New York: Columbia University Press, 1985.

Bowers, Ronald. *The Selznick Players*. Cranbury, NJ: A. S. Barnes, 1976.

Bowser, Eileen. *The Transformation of Cinema, 1907-1915*. New York: Charles Scribner's Sons, 1990.

Brady, Frank. *Citizen Welles: A Biography of Orson Welles*. New York: Charles Scribner's Sons, 1989.

Brownlow, Kevin. *Behind the Mask of Innocence*. New York: Alfred A. Knopf, 1990.

_____. *David Lean: A Biography*. New York: Wyatt/St. Martin's Press, 1996.

_____. *Mary Pickford Rediscovered: Rare Pictures of a Hollywood Legend*. New York: Harry N. Abrams, 1999.

_____. *The Parade's Gone By*. Berkely: University of California Press, 1968.

_____, and John Kobal. *Hollywood: The Pioneers*. New York: Alfred A. Knopf, 1979.

Butler, Ivan. *Silent Magic: Rediscovering the Silent Film Era*. New York: Ungar, 1988.

Cagney, James. *Cagney by Cagney*. Garden City, NY: Doubleday, 1976.

Callow, Simon. *Orson Welles: The Road to Xanadu*. New York: Viking Press, 1995.

Capra, Frank. *The Name Above the Title*. New York: Macmillan, 1971.

Carey, Gary. *Doug and Mary: A Biography of Douglas Fairbanks and Mary Pickford*. New York: E. P. Dutton, 1977.

Catlin, George B. *The Story of Detroit*. Detroit: Detroit News, 1926.

Chaplin, Charles. *My Autobiography*. New York: Simon and Schuster, 1964.

_____. *My Life in Pictures*. New York: Peerage Books, 1974.

Chaplin, Charles, Jr., with N. and M. Rau. *My Father, Charlie Chaplin*. New York: Random House, 1960.

Chaplin, Lita Grey, with Morton Cooper. *My Life with Chaplin: An Intimate Memoir*. New York: Bernard Geis, 1966.

Chown, Jeffrey. *Hollywood Auteur: Francis Coppola*. New York: Praeger, 1988.

Conant, Michael. *Antitrust in the Motion Picture Industry*. New York: Arno Press, 1978.

Cowie, Peter. *Coppola: A Biography*. New York: Charles Scribner's Sons, 1989.

Crafton, Donald. *Before Mickey: The Animated Film 1898-1928*. Cambridge, MA: MIT Press, 1982.

_____. *The Talkies: American Cinema's Transition to Sound, 1926-1931*. New York: Charles Scribner's Sons, 1997.

Crosby, Bing, as told to Pete Martin. *Call Me Lucky*. New York: Simon and Schuster, 1953.

Cross, Robin. *The Big Book of "B" Movies or How Low Was My Budget*. New York: St. Martins Press, 1981.

Crowther, Bosley. *Hollywood Rajah: The Life and Times of Louis B. Mayer*. New York: Henry Holt, 1960.

Culhane, John. *Walt Disney's Fantasia*. New York: Harry N. Abrams, 1983.

Curtis, James. *Between Flops: A Biography of Preston Sturges*. New York: Harcourt Brace Johanovich, 1982.

Dardis, Tom. *Harold Lloyd: The Man on the Clock*. New York: Viking Press, 1983.

Davis, Ronald L. *John Ford: Hollywood's Old Master*. Norman, OK: University of Oklahoma Press, 1995.

DeMille, Cecil B., edited by Donald Hayne. *The Autobiography of Cecil B. DeMille*. Englewood Cliffs, NJ: Prentice-Hall, 1959.

Dick, Bernard F. *City of Dreams: The Making and Remaking of Universal Pictures*. Lexington, KY: University of Kentucky, 1997.

_____. *The Star-Spangled Screen: The American World War II Film*. Lexington, KY: University Press of Kentucky, 1985.

Doherty, Thomas. *Teenagers and Teenpics: The Juvenilization of American Movies in the 1950s*. Boston: Unwin Hyman, 1988.

Donati, William. *Ida Lupino: A Biography*. Lexington, KY: University Press of Kentucky, 1996.

Durgnat, Raymond, and Scott Simmon. *King Vidor: American*. Berkeley, CA: University of California Press, 1988.

Eames, John Douglas. *The MGM Story: The Complete History of Fifty Roaring Years*. New York: Crown, 1975.

_____. *The Paramount Story*. New York: Crown, 1985.

Elsaesser, Thomas, with Adam Barker, eds., *Early Cinema: Space, Frame, Narrative*. London: BFI, 1990.

Essoe, Gabe. *Tarzan of the Movies: A Pictorial History of More Than Fifty Years of Edgar Rice Burroughs' Legendary Hero*. New York: Citadel Press, 1968.

Everson, William K. *American Silent Film*. New York: Oxford University Press, 1978.

Eyles, Allen. *The Western*. Cranbury, NJ: A. S. Barnes, 1975.

Eyman, Scott. *Mary Pickford: America's Sweetheart*. New York: Donald I. Fine, 1990.

Fairbanks, Douglas, Jr., and Richard Schickel. *The Fairbanks Album*. Boston: New York Graphic Society, 1975.

Farber, Stephen, and Marc Green. *Hollywood Dynasties*. New York, Delilah, 1984.

Fell, John L., ed. *Film Before Griffith*. Berkeley, CA: University of California Press, 1983.

Feild, Robert D. *The Art of Walt Disney*. New York: Macmillan, 1942.

Finch, Christopher. *The Art of Walt Disney: From Mickey Mouse to the Magic Kingdoms*. New York: Harry N. Abrams, 1973.

Finler, Joel W. *The Hollywood Story*. New York: Crown, 1988.

Fleischer, Richard. *Just Tell Me When to Cry: A Memoir*. New York: Carroll and Graf, 1993.

Flower, Joe. *Prince of the Magic Kingdom: Michael Eisner and the Re-Making of Disney*. New York: John Wiley and Sons, 1991.

Ford, Dan. *Pappy: The Life of John Ford*. Englewood Cliffs, NJ: Prentice-Hall, 1979.

Freedland, Michael. *The Warner Brothers*. New York: St. Martin's Press, 1983.

French, Philip. *The Movie Moguls: An Informal History of the Hollywood Tycoons*. Chicago: Henry Regnery, 1969.

Friedrich, Otto. *City of Nets: A Portrait of Hollywood in the 1940's*. New York: Harper & Row, 1986.

Gabler, Neal. *An Empire of Their Own: How the Jews Invented Hollywood*. New York: Doubleday, 1985.

Gallagher, Tag. *John Ford: The Man and His Films*. Berkeley, CA: University of California Press, 1986.

Gehring, Wes, D. *Charlie Chaplin's World of Comedy*. Muncie: Ball State University Press, 1980.

_____. *Screwball Comedy: A Genre of Madcap Romance*. New York: Greenwood Press, 1986.

Goldenson, Leonard H., with Marvin J. Wolf. *Beating the Odds: The Untold Story Behind the Rise of ABC: The Stars, Struggles, and Egos That Transformed Network Television By the Man Who Made It Happen*. New York: Charles Scribner's Sons, 1991.

Goldwyn, Samuel. *Behind the Screen*. New York: George H. Doran, 1923.

Gomery, Douglas. *The Hollywood Studio System*. New York: St. Martin's Press, 1986.

_____. *Shared Pleasures: A History of Movie Presentation in the United States*. Madison: University of Wisconsin Press, 1992.

Graham, Cooper C., Steven Higgins, Elaine Mancini, and Joao Luiz Vieira. *D.W. Griffith and the Biograph Company*. Metuchen, NJ: Scarecrow Press, 1985.

Grover, Ron. *The Disney Touch: Disney, ABC and the Quest for the World's Greatest Media Empire*. Burr Ridge, IL: Irwin Professional Publishing, 1996.

Guback, Thomas. *The International Film Industry: Western Europe and America Since 1945*. Bloomington, IN: Indiana University Press, 1969.

Gunning, Thomas. *D.W. Griffith and the Rise of the Narrative Film*. Urbana, IL: University of Illinois Press, 1991.

Hamilton, Ian. *Writers in Hollywood, 1915-1951*. London: Heinemann, 1990.

Hampton, Benjamin B. *A History of the American Film Industry: From Its Beginnings to 1931*. New York: Dover, 1970; reprinted from *A History of the Movies*. New York: Covici, Friede, 1931.

Haver, Ronald. *David O. Selznick's Hollywood*. New York: Bonanza Books, 1980.

Hay, Peter. *MGM: When the Lion Roars*. Atlanta, GA: Turner, 1991.

Hecht, Ben. *A Child of the Century*. New York: Simon and Schuster, 1954.

Henderson, Harold Paulk, *The Politics of Change in Georgia: A Political Biography of Ellis Arnall*. Athens, GA: University of Georgia Press, 1991.

Hendricks, Gordon. *The Edison Motion Picture Myth*. Berkeley, CA: University of California Press, 1961.

Hepburn, Katherine. *The Making of The African Queen: Or How I Went To Africa With Bogart, Bacall and Houston and Almost Lost My Mind*. New York: Alfred A. Knopf, 1987.

Heraldson, Donald. *Creators of Life: A History of Animation*. New York: Drake, 1975.

Herndon, Booton. *Mary Pickford and Douglas Fairbanks: The Most Popular Couple the World Has Known.* New York: W. W. Norton, 1977.

Higham, Charles. *Merchant of Dreams: Louis B. Mayer, M.G.M. and the Secret Hollywood.* New York: Donald I. Fine, 1993.

_____. *Orson Welles: The Rise and Fall of an American Genius.* New York: St. Martin's Press, 1985.

_____. *Warner Brothers.* New York: Charles Scribner's Sons, 1975.

Hirschhorn, Clive. *The Universal Story: The Complete History of the Studio and It's 2,641 Films.* New York: Crown, 1983.

_____. *The Warner Bros. Story.* New York: Crown, 1979.

Holliss, Richard, and Brian Sibley. *The Disney Studio Story.* New York: Crown, 1988.

Huettig, Mae D. *Economic Control of the Motion Picture Industry: A Study in Industrial Organization.* Philadelphia: University of Pennsylvania Press, 1944.

Hurst, Richard M. *Republic Studios: Between Poverty Row and the Majors.* Metuchen, NJ: Scarecrow Press, 1979.

Huston, John. *An Open Book.* New York: Alfred A. Knopf, 1980.

Irwin, Will. *The House that Shadows Built.* New York: Doubleday, Doran, 1928.

Jacobs, Diane. *Christmas in July: The Life and Art of Preston Sturges.* Berkeley, CA: University of California, 1992.

Jacobs, Lewis. *The Rise of the American Film: A Critical History.* New York: Harcourt, Brace, 1939.

James, John Douglas. *The MGM Story.* New York: Crown, 1976.

Jewell, Richard B., and Vernon Harbin. *The RKO Story.* New York: Arlington House, 1982.

Johnston, Alva. *The Great Goldwyn.* New York: Random House, 1937.

Kaminsky, Stuart. *John Huston: Maker of Magic.* Boston: Houghton Mifflin, 1978.

Kapsis, Robert E. *Hitchcock: The Making of a Reputation.* Chicago: University of Chicago Press, 1992.

Kazan, Elia. *A Life.* New York: Alfred A. Knopf, 1988.

Kennedy, Joseph P., ed. *The Story of the Films.* Chicago: A. W. Shaw, 1927.

Keyser, Lester J. *Hollywood in the Seventies.* San Diego: A. S. Barnes, 1981.

Kinney, Jack. *Walt Disney and Assorted Other Characters: An Unauthorized Account of the Early Years at Disney's.* New York: Harmony Books, 1988.

Koppes, Clayton R., and Gregory D. Black. *Hollywood Goes to War: How Politics, Profits, and Propaganda Shaped World War II Movies.* New York: Free Press, 1987.

Korda, Michael. *Charmed Lives: A Family Romance.* New York: Random House, 1979.

Koszarski, Richard. *An Evening's Entertainment: The Age of the Silent Feature Picture, 1915-1928.* New York: Charles Scribner's Sons, 1990.

_____, ed. *Hollywood Directors, 1914-1940*. New York: Oxford University, 1976.

_____, ed. *Hollywood Directors, 1941-1976*. New York: Oxford University, 1977.

Kramer, Stanley, with Thomas M. Coffey. *A Mad, Mad, Mad, Mad World: A Life in Hollywood*. New York: Harcourt, Brace, 1997.

Kuhn, Annette. *Cinema, Censorship, and Sexuality, 1909-1925*. New York: Routledge, 1988.

Kulik, Karol. *Alexander Korda: The Man Who Could Work Miracles*. New Rochelle, NY: Arlington House, 1975.

Lahue, Karlton C. *Dreams for Sale: The Rise and Fall of the Triangle Film Corporation*. Cranbury, NJ: A. S. Barnes, 1971.

Lally, Kevin. *Wilder Times: The Life of Billy Wilder*. New York: Henry Holt, 1996.

Lasky, Betty. *RKO: The Biggest Little Major of Them All*. Santa Monica, CA: Roundtable, 1984.

Lasky, Jesse L., with Don Weldon. *I Blow My Own Horn*. Garden City, NY: Doubleday, 1957.

Lasky, Jesse, Jr. *Whatever Happened to Hollywood?*. New York: Funk & Wagnalls, 1975.

Leaming, Barbara. *Orson Welles: A Biography*. New York: Viking Press, 1985.

Lebo, Harlan. *Citizen Kane: The Fiftieth-Anniversary Album*. New York: Doubleday, 1990.

Leebron, Elizabeth, and Lynn Gartley. *Walt Disney: A Guide to References and Resources*. Boston: G. K. Hall, 1979.

Leff, Leonard J., and Jerold L. Simmons. *The Dame in the Kimono: Hollywood, Censorship, and the Production Code from the 1920s to the 1960s*. New York: Grove Weidenfeld, 1990.

Leff, Leonard J. *Hitchcock and Selznick: The Rich and Strange Collaboration of Alfred Hitchcock and David O. Selznick In Hollywood*. New York: Weidenfeld and Nicholson, 1987.

Le Roy, Mervyn, as told to Dick Kleiner. *Mervyn Le Roy: Take One*. New York: Hawthorn Books, 1974.

Lingeman, Richard R. *Don't You Know There's a War On?: The American Home Front, 1941-1945*. New York: G.P. Putnam's Sons,1970.

MacCann, Richard Dyer. *The First Tycoons*. Metuchen, NJ: Scarecrow Press, 1987.

Madsen, Axel. *William Wyler: The Authorized Biography*. New York: Thomas Y. Crowell, 1973.

Maland, Charles. *American Visions: The Films of Chaplin, Ford, Capra, and Welles, 1936-1941*. New York: Arno Press, 1977.

Maland, Charles J. *Chaplin and American Culture: The Evolution of a Star Image*. Princeton, NJ: Princeton University Press, 1989.

Maltin, Leonard. *Of Mice and Magic: A History of American Animated Cartoons*. Rev. ed. New York: New American Library, 1987.

Maltin, Leonard, and Richard W. Bann. *Our Gang: The Life and Times of the Little Rascals*. New York: Crown, 1977.

Manvell, Roger. *Films and the Second World War*. New York: Dell, 1976.

Marill, Alvin H. *Samuel Goldwyn Presents*. Cranbury, NJ: A. S. Barnes, 1976.

Marx, Arthur. *Goldwyn: A Biography of the Man Behind the Myth*. New York: W. W. Norton, 1976.

Marx, Samuel. *Mayer and Thalberg: The Make-Believe Saints*. New York: Random House, 1975.

Mast, Gerald, ed. *The Movies in Our Midst: Documents in the Cultural History of Film in America*. Chicago: University of Chicago Press, 1982.

McBride, Joseph. *Frank Capra: The Catastrophe of Success*. New York: Simon and Schuster, 1992.

McCabe, John. *Cagney*. New York: Alfred A. Knopf, 1997.

_____. *Charlie Chaplin*. New York: Doubleday, 1978.

McCarthy, Todd. *Howard Hawks: The Grey Fox of Hollywood*. New York: Grove Press, 1997.

McDougal, Dennis. *The Last Mogul: Lew Wasserman, MCA, and the Hidden History of Hollywood*. New York: Crown, 1998.

McGilligan, Patrick. *Fritz Lang: The Nature of the Beast*. New York: St. Martin's Press, 1997.

Merritt, Russel, and J. B. Kaufman. *Walt in Wonderland: The Silent Films of Walt Disney*. Pordenone, Italy: Le Giornate del Cinema Muto, 1992.

Miller, Diane Disney. *The Story of Walt Disney*. New York: Henry Holt, 1957.

Milton, Joyce. *Tramp: The Life of Charlie Chaplin*. New York: Harper Collins, 1996.

Monaco, Paul. *Ribbons in Time: Movies and Society Since 1945*. Bloomington, IN: Indiana University Press, 1987.

Morden, Ethan. *The Hollywood Studio: House Style in the Golden Age of the Movies*. New York: Alfred A. Knopf, 1988.

Mosely, Leonard. *Disney's World: A Biography*. New York: Stein and Day, 1985.

_____. *Zanuck: The Rise and Fall of Hollywood's Last Tycoon*. Boston: Little, Brown, 1984.

Musser, Charles. *The Emergence of Cinema: The American Screen to 1907*. New York: Charles Scribner's Sons, 1990.

_____. *Before the Nickelodeon: Edwin S. Porter and the Edison Manufacturing Company*. Berkeley, CA: University of California Press, 1991.

Naremore, James. *The Magic World of Orson Welles*. New York: Oxford University Press, 1978.

Paley, William S. *As It Happened, A Memoir*. Garden City, NY: Doubleday, 1979.

Pickford, Mary. *Sunshine and Shadow*. Garden City, NY: Doubleday, 1955.

Poitier, Sidney. *This Life*. New York: Alfred A. Knopf, 1980.

Ramsaye, Terry. *A Million and One Nights*. New York: Simon & Schuster, 1926; reprint ed., New York: Touchstone, 1986.

Rebello, Stephen. *Alfred Hitchcock and the Making of Psycho*. New York: Dembner Books, 1990.

Robinson, David. *Chaplin: His Life and Art*. New York: McGraw-Hill, 1985.

_____. *Chaplin: The Mirror of Opinion*. London: Secker & Warburg, 1983.

Sanders, Coyne Steven, and Tom Gilbert. *Desilu: The Story of Lucille Ball and Desi Arnaz*. New York: William Morrow, 1993.

_____. *Hollywood in the Twenties*. Cranbury, NJ: A. S. Barnes, 1968.

Schary, Dore. *Heyday: An Autobiography*. Boston: Little, Brown, 1979.

Schatz, Thomas. *Boom and Bust: The American Cinema in the 1940s*. New York: Charles Scribner's Sons, 1997.

_____. *The Genius of the System*. New York: Henry Holt, 1996.

_____. *Hollywood Genres: Formulas, Filmmaking, and the Studio System*. New York: McGraw-Hill, 1981.

Schickel, Richard. *D. W. Griffith: An American Life*. New York: Simon & Schuster, 1984.

_____. *The Disney Version: The Life, Times, Art and Commerce of Walt Disney*. New York: Simon and Schuster, 1968.

_____. *James Cagney: A Celebration*. Boston: Little, Brown, 1985.

Schrecker, Ellen. *The Age of McCarthyism: A Brief History With Documents*. Boston: St. Martins Press, 1994.

Schulberg, Budd. *Moving Pictures: Memories of a Hollywood Prince*. New York: Simon & Schuster, 1984.

Schumacher, Michael. *Francis Ford Coppola: A Filmmaker's Life*. New York: Crown, 1999.

Schwartz, Lynn, Nancy. *The Hollywood Writer's Wars*. New York: Alfred A Knopf, 1982.

Selznick, Irene Mayer. *A Private View*. New York: Alfred A. Knopf, 1983.

Sennett, Mack, as told to Cameron Shipp. *King of Comedy*. Garden City, NY: Doubleday, 1954.

Shale, Richard. *Donald Duck Joins Up: The Walt Disney Studio During World War II*. Ann Arbor, MI: UMI Research Press, 1982.

Shindler, Colin. *Hollywood Goes to War: Films and American Society, 1939-1952*. Boston: Routledge & Kegan Paul, 1979.

Sinyard, Neil. *Silent Movies*. New York: Gallery Books, 1990.

Shipman, David. *The Story of Cinema*. New York: St. Martin's Press, 1982.

Shows, Charles. *Walt: Backstage Adventures With Walt Disney*. La Jolla, CA: Windsong Books, 1979.

Sikov, Ed. *On Sunset Boulevard: The Life and Times of Billy Wilder*. New York: Hyperion, 1998.

Silverman, Stephen M. *David Lean*. New York, Harry N. Abrams, 1989.

Sinclair, Andrew. *John Ford*. New York: Dial Press/James Wade, 1979.

_____. *Spiegel: The Man Behind the Pictures*. Boston: Little, Brown, 1987.

Sklar, Robert. *Film: An International History of the Medium*. New York: Harry N. Abrams, 1993.

_____. *Movie-Made America: A Cultural History of American Movies*. New York: Vintage Books, 1994.

Smith, Albert E. *Two Reels and a Crank*. Garden City, NY: Doubleday, 1952.

Smoodin, Eric, ed. *Disney Discourse: Producing the Magic Kingdom*. New York: Routledge, 1994.

Solomon, Charles. *The Disney That Never Was: The Stories and Art from Five Decades of Unproduced Animation*. New York: Hyperion, 1995.

_____. *Enchanted Drawings: The History of Animation*. New York: Alfred A. Knopf, 1989.

Spoto, Donald. *The Dark Side of Genius: The Life of Alfred Hitchcock*. Boston: Little, Brown, 1983.

_____. *Stanley Kramer, Film Maker*. New York: Putnam, 1978.

Stanley, Robert H. *The Celluloid Empire: A History of the American Movie Industry*. New York: Communications Arts/Hastings House, 1978.

Sturges, Preston, adapted and edited by Sandy Sturges. *Preston Sturges*. New York: Simon and Schuster, 1990.

Swanson, Gloria. *Swanson on Swanson*. New York: Random House, 1980.

Tabori, Paul. *Alexander Korda: A Biography*. London: Oldbourne, 1959.

Taylor, John. *Storming the Magic Kingdom: Wall Street, the Raiders, and the Battle for Disney*. New York: Alfred A. Knopf, 1987.

Taylor, John Russell. *Hitch: The Life and Times of Alfred Hitchcock*. New York: Pantheon Books, 1978.

_____. *Orson Welles*. Boston: Little, Brown, 1986.

_____. *Strangers in Paradise: The Hollywood Emigres*. London: Faber and Faber, 1983.

Thomas, Bob. *Building a Company: Roy O. Disney and the Creation of an Entertainment Empire*. New York: Hyperion, 1998.

_____. *Selznick*. Garden City, NY: Doubleday, 1970.

_____. *Thalberg: Life and Legend*. Garden City, NY: Doubleday, 1969.

_____. *Walt Disney: An American Original*. New York: Simon and Schuster, 1976.

Thomas, Tony. *Howard Hughes in Hollywood*. Secaucus, NJ: The Citadel Press, 1985.

Thompson, Kristin. *Exporting Entertainment: America in the World Film Market, 1907-1934*. London: British Film Institute, 1985.

Thomson, David. *Rosebud: The Story of Orson Welles*. New York: Alfred A. Knopf, 1996.

Torrence, Bruce, T. *Hollywood: The First Hundred Years*. New York: Zoetrope, 1982.

Trethewey, Richard L. *Walt Disney: The FBI Files*. Pacifica, CA: Rainbo Animation Art, 1994.

Tytle, Harry. *One of "Walt's Boys": An Insider's Account of Disney's Golden Years*. Royal Oak, MI: Airtight Seels Allied Productions, 1997.

Trumbo, Dalton. *Additional Dialogue: Letters of Dalton Trumbo 1942 - 1962*. New York: M.Evans, 1970.

Udelson, Joseph H. *The Great Television Race: A History of the American Television Industry, 1925- 1941*. Alabama: University of Alabama Press, 1982.

Vidor, King. *King Vidor on Film Making*. New York: David McKay, 1972.

Wallis, Hal, and Charles Higham. *Starmaker: The Autobiography of Hall Wallis*. New York: Macmillan, 1980.

Wapshott, Nicholas. *Carol Reed: A Biography*. New York: Alfred A. Knopf, 1994.

Warner, Jack. *My First Hundred Years in Hollywood*. New York: Random House, 1965.

Watts, Steven. *The Magic Kingdom: Walt Disney and the American Way of Life*. Boston: Houghton Mifflin, 1997.

Weales, Gerald. *Canned Goods as Caviar: American Film Comedy of the 1930s*. Chicago: University of Chicago Press, 1985.

Welles, Orson, and Peter Bogdanovich. *This Is Orson Welles*. New York: HarperCollins, 1992.

Whitefield, Eileen. *Pickford: The Woman Who Made Hollywood*. Lexington, KY: University Press of Kentucky, 1997.

Wilkerson,Tichi, and Marcia Borie, *The Hollywood Reporter, the Golden Years*. New York: Coward- McCann, 1984.

Williams, Henry B. *Theatre at Dartmouth 1769-1914: From Eleazar Wheelock to Walter Wanger*. Hanover, NH: Friends of the Dartmouth Library, 1987.

Williams, Martin. *Griffith: First Artist of the Movies*. New York: Oxford University Press, 1980.

Windeler, Robert. *Sweetheart: The Story of Mary Pickford*. New York: Praeger, 1974.

Zierold, Norman. *The Moguls: Hollywood's Merchants of Myth*. New York: Coward-McCann, 1969.

Zinnemann, Fred. *A Life in the Movies: An Autobiography*. New York: Robert Stewart/Charles Scribner's Sons, 1992.

Zukor, Adolph, with Dale Kramer. *The Public Is Never Wrong: My Fifty Years in the Motion Picture Industry*. New York: G. P. Putnam's Sons, 1953.

Index